SEXUAL HARASSMENT

Contemporary Issues

Series Editors: Robert M. Baird
Stuart E. Rosenbaum

Other titles in this series:

Animal Experimentation: The Moral Issues
edited by Robert M. Baird and Stuart E. Rosenbaum

Bigotry, Prejudice, and Hatred: Definitions, Causes, and Solutions
edited by Robert M. Baird and Stuart E. Rosenbaum

The Ethics of Abortion: Pro-Life vs. Pro-Choice
edited by Robert M. Baird and Stuart E. Rosenbaum

Euthanasia: The Moral Issues
edited by Robert M. Baird and Stuart E. Rosenbaum

The Gun Control Debate: You Decide
edited by Lee Nisbet

Morality and the Law
edited by Robert M. Baird and Stuart E. Rosenbaum

Philosophy of Punishment
edited by Robert M. Baird and Stuart E. Rosenbaum

Pornography: Private Right or Public Menace?
edited by Robert M. Baird and Stuart E. Rosenbaum

Suicide: Right or Wrong?
edited by John Donnelly

SEXUAL HARASSMENT

CONFRONTATIONS AND DECISIONS

edited by Edmund Wall

CONTEMPORARY ISSUES

PROMETHEUS BOOKS • *Buffalo, New York*

Published 1992 by Prometheus Books

Sexual Harassment: Confrontations and Decisions. Copyright © 1992 by Edmund Wall. All rights reserved. Inquiries should be addressed to Prometheus Books, 59 John Glenn Drive, Buffalo, New York 14228-2197, 716-837-2475. FAX: 716-835-6901.

96 95 94 93 92   5 4 3 2 1

Library of Congress Cataloging-in-Publication Data

Sexual harassment : confrontations and decisions / edited by Edmund Wall.
    p.   cm.
Includes bibliographical references.
ISBN 0-87975-787-6
1. Sexual harassment of women—United States. 2. Sexual harassment of women—Law and legislation—United States. I. Wall, Edmund. II. Series: Contemporary issues (Buffalo, N.Y.)
HQ1237.5.U6S48   1992
305.42—dc20
                                                            92-25482
                                                                CIP

Printed in Canada on acid-free paper.

Acknowledgments

I owe a large debt to Burleigh Wilkins, University of California at Santa Barbara, for his valuable assistance on this and other projects throughout the years. It was his suggestion two years ago that prompted me to prepare a sexual harassment anthology.

The editorial director at Prometheus Books, Steven L. Mitchell, was very supportive from the beginning.

The suggestions offered on the manuscript by Geoffrey Wallace and Amelia Frank, Office of the Ombudsman, UC Santa Barbara, were greatly appreciated, as was the assistance offered by Ruth Kauffman of the Rape Crisis Center of Santa Barbara. Raymond Huerta, affirmative action coordinator at UC Santa Barbara, graciously offered his knowledge of the subject. The manuscript benefited from the suggestions of Joseph White, Santa Barbara City College. The materials offered by psychologist Keith Mar, who works with the Santa Barbara sheriff's department, were also helpful.

My wife, Robin Wall, was very supportive. I would also like to thank Jerry for his timely assistance during the preparation of this manuscript. Special thanks to Pat for her kind support. Despite all that she has done for me, she never expected anything in return.

Contents

7

Introduction

This anthology not only presents some of the major debates in the current research on sexual harassment, but also attempts to demonstrate the need for further study of this problem. Although significant attention has been given to sexual harassment for approximately the past twenty years, little has been established. Its meaning, its causes, and its remedy seem to elude researchers and public officials. We might expect researchers to have reached a basic understanding of this problem. Surely, we say to ourselves, social science has at least advanced us in the right direction. Unfortunately, what we would expect does not coincide with what has been delivered.

Since the late 1970s there have been numerous scientific studies that have investigated the frequency, causes, and effects of sexual harassment. Yet, the first thing one notices when reviewing these studies is the chaos regarding the description or definition of the problem. In addition to differences in survey techniques, many different definitions have been employed, so that what is considered relevant data for one survey may not be relevant for another. Social scientists admit that for these very reasons comparisons between studies are often misleading.[1]

The absence of a uniform method for organizing sexual harassment studies is imposing enough.[2] However, the problems do not end there. In many studies, the number of respondents is too small, and there is inadequate assurance that the respondents do not share common backgrounds, do not all live in the same geographical location, and do not all have the same profession.

For example, one possible difficulty with studies conducted in the same geographical location is that community mores could color the perceptions of the respondents. Consider the possibility that in some geographical areas a certain style of clothing might seem suggestive and revealing, while in other areas the same garments are seen as routine. Those who find the clothing suggestive may be more inclined to conclude that those who dress in this way are inviting sexual advances. They might also be reluctant to consider sexual advances toward these people sexually harassing. These reluctant bystanders might even say that *they* are being sexually harassed by those who wear the "revealing" garments. The region in which this style of dress is common, on the other hand, might be more inclined to label sexual advances toward these people as "sexual harassment."

One of the most cited studies in the research was done by the U.S. Merit Systems Protection Board in 1981. Their follow-up study, which had the same basic results, was conducted in 1988.[3] It is very impressive to note that over 20,000 people were surveyed. It is not as heartening to find that all of those sampled were federal government employees. Moreover, the definition of sexual harassment employed there was relatively open-ended: "unwanted sexual attention." This definition would fail to exclude the more paranoid respondents at one extreme and the more desensitized respondents at the other. For example, the latter might only view very blatant sexual advances as instances of sexual harassment. Such a definition is not only bound to circumvent genuine cases but also to implicate the innocent.

The importance of an adequate definition of sexual harassment was underscored in October 1991, when Clarence Thomas went before the Senate for confirmation of his seat on the U.S. Supreme Court. Although it was clear that if Anita Hill's charges were true, Thomas did sexually harass her, the media gave considerable coverage to the problem of deciding what constitutes sexual harassment. For example, there hardly seems to be a consensus as to whether or not cursing, sexual jokes, and compliments in the workplace constitute sexual harassment. Anita Hill's allegations not only made many people aware of the importance of the issue, it also introduced them to some of its puzzles such as the problem of formulating a comprehensive definition.

The frequency of sexual harassment has not been authoritatively established. In both studies conducted by the U.S. Merit Systems Protection Board, the rates were found to be approximately 42 percent for female federal employees and 15 percent for male federal employees. This percentage is based on a two-year period. Of course, one needs to read these results with a reminder about the diversity of the sample and the absence of an adequate description of the problem.

After reviewing many of the studies, one cannot avoid the impression that the problem of sexual harassment against men has not been given adequate consideration. Although it is generally accepted that two to three times as many women than men are sexually harassed,[4] it might be that current social attitudes prevent many men from admitting they have been harassed. For example, perhaps a large percentage of men feel that a "real man" could handle the problem on his own. But even if this is not the case, even if only 15 percent of the men will be sexually harassed over the next few years, this is not an inconsiderable number.

There is some evidence that social expectations and other factors affect the number of cases reported to academic and business institutions. Studies seem to indicate that male and female victims are generally reluctant to take action against offenders.[5] Sexual harassment can be a psychologically damaging experience.[6] Social scientists claim that many victims do not want to discuss the harrowing details with authorities without adequate assurance that grievance procedures will be effective and that they, the victims, will not be blamed.[7] The fear of an employer's or instructor's retaliation for reporting a case figures prominently into the concerns among victims.[8] Moreover, the studies indicate a loss of self-confidence among many victims.[9] In fact, it is claimed that some victims blame themselves for the impropriety. These persons feel that there must be something about their general behavior that encourages inappropriate sexual advances.[10] If these findings represent the emotional responses of a considerable percentage of sexual harassment victims, this may be yet another obstacle to the attainment of accurate research data. Nevertheless, social science has at least begun its task.

The first selection, by Linda Rubin and Sherry Borgers, provides an overview of the scientific studies conducted during the 1980s on sexual harassment in academia. Among other things, Rubin and Borgers acknowledge the lack of a common methodology among social scientists, but nevertheless conclude that sexual harassment is a "pervasive problem throughout higher education."

Alan Kors maintains that minorities and women are unjustly favored in university harassment policies. He also objects that the definitions of sexual harassment in such policies can be interpreted to prevent instructors from meeting with students at social gatherings—even if it is to discuss some academic subject.

Nancy Tuana finds that students, especially female students, need special protection against sexual harassment. According to her, even ostensibly innocent social meetings can occur within a coercive context. Unlike Kors, Tuana pays special attention to the power differential between student and instructor, and maintains that at social gatherings words and gestures may be misinterpreted, with the result that the instructor unwittingly yet negligently coerces his or her students.

The next two selections center on sexual harassment in the workplace, but many of the points made in these essays may also apply to the academic setting. Larry May and John Hughes define sexual harassment in terms of a power differential between supervisors and employees and in terms of the discriminatory effects of inappropriate sexual advances. They focus on the harassment of women by men, since this is seen as the typical case.[11] May and Hughes's main thesis is that whenever a male supervisor sexually harasses his female employees with threats or offers, the harassment necessarily constitutes sex discrimination. Edmund Wall, on the other hand, defines sexual harassment as a type of wrongful communication and rejects the notion that a power-differential is part of the definition. Wall also challenges the view that sexual harassment is a form of sexual discrimination.

In the second section of this anthology, Sandra Tangri, Martha Burt, and Leanor Johnson summarize sociological and legal explanations of sexual harassment under three basic headings: the Natural/Biological Model, the Organizational Model, and the Sociocultural Model. The first model suggests that sexual harassment is generally a normal expression of the natural sexual attraction between people.[12] The second describes sexual harassment as the result of the way that work and other organizations are structured. The last attributes the problem to social and economic differences between the sexes.

The selection by Camille Paglia—whose book *Sexual Personae* has drawn much criticism—provides a challenging account of the causes of the problem. Although Paglia's account would fall under the Natural/Biological Model, it is by no means a tidy match. The Natural/Biological Model is rooted in the function of male and female sex drives; it also maintains that sexual attraction and behavior in the workplace are basically legitimate. Paglia, on the other hand, does not limit her description of male and female relations to their sex drives, and her account of sexual attraction is much darker than that offered by the Natural/Biological Model. Essentially, Paglia argues that mysterious, natural forces are not only largely responsible for the harassment of women by men, but for violent crimes in general. This does not square at all with Catharine MacKinnon's feminist account, which maintains that the problem has arisen primarily because of social beliefs and practices. MacKinnon's views on sexual harassment, which more or less fit the Sociocultural and Organizational Models, have been influencing social theorists, legal scholars, and public officials since the mid-1970s.

According to MacKinnon, genuine progress can be made in the struggle against sexual harassment, if society alters many of its beliefs as well as many of the social conditions that it has created. Paglia, on the other hand, believes that, at best, society can provide external constraints on the forces that *naturally* propel men to be violent.

Paglia's view does not fit today's scientific models very well. However, the prevailing view among social scientists lines up well with MacKinnon's account. They view the problem against the background of the present social structure, taking account of the influence of social roles on behavior as well as the part played by other societal factors. It is, therefore, almost shocking to hear Paglia tell us that underneath the social structure we find something that science cannot categorize.

The third section presents some of the controversy over Title VII of the 1964 Civil Rights Act, which, among other things, outlaws sex discrimination. Catharine MacKinnon has been instrumental in persuading the legal establishment to view sexual harassment as a form of sex discrimination. Moreover, she helped to persuade public policymakers that the Civil Rights Act should be used to remedy what has come to be known as "hostile environment" sexual harassment. Unlike *quid pro quo* sexual harassment, which involves possible tangible losses to the victim such as job termination or demotion, hostile environment cases center on the atmosphere in the workplace. The idea behind it is that the work environment can be polluted by inappropriate sexual advances and sexist attitudes, which will in turn disrupt the functions of the workplace.

Before the Civil Rights Act became a legal tool for protecting women from sexual harassment, tort law (or the law of private harms) ostensibly provided this protection. In certain types of harassment cases, workers could invoke tort law and bring charges of assault and battery. However, MacKinnon finds the legal reasoning behind tort law to be very inadequate and sexist. She argues that Title VII of the Civil Rights Act affords better protection for women.

J. P. Minson argues that tort law is not as inadequate as MacKinnon believes, and that a combination of tort and Title VII approaches would be wise. As Minson sees it, MacKinnon makes too rigid a distinction between the private and public (i.e., social) spheres, labeling sexual harassment as a "social" problem. Minson argues that even if sexual harassment is a social problem to be remedied by Title VII, tort law and other private solutions should also be applied. Minson believes that to avoid private solutions (such as those devised by corporate management) is to turn Title VII into a legal behemoth. By Minson's argument, MacKinnon's application of Title VII is antidemocratic.

Ellen Frankel Paul's position is even more at odds with MacKinnon's. She calls for the use of revised tort law *instead* of Title VII anti-discrimination law. Paul argues that both *quid pro quo* and hostile environment protections are unfair to employers. Moreover, she objects that the hostile environment approach overprotects workers by failing to distinguish genuine harm from merely offensive behavior.

The selections by Paul, Minson, and MacKinnon provide philosophical debates about Title VII. The selection by William Woerner and Sharon Oswald briefly tells us what the law has actually done with Title VII. The authors highlight some of the important legal cases and offer a brief description of the evolution of sexual harassment law.

The next selection is from an important case, *Vinson* v. *Taylor*, that is not summarized by Woerner and Oswald. This 1985 case, which includes a decision by a federal appeals court, was reviewed a year later by the U.S. Supreme Court as *Meritor Savings Bank* v. *Vinson*, a brief description of which occurs in Woerner and Oswald's selection. The decision of the *Vinson* v. *Taylor* court, delivered by Chief Judge Spottswood Robinson, III, more or less coincides with MacKinnon's position. It finds that the sexual harassment against Vinson was a form of sex discrimination. The court defends the distinction between *quid pro quo* and hostile environment sexual harassment cases, arguing that a plaintiff can have legal grounds for action in either type of case. In this case the plaintiff/appellant, Mechele Vinson, was an assistant branch manager at a bank. She accused her supervisor Sidney Taylor, the bank's vice president, of repeatedly harassing, assaulting, and raping her. Taylor successfully denied all of these accusations in a district court, but the case was reviewed by the appeals court. Judge Spottswood Robinson, III, and others found that this was indeed a case of hostile environment sexual harassment. Moreover, unlike the district court, the appeals court ruled that whether or not Vinson voluntarily consented to sexual relations with her supervisor was not relevant. What mattered was whether or not the supervisor's sexual advances were "unwanted" by Vinson and whether or not they unreasonably interfered with her work performance. The court also decided that Vinson's own workplace conduct was not admissible evidence for the defense.

Taylor sought another hearing before the appeals court. After this was denied, a dissenting opinion was expressed by Judge Robert Bork. Unlike Robinson, Bork maintains that facts about whether or not Vinson voluntarily consented to sexual relations with Taylor *is* evidence of Taylor's guilt or innocence. Bork also disagrees with Robinson as to the admissibility of Vinson's workplace behavior. He believes that it does constitute evidence as to whether or not Vinson solicited Taylor's sexual advances, or consented to them.[13] Bork concludes that the *Vinson* court overextended Title VII. According to him, Congress did not even intend Title VII to apply to cases in which individuals are sexually harassed.

Very recently the debate over Title VII has become even more intense. Before it became law in 1991, the new Civil Rights Act was greatly contested both inside and outside of the congressional arena. We have yet to see how the courts are going to interpret the new legislation specifically for Title VII cases involving sexual harassment, but the act at least appears to shift the burden of proof from the employee to the employer in "disparate impact" discrimination cases. In such cases an employee/plaintiff alleges that an employment practice results in a statistical disparity with regard to race, gender, or ethnicity. Previously, an *employee* would have to prove that the employment practice that led to a statistical disparity had no "business justification."[14] This requirement was based upon the U.S. Supreme Court's opinion in *Wards Cove Packing Co. v. Atonio.*[15] In effect, the new legislation overturns this important part of the Supreme Court decision by requiring the *employer* to prove that the practice resulting in a statistical disparity was "consistent with business necessity."[16] The act also specifically affects the way that Title VII sex discrimination cases may be handled in the future. It now allows victims of sexual harassment to be awarded limited compensatory and punitive damages, if they can prove they were intentionally discriminated against. Previously, the courts could only award such victims lost pay, benefits, and some remuneration for legal expenses.[17]

Among other concerns, such as the possibility of a retroactive application of the new legislation, opponents argue that employers will now have to institute quota systems in order to protect themselves against potential legal action. Proponents of the legislation, on the other hand, welcome the protection that may now be provided to women and minorities in light of what they take to have been a defeat in *Wards Cove.* This long-standing rift in our society is not about to subside, as many anxious citizens await upcoming court decisions.

The use of a "reasonable woman standard" in sexual harassment law also causes disagreement among social and legal theorists. The legal establishment is dogged by the dilemma of trying to make objective determinations when there are wide differences in perceptions as to what constitutes sexual harassment. In many of their efforts to determine what constitutes a crime, the courts historically have employed a reasonable man standard, i.e., they have tried to determine how a reasonable man would react to a defendant's behavior and have used this information to help decide a case. The courts now use either a reasonable person standard or reasonable woman/victim standard when they consider cases of alleged hostile environment sexual harassment.[18] In deciding whether or not a plaintiff was subjected to a hostile environment, the courts try to determine how a typical person, woman, or victim would be affected by a defendant's sexual advances, proposals, etc.

Although Stephanie Riger does not refer explicitly to a reasonable woman standard for sexual harassment determinations, she believes that social policies need to be rewritten in light of the experiences of women. Her paper attempts to account for the fact that few sexual harassment complaints are actually reported. Riger accounts for this by saying that gender bias afflicts definitions and grievance procedures. Since men are more or less in control of the sexual harassment policies that are needed to protect women, and since many studies show that women and men do not agree on what is appropriate and inappropriate behavior, Riger suggests a reformulation of harassment policies that includes women's perceptions of the problem.

Douglas Baker, David Terpstra, and Bob Cutler believe that gender differences in perceptions of sexual harassment have been exaggerated.[19] They warn their readers about problems with current studies that claim wide gender differences, but admit that their own study, which basically finds no such differences, is also inconclusive.

The editors of the *New Republic* see a danger in using the reasonable woman standard for hostile environment cases of sexual harassment. They not only reject the reasonable woman standard in favor of a gender-neutral test, but also urge the law to omit hostile environment claims altogether. They maintain that the combination of the reasonable woman standard and hostile environment guidelines threatens the right to free speech.

Nancy Ehrenreich's essay is considerably more pessimistic than the other selections in this section. Although she sees the reasonable woman standard as currently preferable to either the reasonable man or reasonable person standard in sexual harassment law, she does not expect an effective treatment of the problem unless society is restructured to alleviate pervasive bias. Among other things, Ehrenreich believes that in the battle against social inequities, some men will have to forfeit a portion of their social and economic power to women and minorities. She contends that the reasonable woman standard, like any other social principle or standard, will be interpreted according to the socioeconomic backgrounds of those who make and enforce public policy. Given the depth of the social and economic inequities in society, Ehrenreich believes that all women and men are victims of their respective social and economic classes. As such, she finds them, at least for now, to be incapable of constructing any equitable social standards.

Establishing acceptable social standards to address sexual harassment is certainly no easy task, but the military has yet to establish any such standards at all. Recently the public was shocked to learn about what took place at last September's Tailhook convention, an annual meeting of Navy aviators that was scheduled at the Las Vegas Hilton. The convention was riddled with cases of sexual assault and other odious behavior perpetrated by male junior officers against female officers. In the future one would expect the military to direct considerably more attention to this very difficult issue. In any case the problem of sexual harassment in the military community is a fertile area for social research and philosophical investigation. Indeed, as we have seen, the same opportunities present themselves to social scientists and philosophers who consider the problem in a civilian context.

NOTES

1. In addition to Rubin and Borgers, Part One, below, see Amy Somers, "Sexual Harassment in Academe: Legal Issues and Definitions," *Journal of Social Issues* 38, no. 4 (1982): 223–32; Marilynn B. Brewer, "Further Beyond Nine to Five: An Integration and Future Directions," *Journal of Social Issues* 38, no. 4 (1982): 149–58; James E. Gruber, "Methodological Problems and Policy Implications in Sexual Harassment Research," *Population Research and Policy Review* 9, no. 3 (1990): 235–37; Louise F. Fitzgerald and Matthew Hesson-McInnis, "The Dimensions of Sexual Harassment: A Structural Analysis," *Journal of Vocational Behavior* 35 (1989): 309–310; Louise F. Fitzgerald et al., "The Incidence and Dimensions of Sexual Harassment in Academia and the Workplace," *Journal of Vocational Behavior* 32 (1988): 152–56; Kenneth M. York, "Defining Sexual Harassment in Workplaces: A Policy-Capturing Approach," *Academy of Management Journal* 32, no. 4 (1989): 831.

2. Recently Gruber and Fitzgerald, *supra,* have separately begun work on an adequate definition and common methodology for sexual harassment research.

3. In their national survey of sexual harassment among federal employees, the U.S. Merit Systems Protection Board found that 42 percent of all women surveyed had experienced various forms of "unwanted sexual attention" within the 24 months prior to the study. The figure was 15 percent for men. These findings are reported in U.S. Merit Systems Protection Board, *Sexual Harassment in the Federal Workplace: Is It a Problem?* (Washington, D.C.: U.S. Government Printing Office, 1981). See, also, U.S. Merit Systems Protection Board, *Sexual Harassment in the Federal Government: An Update* (Washington, D.C.:

U.S. Government Printing Office, 1988). In Barbara A. Gutek's "Experience of Sexual Harassment; Results from a Representative Survey" (Paper presented at the 89th Annual Convention of the American Psychological Association, Los Angeles, August 1981), we find that the results from a large survey of private-sector workers in the Los Angeles area reflect a rate of 53.1 percent among women respondents. For sexual harassment figures on college campuses, see Donna J. Benson and Gregg E. Thomson, "Sexual Harassment on a University Campus: The Confluence of Authority Relations, Sexual Interest, and Gender Stratification," *Social Problems* 29, no. 3 (1982): 241. From a sample of UC Berkeley undergraduate women Benson and Thomson found the incidence rate to be 30 percent. In "Sexual Harassment on Campus: Individual Differences in Attitudes and Beliefs," *Psychology of Women Quarterly* 14 (1990): 64, Natalie J. Malovich and Jayne E. Stake's review of the research finds that among undergraduate as well as graduate women, rates of sexual harassment are between 30–53 percent. For undergraduate men, they place the rate at 12.6 percent.

4. See n. 3.

5. In addition to Tangri, Burt, and Johnson, Part Two, see Rubin and Borgers, Part One; and Riger, Part Three, see Joy A. Livingston, "Responses to Sexual Harassment on the Job: Legal, Organizational, and Individual Actions," *Journal of Social Issues* 38, no. 4 (1982): 16–17. See also Fitzgerald et al., "The Incidence and Dimensions of Sexual Harassment in Academia and the Workplace," p. 162.

6. In addition to Riger, Part Three, see Inger W. Jensen and Barbara A. Gutek, "Attributions and Assignment of Responsibility in Sexual Harassment," *Journal of Social Issues* 38, no. 4 (1982): 129–30. See, also, Fitzgerald et al., "The Incidence and Dimensions of Sexual Harassment in Academia and the Workplace," p. 154; Livingston, "Responses to Sexual Harassment on the Job: Legal, Organizational, and Individual Actions," pp. 16–17; Benson and Thomson, "Sexual Harassment on a University Campus," p. 246.

7. In addition to Riger, Part Three, and Rubin and Borgers, Part One, see Fitzgerald et al., "The Incidence and Dimensions of Sexual Harassment in Academia and the Workplace," p. 162.

8. In addition to Tangri, Burt, and Johnson, Part Two, and Rubin and Borgers, Part One, see Benson and Thomson, "Sexual Harassment on a University Campus," pp. 243–48.

9. In addition to Riger, Part Three, and Rubin and Borgers, Part One, see Benson and Thomson, "Sexual Harassment on a University Campus," p. 246, and Livingston, "Responses to Sexual Harassment on the Job," pp. 16–17.

10. In addition to Riger, Part Three, see Jensen and Gutek, "Attributions and Assignment of Responsibility in Sexual Harassment," pp. 126–30.

11. In addition to Riger, Part Three; Tangri, Burt, and Johnson, Part Two; and Rubin and Borgers, Part One, see Fitzgerald et al., "The Incidence and Dimensions of Sexual Harassment in Academia and the Workplace," pp. 159–69, 172–73.

12. See Richard Hagen, *The Bio-Sexual Factor,* 1st ed. (Garden City, N.Y.: Doubleday, 1979).

13. In *Meritor Savings Bank, FSB* v. *Vinson,* 40 EPD, 36,159 at 42,579, the U.S. Supreme Court agreed with Bork's dissenting opinion that Vinson's workplace behavior was relevant, but only as evidence that the sexual advances were wanted or unwanted, not as evidence that she did or did not voluntarily consent to sexual relations with Taylor. Thus, the Supreme Court also agreed with the federal appeals court that the issue of voluntariness is not relevant to Title VII sexual harassment claims.

14. Vincent J. Apruzzese, "Selected Recent Developments in EEO Law: The Civil Rights Act of 1991, Sexual Harassment, and the Emerging Role of ADR," *Labor Law Journal,* 43, No. 6 (1992), pp. 325–26; Elizabeth Drew, "Letter from Washington," *The New Yorker* (June 17, 1991), p. 104.

15. 109 US SCt 2115 (1989), 50 EPD 39,021.

16. Apruzzese, "Selected Recent Developments in EEO Law," p. 326; Drew, "Letter from Washington," pp. 104–105.

17. Apruzzese, "Selected Recent Developments in EEO Law," p. 336; Drew, "Letter from Washington," p. 106.

18. See Woerner and Oswald, Part Three.

19. See also York, "Defining Sexual Harassment in Workplaces: A Policy-Capturing Approach," pp. 845–46, as well as Malovich and Stake, "Sexual Harassment on Campus: Individual Differences in Attitudes and Beliefs," pp. 78–80.

Part One

Definitions and Policy Descriptions

1

Sexual Harassment in Universities During the 1980s

Linda J. Rubin and Sherry B. Borgers

Sexual harassment is a pervasive problem throughout higher education. Till defined academic sexual harassment as "the use of authority to emphasize the sexuality or sexual identity of a student in a manner which prevents or impairs the student's full enjoyment of educational benefits, climate, or opportunities."[1] Many universities have adopted a definition similar to this in order to censor behaviors that represent unwanted sexual attention toward students. This is an attempt to prevent this unwanted attention from negatively affecting the student's academic performance, opportunities, and personal adjustment. There is no easy way to categorize students who are affected by this since individuals of all ages, sexes, socioeconomic classes, and ethnic groups have experienced the problem. Although there is general agreement that sexual harassment has been and continues to be a problem in academia, the research studies have been conducted in isolation and no comprehensive synthesis exists. The purpose of this review is to synthesize the current research concerning instructor-student sexual harassment in university settings. . . .

From *Sex Roles* 23, no. 7/8 (1990): 397, 399–411. Reprinted by permission of Plenum Publishing Corporation.

PROBLEM OF DEFINITION

A clear definition of sexual harassment has yet to be commonly accepted in the psychology research. The majority of studies conducted on sexual harassment have generated their own definitions and lists of specific behaviors identified as harassment.

The most common cited definition[2] identified five types of sexual harassment: generalized sexist remarks or behaviors; inappropriate and offensive, but essentially sanction-free, sexual advances; solicitation of sexual activity or other sex-linked behavior by promise of rewards; coercion of sexual activity by threat of punishment; and sexual assaults. The identification of these behaviors as harassment was based upon the descriptive information provided by a sample of respondents from several types of educational institutions. Due to the extremely limited response rate of this sample (n = 259/8000), it was difficult to draw any definitive conclusions. Thus, these widely cited results must be used with great caution because of the unacceptably low return rate.

In an attempt to distinguish between factors that clearly define sexual harassment and those that lead to disagreement or an ambiguous definition, Reilly, Carpenter, Dull, and Bartlett[3] assessed student and faculty perceptions at the University of California, Santa Barbara. The researchers reported a high degree of consensus in defining cases of harassment among all respondents of both sexes. More specifically, extreme cases of sexual harassment and cases that were clearly not harassment were recognized with consistency. Behaviors or statements involving coercion, intimacy, or sexuality on the part of the instructor contributed significantly to the judgment of an incident as sexual harassment. In contrast, a prior relationship between the instructor and the student or provocative actions on the part of the student tended to increase consensus that the incident did *not* describe harassment. If, however, a prior relationship existed and the student refused to date the instructor, then ratings for harassment significantly increased.

In a replication and expansion of the Reilly et al. study, Weber-Burdin and Rossi[4] surveyed undergraduates attending the University of Massachusetts. As in the Santa Barbara study, these findings indicated a remarkable similarity between the two studies. It seems that the "definiteness" of sexual harassment is likely to be influenced by the actions of both participants, whereas the "seriousness" of sexual harassment is more likely to be affected by the male instructor's behavior.

Overall, the Reilly et al. and Weber-Burdin and Rossi studies yielded similar findings. It seems that actions by either person in the vignettes influenced perceptions of sexual harassment and that moderate levels of harassment created confusion in perceptions. Since these are analog studies, it is difficult to know whether responses to these vignettes actually reflect the behaviors of students when they are confronted with a real sexual harassment situation.

At Iowa State University, Adams, Kottke, and Padgitt[5] conducted a study to determine what behaviors are defined as sexual harassment. There was a high degree of consensus for the three most overt sexual behaviors; more than 90 percent of all respondents believed physical advances, sexual propositions, and bribery were clearly forms of sexual harassment. Although more variation existed in the responses to the less severe behavioral categories (i.e., sexist comments, undue attention, verbal sexual advances, body language, invitations), the majority of both female and male students still identified verbal sexual advances, body language, and invitations as harassment. Although the response rate for this study was only 37 percent, it included a representative distribution of men and women as well as graduate and undergraduate students.

Extreme cases of harassment and the clear absence of harassment are readily identified. However, moderate levels of harassment create confusion in perception.[6] This finding is supported by Sullivan and Bybee,[7] who found that students perceived two distinct levels of harassment: mild and severe. The moderate level was not clearly distinguishable from the other two levels; this issue needs more study. Furthermore, the milder forms of harassing behaviors are less likely to be defined as sexual harassment.[8] According to Reilly et al. and Weber-Burdin and Rossi, this confusion may be introduced, at least in part, by prior relationships between instructors and students. It seems that faculty and students are unclear about whether or not "some" sexual behaviors are acceptable.

Numerous studies have defined sexual harassment by labeling specific behaviors, along a continuum, that identify harassment by type and severity.[9] The specific behaviors identified as sexual harassment range in number from three to eight, and increase in severity from mild to severe. Although variations exist in the language used to describe these behaviors, the eight behaviors outlined by Adams, Kottke, and Padgitt are representative: sexist comments, undue attention, verbal sexual advances, body language, invitations, physical advances, explicit sexual propositions, and sexual bribery.

In order to determine whether or not a preestablished set of social definitions and norms regarding sexual harassment actually exists, Padgitt and Padgitt[10] investigated the cognitive structure of sexual harassment among university students. Using the continuum approach, the researchers assumed that conformity in the succession of sexually harassing behaviors would be indicative of an existing cognitive structure among the population. The eight behaviors chosen for potential placement on the continuum were sexist comments, undue attention (e.g., flirting), verbal sexual advances, body language (e.g., leering), personal invitations, physical advances, explicit sexual propositions, and sexual bribery. Although, conceptually, the difference between "offensive" behaviors and "harassing" behaviors may be unclear for some respondents, evidence supporting a continuum was found for both types of behavior. The women were highly consistent in describing behaviors that were perceived to be harassing as also offensive; men were less consistent in their perceptions. Both continuums identified clear patterns for both sexes; however, men and women did differ in their perceptions of where offensiveness begins and where sexual behaviors become harassment. Based upon the evidence of a continuum, the researchers concluded that, in general, a preestablished set of definitions exists for sexual harassment and that "these behaviors do systematically convey meaning to male and female students."[11]

One of the major problems with this body of literature is the lack of a commonly accepted definition of sexual harassment. Most researchers operationally define sexual harassment along a continuum, and the behaviors on this continuum differ by type and severity. However, these similarities have not been sufficient to create a cohesive body of literature in this area. If a clear set of preestablished definitions exist,[12] then they need to be explicitly stated, commonly accepted, and actively employed in research, counseling, and policy. Our effectiveness in each of these areas can only improve with agreement on the basic question of definition.

INCIDENCE

The frequency of sexual harassment is commonly addressed in the literature; however, reported frequencies vary depending on the definition given by the researcher. In addition, an enormous amount of ambiguity exists when individuals are forced to deal directly with sexual harassment in their own lives. Because of this ambiguity, it is likely that the actual incidence of all forms of sexual harassment is underreported.

Till[13] concluded that incidents of sexual harassment were not confined to any particular type of institution. Rather, harassing behaviors occurred at large and small public institutions, private institutions, vocational schools, and religiously affiliated schools. However, the research conducted on the incidence of sexual harassment has focused primarily on large public institutions. Each study that presented data on the incidence of sexual harassment is described individually in order to identify the specific population under consideration.

In a widely cited study, Benson and Thomson[14] sought detailed accounts of sexual harassment experiences among 269 randomly selected female students in their senior year at Berkeley. Fifty-nine percent of the respondents estimated that sexual harassment occurs "occasionally" and more than one-third of the sample indicated that they were personally acquainted with at least one victim of sexual harassment. Furthermore, 29.7 percent of the respondents reported that they had personally experienced some form of sexual harassment from male instructors during their college careers. Instances of overt sexual bribery were assumed to be rare as there were only three cases reported by these respondents.

Lott, Reilly, and Howard[15] surveyed 927 male and female students, faculty, and staff at the University of Rhode Island. Of the respondents, 13 percent reported personal knowledge of a sexual assault on someone else. When asked about personal experience, 8 percent of the males and 7.1 percent of the females reported at least one incident of sexual assault. Personal knowledge of the sexual intimidation of another person was reported in 68 cases (7.3 percent); this, however, was self-report and hearsay. In contrast, only twelve incidents (1.3 percent) were personally experienced by respondents. Significantly more females than males believed women were often sexually insulted. The perceptions of sexual insults directed toward men were similar for female and male respondents. Only 30 percent of the women reported never being sexually insulted by a man on campus whereas 82 percent of the men reported never being sexually insulted by another man.

In a 1986 study, Reilly, Lott, and Gallogly[16] observed 393 juniors, seniors, and graduate students. Both men and women reported witnessing sexually harassing behaviors in classrooms, most often from male professors. Outside the classroom and in job-related situations, women received sexual advances more often than men. In all situations, some male students reported sexual harassment from other men whereas female students rarely reported such behavior by other women.

Wilson and Kraus[17] conducted a study on the sexual harassment of undergraduate and graduate students at East Carolina University with 108 males and 226 females, but reported only the results for females, an obvious weakness. They found that 33 percent of the female students reported being sexually harassed by male teachers. The percentage breakdown of respondents who experienced each of the seven types of harassment is as follows: 20.2 percent verbal harassment; 15.4 percent leering or ogling;

13.6 percent remarks about clothing, body, or sexual attitudes; 8.9 percent unwanted touching, patting, or pinching; 4.9 percent subtle pressures for sexual activity; 2.2 percent demanding sexual favors; and .9 percent physical assault. Overall, the most severe types of harassing behaviors were experienced less frequently than were the milder forms. Those authors also examined nine variables (e.g., feminist beliefs, grade point average, femininity/masculinity) for female students reporting episodes of sexual harassment. Information regarding the motivation of the offender might also help provide some understanding of this issue.

Maihoff and Forest[18] conducted a study at Michigan State University that was designed to assess the incidence of sexual harassment and the degree of disapproval among women students. The 478 respondents were either juniors, seniors, or graduate students. Twenty-five percent of the respondents reported at least one incident of sexual harassment. The reported results focused mainly on harassing behavior between the women students and their work supervisors or co-workers. Not all questions asked about sexual harassment in a work setting were asked about an academic setting. Therefore, it is difficult to draw specific conclusions about instructor-student sexual harassment.

In related articles, Metha and Nigg[19] reported their findings on the sexual harassment of male and female students, faculty, and staff at Arizona State University. A substantial proportion of the respondents indicated that sexual harassment may be a problem in the university community. Nine percent of all respondents had experienced some form of sexual harassment at the university; 13 percent of the women and 5 percent of the men had been victims. Of those individuals who reported being harassed, 43 percent reported a negative impact on their education or career, but only 18 percent of the men and 20 percent of the women made formal complaints.

In 1983 the Metha and Nigg study only reported results for women. The reported incidence was 13.3 percent for students, 13.7 percent for faculty, and 11.2 percent for staff members. More complete information from these studies would be useful, especially regarding male responses.

Cammaert[20] concluded that the findings of sexual harassment on frequency from one Canadian campus were comparable to the results found in the United States. Eighty-six graduate and 264 undergraduate women participated; 23 percent of the graduates and 30 percent of the undergraduates reported that they had encountered sexually inappropriate behaviors. Verbal harassment was said to have occurred "a few times" by 38 percent of the undergraduates and 36 percent of the graduate students. Nonverbal harassment reportedly occurred "a few times" by 44 percent of the undergraduate and 19 percent of the graduate students. In this study, more precise language would be helpful.

McCormack[21] studied sexual harassment by focusing on students in the sciences. Undergraduate and graduate students of both sexes were randomly surveyed at sixteen universities. Nine percent of the participants stated that they had been harassed; 2 percent of the men and 17 percent of the women reported harassment by a teacher. According to McCormack, students experience more sexual harassment at the undergraduate level than at the high school level.

Schneider[22] surveyed 356 randomly selected graduate women at a major East Coast public university. This sample represented a wide cross section of graduate students across a range of ages, marital status, academic departments, graduate status (i.e., master's, doctoral), length of time in their programs, and number of years of departmental funding. At least one experience of sexual harassment was supported by 60 percent of this sample. The author also found a clear pattern of unmarried women as the more frequent victims of pressured sexual relations. Thirteen percent of the women had consensually dated a faculty member, and 9 percent reported pressure to date or have sex with a faculty member. The majority (86 percent) of those women receiving pressure refused the sexual advances.

Fitzgerald et al.[23] surveyed two universities (No. 1, 903 women and 491 men; No. 2, 843 women and 362 men), and concluded that sexual harassment is widespread and commonly experienced by women students. These authors also sampled female faculty, staff, and administrators, and found that the administrators reported more experiences of sexual harassment. The instrument used was carefully constructed and built upon the results of similar studies. Over 31 percent of women students reported some form of sexual harassment and 15 percent of the students experienced seductive sexual approaches from their professors. The authors noted that these were conservative estimates. Direct sexual coercion appears much less widespread.

In two studies, which are related to the topic of sexual harassment, researchers examined sexual behavior between psychology educators and graduate students. Instead of identifying the experience as sexual harassment, the terms "sexual contact" and "sexual intimacy" were used. The behaviors examined in these studies would correspond to the more severe forms of harassment described in other studies. They were specifically defined as intercourse or genital stimulation. The term "educators" is intended to refer to instructors, supervisors, and advisors.

The first of those two studies was conducted by Pope, Levenson, and Schover.[24] These researchers surveyed 481 male and female psychologists who were members of the American Psychological Association (APA) Division 29 (Psychotherapy). Reportedly, 10 percent of the respondents had experienced sexual contact with psychology educators while they were graduate students. As educators, 13 percent of the respondents reported sexual contact with their students. Despite these findings, only 2 percent of the respondents believed sexual relationships between educators and students could be beneficial. Significantly more women than men reported sexual contact as students; significantly more men than women reported such contact as educators. These sex differences fit into the pattern demonstrated in other sexual harassment research.

The second study that focused on sexual contact between psychology educators and graduate students was conducted by Glaser and Thorpe.[25] The 464 participants were all female members of APA Division 12 (Clinical Psychology). Overall, 17 percent of the respondents indicated that they had experienced sexual contact with psychology educators while they were graduate students. A sizable minority (31 percent) of the women reported sexual advances by psychology educators that did not lead to actual sexual contact. It appears that the frequency of sexual contact between psychology educators and their students is comparable to the instructor-student sexual harassment that is found in the universities in general.

When examining the incidence of sexual harassment in universities a pattern emerges—it exists as a common occurrence in our universities. While reported frequencies vary, it is suggested that 30 percent may be a reliable estimate.[26] This is not a new problem but one that apparently continues to exist for large numbers of women in our universities.

REACTIONS TO SEXUAL HARASSMENT

Considering the high incidence of instructor-student sexual harassment in academia, it is important to know how students behave to manage harassing situations. Information regarding the effectiveness of such strategies will help researchers, counselors, and policymakers improve their interventions.

Sullivan and Bybee[27] examined factors that may predict reporting behaviors in victims of sexual harassment. The 219 female undergraduate students at Michigan State University were given standardized scenarios that described one of nine incidents of sexual harassment. The scenarios were manipulated for harasser-victim power differential and for severity of harassment. Subjects were asked to respond to the scenario by rating their perceptions of the severity, the likelihood of occurrence, and various factors associated with reporting procedures. As expected, female students were more likely to report incidents of severe harassment than incidents of mild harassment. It is important to note that the following four factors significantly contributed to the students' predicted reporting behaviors: severity of harassment, fear of not being believed, beliefs in the effectiveness of reporting, and fear of the reporting procedures. In addition, female students were more likely to report sexual harassment to a woman rather than a man and to someone outside the harasser's department.

As previously mentioned, a discrepancy seems to exist between what students believed they would do and what they actually do when confronted with a sexually harassing situation. According to Adams et al.,[28] most subjects stated that they would report such incidents; however, not one actual victim made an official complaint. Reasons cited in their study included fear of retaliation, fear of not being believed, fear of being accused of provocation, and lack of knowledge regarding how to go about making a report.

Benson and Thomson[29] asked sexual harassment victims how they attempted to manage their situations. Thirty percent of the students did not discuss the harassment with the instructor. In the majority of these cases, the unwanted sexual attention continued. A sizable minority (44 percent) of the victims discontinued all contact with the instructor. Reportedly, 70 percent of the victims did communicate their displeasure "in various ways" to the instructor and were more effective in stopping the harassment. The 70 percent figure seems to be a high rate of confrontation between students and instructors. Since the authors have not identified what behaviors the phrase "in various ways" refer to, it is impossible to know which specific behaviors were effective in stopping the harassment.

According to Cammaert,[30] the most common strategy employed to handle sexual harassment situations was to ignore the perpetrator. Although emotional side effects such as anger, frustration, depression, and anxiety were found for severe types of harassment, very few victims reported the incident to a person or an organization with the authority to act on the problem.

Many students who have experienced sexual harassment do not know where to go for information, counseling, or to make a formal complaint.[31] Metha and Nigg also reported that only 18 percent of the male victims and 20 percent of the female victims actually made formal complaints. The men tended to be more satisfied with the formal reporting process than were the women.

While the majority of women disapprove of sexually harassing behaviors, they have found such behaviors to be unavoidable and thus take them for granted.[32] It appears women may forego reporting procedures as the harassment is accepted, and the reporting procedures are either feared or are expected to make no real difference. Perhaps if the reporting process was demystified and women felt reporting actually improved their situations, they would be more willing to take the risk of making a formal complaint.

GENDER DIFFERENCES

Both men and women have witnessed sexually harassing behaviors in classrooms.[33] In the majority of sexual harassment situations, the harasser is male, an authority figure, and older than his students. The victim is often a younger female of subordinate status. This pattern of interaction has been documented in several studies.[34] This is not surprising as it reflects traditional sex role differences that are evident in our culture.

Fitzgerald et al.[35] stated that male students are quite unlikely to be harassed. In a few instances, male students have reported sexual harassment from other men whereas female students have rarely reported such behaviors by other women. Women described more negative consequences than men, except in cases when males were sexually harassed by other males.[36]

Due to the higher rate of victimization, more information exists on female perceptions of sexual harassment than on male perceptions. Nevertheless, when men and women are compared, the existing evidence demonstrates important sex role differences. For instance, women are more likely than men to identify specific behaviors as sexual harassment.[37] Furthermore, women and men have substantially different attitudes regarding the acceptability of sexual behaviors. Males are significantly more accepting of harassing behaviors than are females.[38] In general, men are reported to believe sexual behaviors at school are more natural, more expectable, and less problematic than do women.[39] Men also tend to believe women contribute to their own harassment.[40] This notion may be perpetuated by observations that women often put up with sexual harassment, blame themselves, and view it as inevitable.[41]

In superior-subordinate relationships, like that of the instructor and the student, the power *always* rests with the person of authority. Thus, in instructor-student relationships, ethical behavior must ultimately be the responsibility of the teacher. These findings regarding assignment of responsibility for sexual harassment demonstrate the need to reeducate both female and male faculty and students regarding their attributions in harassing situations.

There also exists a difference in terms of beliefs about how sexual harassment should be handled.[42] Males are more likely to believe individuals should deal with it on their own. Females are more likely to believe it should be handled in conjunction with the university. Once again, it may be difficult for female students to deal effectively with sexual harassment on their own as they have very little power in the offending relationship with which to work.

INDIVIDUAL DIFFERENCES

Individual differences affect our perceptions of sexual harassment. In addition to the sex differences that were discussed in the previous section, Fitzgerald et al.[43] discussed two mediating variables: age and severity of the incident. Predictably, there was less tolerance for the more severe incidents. It has been suggested that female graduate students experience more harassment than female undergraduate students;[44] this may be due to the fact that graduate students have closer associations with their instructors. Another plausible explanation is that younger persons are more tolerant of these behaviors than older persons.[45] It has also been found by Maihoff and Forrest[46] that situational variables play a large role when it comes to evaluating specific behaviors; thus women do not unequivocally disapprove of all forms of sexual harassment.

The following factors have *not* been found to contribute to sexual harassment: feminist beliefs,[47] length of education,[48] family background characteristics,[49] and self-confidence.[50] However, a loss of self-confidence and disillusionment with male faculty have been found to be direct costs of sexual harassment.[51] Most studies have focused on definition and incidence rather than individual differences. More research in this area is needed.

CONCLUSIONS AND IMPLICATIONS

There are several conclusions to be drawn from this review. It is important to recognize that sexual harassment exists on all types of university campuses. There is some consistency in identifying sexual harassment when it occurs, although different labels and categories may be used. There is a need for a commonly accepted definition and a standardized instrument so that comparable results can be obtained; Fitzgerald et al. are developing such an instrument. Once an instrument is developed, a national profile needs to be established.

Until the problem of sexual harassment is resolved, students and faculty need access to information about coping strategies. Individuals must be taught how to cope with this harassment since institutional change is very slow. University counseling centers might offer workshops that focus on strategies for coping with sexual harassment and affirmative action offices might focus on prevention as well as remediation.

The quality of the research needs to be improved. Researchers must randomly select samples of both females and males. Efforts need to be made to increase the return rates of studies. Also, findings need to be reported in their entirety. Many of the studies use an analog methodology and do not examine actual behaviors. As earlier indicated, a common definition and standardized instrument are needed if research is to be useful to educators and policymakers.

Another important finding is that in many cases sexual harassment often goes unreported, especially the less severe forms.[52] In fact, the most common strategy is to ignore the perpetrator.[53] The incidents that are reported are likely to be the more severe ones and these are experienced less frequently.[54] There is a discrepancy in that students believe they will report the incidents but fail to do so. The reporting process clearly needs to be demystified; information should be readily available concerning where to go and how to file a complaint. Since female students are more likely to report sexual harassment to a woman outside the harasser's department,[55] it seems institutions need to be sensitive to this fact. Offices such as counseling centers and student assistance centers might help make these procedures more public.

The variables that affect reporting are also important to note. Many of the findings suggest that females and males have different experiences in and attitudes about sexual harassment. Kenig and Ryan[56] found that females and males differed significantly in their judgments, with women more likely to define behaviors as harassing and men more likely to believe victims have contributed to their own problem. Perhaps women are less tolerant of harassment because they are more often the victims. Men may be more satisfied with the reporting procedures because they have less need to use them. Such differences in gender are too important to be ignored.

Individual differences in age and status also need to be addressed. In academia, the majority of persons with occupational prestige are males who are older than their students. The differential power and status between educators and students is a central component in sexual harassment and must be addressed by educators and policymakers. Institutions need to be alert to the possible misuse of this status and power.

Faculty members need to take responsibility when they see their colleagues engaging in harassing behaviors. To ignore these behaviors is unethical for those of us in areas where emphasis is on the welfare of the individual. It is disturbing to note that the incidence of instructor-student sexual contact in the field of psychology is comparable to other areas. There is no indication that psychologists are any more ethical in conduct or sensitivity to the issue than instructors in other fields. Commitment must be to the education of students, not to the protection of unethical colleagues. Also, the individuals affected need to be encouraged to take responsibility for reporting incidents of sexual harassment.

Finally, it can be concluded that there are costs both to the individual and to the institution. The victim loses self-confidence, academic and work opportunities, letters of recommendation, and grades. In general, the student's professional development is hindered and the university acquires a negative image. Universities must examine their procedures and evaluate their usefulness. More education and responsiveness in the area of sexual discrimination are needed. The overall distribution of females and males in the university system needs to be improved. Sexual harassment cannot remain a hidden issue; educators need to solve this problem rather than to accept it.

In summary, it is noted that the status of sexual harassment during the 1980s has not shown that much of an improvement over the past 15 years. In the 1970s it was established that sexual harassment is illegal. Perhaps the 1990s is the time to make it clear that any form of sexual harassment is not only illegal but also unacceptable.

NOTES

1. F. J. Till, *Sexual Harassment: A Report on the Sexual Harassment of Students* (Washington, D.C.: Report of the National Advisory Council of Women's Educational Programs 1980), p. 7.

2. Ibid.

3. T. Reilly, S. Carpenter, V. Dull, and K. Bartlett, "The Factorial Survey: An Approach to the Defining of Sexual Harassment on Campus," *Journal of Social Issues* 38 (1982): 99–110.

4. E. Weber-Burdin and P. H. Rossi, "Defining Sexual Harassment on Campus: A Replication and Extension," *Journal of Social Issues* 38 (1982): 111–20.

38   Part One: Definitions and Policy Descriptions

5. J. W. Adams, J. L. Kottke, and J. S. Padgitt, "Sexual Harassment of University Students," *Journal of College Student Personnel* 24 (1983): 484–90.

6. Reilly et al., "The Factorial Survey: An Approach to the Defining of Sexual Harassment on Campus," pp. 99–110, and Weber-Burdin and Rossi, "Defining Sexual Harassment on Campus; A Replication and Extension," pp. 111–20.

7. M. Sullivan and D. I. Bybee, "Female Students and Sexual Harassment: What Factors Predict Reporting Behavior," *Journal of the National Association for Women Deans, Administrators, and Counselors* 50 (1987): 11–16.

8. Adams et al., "Sexual Harassment of University Students," pp. 484–90.

9. Ibid.; D. J. Benson and G. E. Thomson, "Sexual Harassment on a University Campus: The Confluence of Authority Relations, Sexual Interest and Gender Stratification," *Social Problems* 29 (1982): 236–51; L. P. Cammaert, "How Widespread Is Sexual Harassment on Campus?" *International Journal of Women's Studies* 8 (1985): 388–97; S. Kenig and J. Ryan, "Sex Differences in Levels of Tolerance and Attribution of Blame for Sexual Harassment on a University Campus," *Sex Roles* 15 (1986): 535–49; B. Lott, M. E. Reilly, and D. R. Howard, "Sexual Assault and Harassment: A Campus Community Case Study," *Signs: Journal of Women in Culture and Society* 8 (1982): 296–319; N. Maihoff and L. Forest, "Sexual Harassment in Higher Education: An Assessment Study," *Journal of the National Association for Women Deans, Administrators, and Counselors* 46 (1983): 3–8; S. C. Padgitt and J. S. Padgitt, "Cognitive Structure of Sexual Harassment: Implications for University Policy," *Journal of College Student Personnel* 34 (1986): 34–39; B. E. Schneider, "Graduate Women, Sexual Harassment, and University Policy," *Journal of Higher Education* 58 (1987): 46–65; and J. R. Wilson and L. A. Kraus, "Sexual Harassment in the University," *Journal of College Student Personnel* 24 (1983): 219–24.

10. Padgitt and Padgitt, "Cognitive Structure of Sexual Harassment; Implications for University Policy," pp. 34–39.

11. Ibid., p. 37.

12. Ibid., pp. 34–39.

13. Till, *Sexual Harassment.*

14. Benson and Thomson, "Sexual Harassment on a University Campus: The Confluence of Authority Relations, Sexual Interest and Gender Stratification," pp. 236–51.

15. Lott, Reilly, and Howard, "Sexual Assault and Harassment: A Campus Community Case Study," pp. 296–319.

16. M. E. Reilly, B. Lott, and S. M. Gallogly, "Sexual Harassment of University Students," *Sex Roles* 15 (1986): 333–358.

17. Wilson and Kraus, "Sexual Harassment in the University," pp. 219–24.

18. Maihoff and Forest, "Sexual Harassment in Higher Education: An Assessment Study," pp. 3–8.

19. A. Metha and J. Nigg, "Sexual Harassment: Implications of a Study at Arizona State University, *Women's Studies Quarterly* 10 (1982): 24–26, and

Metha and Nigg, "Sexual Harassment on Campus: An Institutional Response," *Journal of the National Association for Women Deans, Administrators, and Counselors* 46 (1983): 9–15.

20. Cammaert, "How Widespread Is Sexual Harassment on Campus?" pp. 388–97.

21. A. McCormack, "The Sexual Harassment of Students by Teachers: The Case of Students in Science," *Sex Roles* 13 (1985): 21–32.

22. Schneider, "Graduate Women, Sexual Harassment, and University Policy," pp. 46–65.

23. L. F. Fitzgerald et al., "The Incidence and Dimensions of Sexual Harassment in Academia and the Workplace," *Journal of Vocational Behavior* 32 (1988): 152–75.

24. K. S. Pope, H. Levenson, and L. R. Schover, "Sexual Intimacy in Psychology Training; Results and Implications of a National Survey," *American Psychologist* 34 (1979): 682–89.

25. R. D. Glaser and J. S. Thorpe, "Unethical Intimacy: A Survey of Sexual Contact and Advances between Psychology Educators and Female Graduate Students," *American Psychologist* 41 (1986): 43–51.

26. B. Dziech and L. Weiner, *The Lecherous Professor* (Boston: Beacon Press, 1984).

27. Sullivan and Bybee, "Female Students and Sexual Harassment: What Factors Predict Reporting Behavior," pp. 11–16.

28. J. W. Adams et al., "Sexual Harassment of University Students," pp. 484–90.

29. Benson and Thomson, "Sexual Harassment on a University Campus," p. 236–51.

30. Cammaert, "How Widespread Is Sexual Harassment on Campus?" pp. 388–97.

31. Metha and Nigg, "Sexual Harassment: Implications of a Study at Arizona State University," pp. 24–26.

32. Schneider, "Graduate Women, Sexual Harassment, and University Policy," pp. 46–65.

33. Reilly et al., "Sexual Harassment of University Students," pp. 333–58.

34. Benson and Thomson, "Sexual Harassment on a University Campus: What Factors Predict Reporting Behavior," pp. 236–51; Kenig and Ryan, "Sex Differences in Levels of Tolerance and Attribution of Blame for Sexual Harassment on a University Campus," pp. 535–49; Metha and Nigg, "Sexual Harassment on Campus: An Institutional Response," pp. 9–15; Reilly et al., "Sexual Harassment of University Students," pp. 333–58; and Wilson and Kraus, "Sexual Harassment in the University," pp. 219–24.

35. Fitzgerald et al., "The Incidence and Dimensions of Sexual Harassment in Academia and the Workplace," pp. 152–75.

36. Reilly et al., "Sexual Harassment of University Students," pp. 333–58.

37. Adams et al., "Sexual Harassment of University Students," pp. 484–90;

Kenig and Ryan, "Sex Differences in Levels of Tolerance and Attribution of Blame for Sexual Harassment on a University Campus," pp. 535–49; and Padgitt and Padgitt, "Cognitive Structure of Sexual Harassment," pp. 34–39.

38. Lott et al., "Sexual Assault and Harassment: A Campus Community Case Study," pp. 296–319; Metha and Nigg, "Sexual Harassment: Implications of a Study at Arizona State University," pp. 24–26; and Reilly et al., "Sexual Harassment of University Students," pp. 333–58.

39. Lott et al., "Sexual Assault and Harassment: A Campus Community Case Study," pp. 296–319.

40. Kenig and Ryan, "Sex Differences in Levels of Tolerance and Attribution of Blame for Sexual Harassment on a University Campus," pp. 535–49.

41. I. W. Jensen and B. A. Gutek, "Attributions and Assignment of Responsibility in Sexual Harassment," *Journal of Social Issues* 38 (1982): 121–36, and Reilly et al., "Sexual Harassment of University Students," pp. 333–58.

42. Kenig and Ryan, "Sex Differences in Levels of Tolerance and Attribution of Blame for Sexual Harassment on a University Campus," pp. 535–49.

43. Fitzgerald et al., "The Incidence and Dimensions of Sexual Harassment in Academia and the Workplace," pp. 152–75.

44. Ibid.

45. Lott et al., "Sexual Assault and Harassment: A Campus Community Case Study," pp. 296–319.

46. Maihoff and Forest, "Sexual Harassment in Higher Education: An Assessment Study," pp. 3–8.

47. Wilson and Kraus, "Sexual Harassment in the University," pp. 219–34.

48. McCormack, "The Sexual Harassment of Students by Teachers: The Case of Students in Science," pp. 21–32.

49. Ibid.

50. D. Lester et al., "Is Personality Related to Judgments about Sexual Harassment?" *Psychological Reports* 59 (1986): 1114.

51. Benson and Thomson, "Sexual Harassment on a University Campus," pp. 236–51.

52. Adams et al., "Sexual Harassment of University Students," pp. 484–90, and Metha and Nigg, "Sexual Harassment: Implications of a Study at Arizona State University," pp. 24–26.

53. Cammaert, "How Widespread Is Sexual Harassment on Campus?" pp. 236–51.

54. Wilson and Kraus, "Sexual Harassment in the University," pp. 219–24.

55. Sullivan and Bybee, "Female Students and Sexual Harassment: What Factors Predict Reporting Behavior," pp. 11–16.

56. Kenig and Ryan, "Sex Differences in Levels of Tolerance and Attribution of Blame for Sexual Harassment on a University Campus," pp. 535–49.

2

Harassment Policies in the University

Alan Charles Kors

Current discussions of efforts to protect people from behaviors defined as "harassment" occur in a minefield of passionate debates about rights, individual and group identities, a proper understanding of discrimination, and the nature and limits of power. This is a remarkable set of issues in any time; in our time, it reflects and crystallizes the deepest moral, social, and political concerns.

At universities, harassment policies raise questions of the restriction of freedom of speech and expression precisely at institutions that, nominally at least, have defined unfettered first amendment freedoms as vital to the well-being both of education and society. Ironically, some who supported the "free-speech movement" in the 1960s with passionate conviction now favor, with equal conviction, Herbert Marcuse's notion that a content-neutral definition of free speech constitutes "repressive tolerance." The enactment of academic harassment policies has left paradox and dissonance in its wake.

It is essential that extraordinarily broad freedom of speech and expression be preserved; "hate speech" is less threatening to human liberation from ignorance and abusive power than the legitimization of expedient restrictions upon that freedom. Even without the new harassment policies, our existing laws and codes protect individuals—or, more

From *Society* 28, no. 4 (1991): 22–25, 28, 29. Copyright © 1991. Reprinted by permission of Transaction.

precisely, if enforced, would protect individuals—from terrorist threats, molestation, assault, property damage, vandalism, conspiracy to deprive individuals of constitutional rights, and invidious discrimination. Fair persons disagreeing with these propositions still would not want to advance covertly policies that mask partisan political agendas under the guise of enhanced protection of individuals. In the politicized world of current academia, the perceived or real need to protect individuals from illegal or immoral behaviors is being used as a pretext for, at best, privileging one very particular ideological agenda and school of social thought, and, at worst, for creating a repressive apparatus that seeks to censor, directly or indirectly, unwelcome interpretations of the world. It is important for open minds to consider the context and actual implications of the "harassment" issue at our universities.

Since the 1960s in America, those judged (rightly or wrongly) to think most deeply about the consequences of both the end of legal racial segregation and the rapid movement of women into all areas of public life have defined (for academic, legal, and journalistic minds, at least) the criteria of the moral progress or regression of our society. Part of that power is moral: the ability to appeal to consistent application or extension of American ideals of fairness, decency, and ethical community. Part of that power is political and legal: the ability to influence legislative and judicial outcome. Part of that power is rhetorical: the ability to control a symbolic environment in which we judge as much by labeling, metaphor, and *ad hominem* argument as by complex analysis and nuanced judgment. The control of symbolic environment is dramatic, given human tendency to transform almost all issues into symbolic terms. Such control manifests itself most effectively in the ability to define "crises" in relation to which the moral qualities of the actors in society will be determined. Racial and sexual "harassment" currently stands as one of those "crises" by which we are asked to evaluate our society's moral character. If we believe human relations and social work industries, the nation and, in particular, our college campuses are faced with a rising tide of hatred, violence, and other abuses and crimes directed against women, blacks, and gays. This claim has not been empirically confirmed by the sorts of evidence thus far presented.

It is far more likely that in the improved climate on campuses for all of these groups, incidents that would have been ignored in years past are now noted, reported, and protested. Indeed, given the tendency of universities to divide individuals by the attributes of race, sex, and sexual preference, to sensitize them to seeing almost all instances of human unkindness as manifestations of "racism, sexism, and homophobia," to give individual members of these groups official politicized voices and official histories of their oppression, the wonder is that American universities remain about the best places in the world to be, for example, for a gay, black female. Since the "multiculturalism" academics increasingly advocate these days is more the multiculturalism of Beirut than of Martin Luther King's "dream," universities perhaps actually will succeed in producing one day soon the civil wars they claim to administer. Nonetheless it is seemingly unchallenged dogma that a crisis of harassment is upon us.

The notion of "harassment" nominally operative in harassment policies arose from a commonsensical but equivocal extension of anti-discrimination legislation. What good was it to prevent job discrimination if an employer engaged in (or tolerated) behavior toward the new employees that prevented them from performing their jobs? The difficulty, requiring Solomonic wisdom, of course, was to delineate such behavior in a manner consistent with both anti-discriminatory goals and respect of individual rights and psychological differences. In matters of nuanced behavior and the infinite complexities of male and female interaction, finding a "reasonable person" criterion of what is "harassment" and what is the sort of rudeness or eccentricity, to which we all must at times adapt, is problematic. Difficulty, however, does not obviate perceived moral or legal obligation, and society now attempts to tune quite finely, in this time, the regulation of the behavioral and verbal expression of biases, prejudices, secular and religious values, romantic and sexual desires, flirtatious personalities, affinities and antipathies. Having committed itself to outlawing invidious (and indeed many other modes of) employment discrimination, society is seeking to outlaw those conditions that it sees as producing the same effect. To offer the paradigmatic cases, society decided, quite properly, that to hire someone black and burn a cross at his or her workplace, or to hire a woman and insist on sexual favors in return for fair evaluation of her work is the equivalent of employment discrimination. Protection is offered almost universally on the basis of race and sex, usually on the basis of religion and national origin, and often on the basis of sexual preference.

Paradigms rarely do justice to the actuality of behavior, however, and many less obvious judgments have been made over recent years concerning what constitutes such harassment, many of them inconsistent and ambiguous. Nonetheless, the broad intent of such decisions seems clear. A body of laws, administrative rulings, arbitrations and court decisions has established a doctrine that seeks to protect people from verbal or behavioral harassment that "threatens employment status," "interferes with work performance" or "creates an intimidating or offensive environment."

Employers increasingly are obliged to have policies in place that work to guarantee such protection. In recent years, a growing number of universities have adopted such policies not only for their nonacademic employees, but for their faculty and students as well. Whatever the problem of these harassment policies outside of the university, in the academy, and relating to academic life, they raise problems of a serious and disturbing nature.

In general, university harassment policies at major institutions, both private and public, offer protection to people on grounds of race, sex (or "gender," as we curiously say today), ethnicity, religion, and, often, sexual preference. In almost all cases, they extend protection to the interactions of administrators, faculty, staff, graduate students, and undergraduates in all possible permutations. At the University of Pennsylvania, for example, the policy in place since 1986 until the time of this writing defines racial harassment as:

Any behavior, verbal or physical, that stigmatizes or victimizes individuals on the basis of race, ethnic or national origin, and that (1) involves a stated or implicit threat to the victim's academic or employment status; (2) has the purpose or effect of interfering with an individual's work or performance; and/or (3) creates an intimidating or offensive academic, living, or work environment.

Policies relating to sexual harassment often are modified by the seemingly explicit phrase "unwanted sexual attention." Thus, the University of Pennsylvania's policy specifies:

The term "sexual harassment" refers to any unwanted sexual attention that (1) involves a stated or implicit threat to the victim's academic or employment status; (2) has the purpose or effect of interfering with an individual's academic or work performance; and/or (3) creates an intimidating or offensive academic, living, or work environment.

Since it is, above all else, the threats to first amendment rights of free speech that concern me here, I do not wish to devote too much attention to the "unwanted sexual attention" clauses of harassment policies, but several things should be noted about them. First, it is by no means clear that absent such harassment policies universities ever were unable to penalize, censure, or terminate employment on the grounds of sexual extortion and abuse of authority before they had harassment policies. Women at universities (and indeed everywhere) obviously should be protected from all physical sexual coercion, all pressures to trade intimacy for better grades or job promotions, all molestation, and indeed from all invidious discrimination that evaluates their work and their careers by anything other than appropriate, in this case, academic standards. Second, in the context of undergraduate sexual and academic political lives, it requires, to understate the case, great fairness, indeed, to interpret such a phrase as "unwanted sexual attention" in a manner that does not demean and dismiss every defense of any given male's behavior as "blaming the victim."

Not only "feminists" and "non-feminists," but also different schools of feminist thought, would define the terms "attention," "sexual," and "unwanted"—quite differently (perhaps categorically so), and it would be blindness not to see the willful dangers of that. In official literature distributed at the University of Pennsylvania, "jokes" (nothing added) and "questioning about one's private personal life" are cited as examples of that "unwanted sexual attention." In the reports of a committee that planned "diversity education" for freshmen at the University of Pennsylvania (sexism, racism, and heterosexism were mandatory topics for all dormitories with freshmen; "classicism," "ableism," and religious intolerance were optional topics), special attention was devoted to explaining harassment to incoming students. "Sexual harassment" was defined as "direct sexual advance from someone in authority or creation of an intimidating environment." Among the examples listed were "flirting" on the part of a teaching assistant, "many explicit sexual jokes," "nude slides in class presentations," and "stupid women" jokes. Sexual discrimination, which also is illegal at the University of Pennsylvania, was defined as "behavior and policies that disadvantage people on the basis of their sex," and examples included "seeming invisibility of women," "women's names not remembered/not introduced," "double standards in sexuality and socialization," and "body image: eating disorders, clothes." . . .

On closer inspection it turns out that the "unwanted" in the policy was not that of ordinary meaning. Declaring that "any sexual relations between any teacher [professor or graduate student TA] and a student [graduate or undergraduate]" will be presumptively a violation of its policy, the University explains itself as follows: "What might appear to be consensual, even to the parties involved, may in fact not be so." It is not unreasonable to gloss such a passage in light of the goal of the committee on diversity education to disclose to undergraduates the ways in which the oppressed—women, blacks, and gays—internalize the values of their oppressors. A "glossary of terms" that circulated, with the advice that "facilitators" define words so that freshmen have a common language, offered them "Psychological Captivity" as a state in which "prejudiced images and attitudes, ['perpetuated by dominant society'], influence the behavior of subordinates." Thus, self-assortment on the basis of shared interests and similar sensibilities, a dear side of the sixties, now gives way to . . . the view that voluntary, and even loving voluntary, intimacy is presumptively "harassment." Some universities even forbid "dating" in such circumstances, which raises dark questions about asking a student out for coffee or a drink to talk about Wittgenstein, God, death, or, for that matter, liberty.

Few share, at least publicly, the belief that the subjectively consensual private life of citizens, old enough to vote, is no business of any employer, even of the moral paragons who administer universities. The ostensible justification for such proscription is "the integrity of the classroom." Note, however, that it never was declared a threat to the "integrity" of that classroom in the 1960s for the current purveyors of such policies to sit up in consciousness-raising groups with students whose papers they would grade (or with professors who would grade their papers) the next day, or to be gassed on the barricades next to them, or to invite students whose exams they would analyze to join them on a march to Washington. That was liberation! And no one dared to ask about their intimate lives. In today's Animal Farm universities, however, it is "women good/men bad," and those ersatz women with false consciousness who do not understand this yet need be protected from themselves, even by those who earlier married their own students or professors. There is more to the definition of "harassment" at universities than meets the eye. We see this above all when we turn to questions of speech. . . .

Simply stated: You may say anything you wish at most American universities about whites, males, heterosexuals, Catholics, Jews as Israelis, or Jews as white Americans, members of the Unification Church, evangelical Protestants, and, offend them as you will, Episcopalians, the least protected sensitivity in the land. You may not offend militant blacks, politicized Hispanics, radical feminists, or activist gays. From the left, you may call moderate blacks "Oreos" or "Uncle Toms" with impunity—that is social criticism, not harassment! You may equally abuse antifeminist women as "barbie dolls," "mall chicks," and "psychological captives" with impunity (that is analysis, not stigmatization that "creates an offensive environment"!) You may tell white students whose parents died fighting for freedom that their mothers and fathers were, depending on contexts, oppressors, racists, sexists, or baby-killers (in Vietnam, though not in abortion clinics). You may exhibit a cross in urine. If the issue is the sensibilities of white, male, heterosexuals, however vulnerable their egos, universities will talk about the perils of freedom, and, indeed, correctly so! If the issue is the sensibilities of politically correct minorities (evangelicals and "Moonies" need not apply), universities will talk about the vulnerability of egos and the absurdity of an ahistorical definition of freedom. Why?

The answer lies in the notion of "repressive tolerance," and the increasingly institutionalized belief on American campuses that "historically oppressed groups," to wit, women, gays, blacks, and Hispanics—who, mysteriously, have also become "non-European" in origin and culture— exist on campuses not as free individuals, but as mere instances of American oppression. Having suffered, respectively, eons, millennia, centuries, and decades of American oppression, they shall be spared further offense by those look-alike, think-alike, oppress-alike white, heterosexual, unfeeling males by whom they are surrounded abusively on American campuses. The goal of progressive education is to bring the historically oppressed to consciousness of their official group-identity, their official group-history, and their official group-rights, rights that arise not from any modal or content-neutral understanding of due process or freedom, but from the requirements of their ideological and political "empowerment." Although administrations may enact or accept harassment policies that limit freedom of speech and expression out of pure administrative expediency, the motive force behind such policies is the desire of the self-appointed voices of the "oppressed"—recognized or not as such by their wards—to render the drama of oppression and liberation in vivid, symbolic terms. . . .

3

Sexual Harassment in Academe: Issues of Power and Coercion

Nancy Tuana

. . . The importance of a full understanding of the nature of sexual harassment is underscored by the fact that it is a precondition for the development and implementation of university and college codes of conduct for faculty members regarding sexual harassment, statements concerning the nature of academic sexual harassment in student handbooks, university sponsored workshops on academic sexual harassment, and so on. It is to such an analysis that this paper is addressed.

To aid in this analysis, I shall employ the victim-based definition compiled by the National Advisory Council on Women's Educational Programs in their report on the sexual harassment of postsecondary students.[1] As a result of their survey the Council was led to the following working definition:

> Academic sexual harassment is the use of authority to emphasize the sexuality or sexual identity of a student in a manner which prevents or impairs that student's full enjoyment of educational benefits, climate, or opportunities.[2]

. . . The term "harass" means to annoy or to coerce. Sexual harassment then, involves actions with sexual overtones that are annoying and

From *College Teaching* 33, no. 2 (1985): 53-57, 61-63. Reprinted with permission of the Helen Dwight Reid Educational Foundation. Published by Heldref Publications, 1319 Eighteenth Street, N.W., Washington, D.C. 20036–1802. Copyright © 1985.

attempts to coerce sexual activity. Given the meaning of the term "harass," I would refine the above definition of sexual harassment to read as follows:

> Academic sexual harassment is the use of authority to emphasize the sexuality or sexual identity of a student in a manner which is coercive or annoying and which thereby prevents or impairs that student's full enjoyment of educational benefits, climate, or opportunities.

. . . Let me stress that my intention in this paper will be to deal *only* with academic sexual harassment, that is, sexual harassment resulting from an abuse of institutional authority. Institutional authority is that power resulting from one's position in the academic institution. Although there are other types of sexual harassment (where one's power is derived from other sources), this analysis is motivated by the intention to clarify that type of sexual harassment governed by university codes of conduct.

In developing this analysis, I shall choose relatively non-controversial examples to illustrate the various manifestations of academic sexual harassment. Because of this, I acknowledge that this inquiry will not fully clarify certain controversial cases; especially those in which institutional authority is not the only source of power employed in the harassment: Since an analysis of the more complex and controversial situations presupposes a full understanding of the nature of sexual harassment in the less controversial cases, this essay will serve as a foundation for further analyses.

COERCION OF SEXUAL ACTIVITY BY THREAT OF PUNISHMENT

> No one believed that it happened to me. I received a D in a class that was a pre-med class. I was sure that I had at least a C or B, so I went to the professor's office to see why he gave me a D. He refused to discuss the matter with me unless I went to bed with him. Then he would raise the grade to a C. I went to the dean because a D in this class would keep me out of medical school. The dean just laughed at me and said that the professor was a respectable member of the faculty and that false accusations like this would wreck his reputation. I changed majors the next semester, but my reasons were more than sexual harassment. I was left with the fear that this professor was going to rape me because he became quite aggressive while I was in the office with him.[3]

According to the above definition, academic sexual harassment involves the use of the power one has as an authority to engage in sexual actions or sexually related actions which harm or annoy another. The above case offers an example of a situation in which a male faculty member is employing his power over a student to exact sexual actions from her, where such actions result in harm to the student.

The power possessed by an instructor over students in class is the power to evaluate their work, that is, to give them a grade, where such evaluation is based upon criteria which, for the most part, the instructor has designed. The power is accentuated if that instructor is also in the position to make or influence political decisions about that student (whether they are granted an assistantship, recommended for a job, etc.) or is the only instructor who has knowledge of a subject matter in which the student is particularly interested.

In the above example, the instructor is using the power he has to evaluate the student to attempt to coerce the student to participate in sexual actions with him. The instructor wants to engage in sexual acts with the student. This is a situation where the student does not want to participate in such actions with the instructor. Thus any sexual acts which the student submits to would be against her will. In cases such as this one, the faculty member employs his power to get or attempt to get the student to submit to his requests for sexual contact.

In addition, faculty members rely on the power of their position to assure their own safety from reprisals. Students believe, unfortunately all too justly, that in such situations it is their word against the instructor's, and they believe that their complaint will not be taken seriously. Too often complaints of sexual harassment filed by students are seen as an attempt to "get back at" an instructor who justly gave them a low grade. In addition, the student is often seen as responsible for the sexual interest of the instructor.

The view of blaming the victim was perhaps most blatantly voiced by Phyllis Schlafly to the Senate Labor and Human Resources Committee: "Virtuous women are seldom accosted by unwelcome sexual propositions or familiarities, obscene talk or profane language." She concludes that sexual harassment only happens when ". . . a nonvirtuous woman gives off body language which invites sexual advances, but she chooses to give her favors to Man A and not to Man B and he tries to get his share too."[4] This opinion is often echoed in studies done on sexual harassment, and in the word and attitudes of school administrators.[5] In addition, students often fear reprisals from the faculty members if they do report him or her, and students fear that their complaint will result in a questioning of their character and will call attention to their sex and away from their merit.[6]

The above case illustrates a case of attempted coercion. The student did not submit to sexual relations with the instructor in order to get the grade that she deserved in the class. This case also gives a working outline of the criteria which hold in the typical case of sexual harassment involving coercion. In such a case the student, although not desiring a sexual relationship with the instructor, submits to the request in order to retain the grade earned for the class. We thus have a list of five criteria which will hold in cases of coercion: ("F" = the instructor, "S" = the student, and "C" = have sexual contact with the instructor:

1. F wants S to C
2. S does not want to C
3. F threatens S with harm if S does not C
4. S does C
5. S does C only because of F's threat.

In the case of attempted coercion only 1–3 hold. The instructor attempts to coerce the student but is not successful.

To understand fully the nature of sexual harassment involving coercion, it will be necessary to analyze the above criteria. In order for an act to be coercive, I am claiming that the victims must be threatened with harm unless they partake in an action they would not do otherwise. At this point it will be helpful to consider whether the intention to harm is relevant. According to the third criterion, F threatens S with harm if S does not C. The important question is the relevance of F's intention to harm S if S does not consent to sexual contact.

I contend that as long as S has good reason to believe that F may intend harm, the intention to harm is not relevant. Regardless of whether F intends to follow through with the threat, he or she has still threatened S. What is limiting S's option, and forcing a choice between perhaps medical school and having sex with someone unwillingly, is F's threat. If S overheard F talking to a colleague about S saying that they were going to attempt to coerce S, but that they would be unable to follow through with the threat since they were about to be fired, then the threat would not be coercive since S would have no reason to believe that their options were in fact limited by F.*

Barring this type of unusual situation, if an instructor makes such a threat, the student knowing that an instructor has the power to carry through with the threat, and having no reason to doubt that they will

---

*"They" is used here, and elsewhere when unavoidable, instead of the very awkward "he or she" repeated *ad nauseam*.

do so if rebuffed, has been coerced by F if they have sexual contact. Thus F's intention to harm in such a case is irrelevant to the question as to whether or not S was coerced. Whether or not there is the intention to harm may be relevant to the moral gravity of the action of coercion, but such an intention is not a necessary condition for coercion.

The point here is that in saying that S's grade would be lowered or not raised to the level they deserved, F was threatening S whether or not F in fact intended to lower S's grade. The intention to harm is irrelevant to a threat having been made. The threat *results from* the fact of saying "I will not give you the grade you deserve unless you have sex with me."

Thus we see that S can be threatened even though F does not intend to follow through with the harm. Moreover, the threat can be either explicit or implicit. If F says "I will give you a D unless you have sex with me," the threat is explicit. In many cases however, the threat is implicit. Consider the following case:

> This occurred during my senior year [in] a one-on-one graduate studies course. This man asked me for dates repeatedly until I accepted one including his . . . [children] and my son. I rebuffed his attempted kiss and future requests for dates as gracefully as I could, but it was obvious that he was angry. . . . I had an "A" going into the final exam. One day before the exam he assigned me to read another book for the exam. I felt this was unreasonable, but attempted to purchase the book in order to skim it. I discovered that the book was out of print and entirely unavailable. I returned to his office to ask for help, but he offered no solution, only renewed his efforts to take me out. I avoided the request saying I had to study. I studied well and received a perfect score on the first three pages. The fourth page consisted of three essay and more short answer questions on the book he had assigned the day before. He called me at home that evening to tell me that I had failed the exam since the last portion was heavily weighted. I flirted and agreed to go out with him, at which point he announced that he knew I was a capable student who well deserved the "B" he would turn in as my grade.[7]

In this case the instructor has not explicitly said that unless the student had sex with him he would see to it that she received a grade lower than she deserved. But in a case such as this a threat has clearly been made. The student knew that the additional assignment was unjust. The student also knew that the instructor desired sexual contact with her. Given this the student had good reason to believe that the instructor would give her a grade lower than she deserved unless she catered to the instructor's desires.

The category of coercion or attempted coercion of sexual activity through threat of punishment thus can be seen as forming a continuum of types of situations. At one end of the continuum is the instructor who explicitly threatens to lower a student's grade unless that student permits sexual contact, and intends to do so should the student refuse. The second type of harassment involves an explicit threat without the intention to carry through. If an instructor threatens to lower a student's grade if he or she does not consent to sexual contact, but does not intend to carry through with the threat should the student refuse, such a case of sexual harassment would fall under this category. Third, the threat of harm is implicit, and the instructor intends to carry through with the harm should the student fail to do as desired. The above example of the instructor who failed a student on an unfair final illustrates this type of case. In addition, an instructor can implicitly threaten a student while having no intention to harm the student.

What all of the above four types of sexual harassment involving coercion share is that the threat is intended. In each case the instructor intends to threaten the student with certain harm if his or her wishes are refused. I contend that in addition to these four, there is an additional category which constitutes coercion or attempted coercion of sexual activity through threat of punishment. Unlike the other four categories the threat in this case is unintended.

UNINTENDED THREAT

Consider a situation in which an instructor desires to have a sexual relationship with one of her students. That student has to come to talk to her during her office hours concerning his grade. Although the student is carrying a "C" average, the teacher is concerned about his course work since she believes that the student is not fully applying himself. So she gives him a typical teacher pep talk, something like this:

"Troy, I've been listening to your comments in class and I can see from them that you are a very intelligent student who is able to make very astute connections between the ideas being discussed. However, your papers show little familiarity with the readings assigned. If you want a decent grade in this class you are going to have to demonstrate to me that you are really concerned about these issues, that you have applied yourself properly, and that you have fully satisfied my requirements for the class. I am not going to let you slip through in this class. Either you work up to my standards or I will fail you."

Let us assume that the instructor's intentions are to get a bright, but for some reason unmotivated, student to apply himself more seriously. That night the instructor recognizes the student at the local pub, sits down beside him, buys him a drink, and proceeds to tell him of her sexual attraction to him. Assume here that the instructor's intention is to make the student aware of her growing attraction and to see if there is a chance that it might be requited. The student, however, remembering the sternness of the instructor's comments and her warning that if he does not work up to standards, she will fail him, sees the confession of the instructor as containing a veiled threat that if he does not participate in sexual acts with her, he will fail the class.

In this case the instructor, without intending to do so, has threatened the student. If the student then agrees to a sexual relationship with the instructor because of the threat he believes has been made against him, he would be acting in a manner he would not otherwise have chosen. *His choice would have been determined by the harm he believes is threatened by the instructor.*

I have tried to map out an example of a situation in which it was reasonable for the student to believe that he had been implicitly threatened. It is my contention that if a student has good reason to believe that he or she has been threatened by an instructor in order to procure sexual contact because of something that the instructor has said or done, then even if the instructor has not intended the threat, *the student has been harassed.* The notion of "having good reason to believe" is complex, and I shall not here attempt to outline clear criteria for it, but I believe that I can clarify this notion more fully.

An important point to remember is that faculty members in taking their jobs sign a contract which binds them to a set of obligations. One group of these requirements concerns professional ethics. Many universities, including my own, have adopted the American Association of University Professors' statement of professional ethics to make these requirements explicit. Concerning the relationship of instructors to their students, the bulletin says the following:

As teachers, professors encourage the free pursuit of learning in their students . . . they demonstrate respect for students as individuals, and adhere to their proper role as intellectual guide and counselor. They make every reasonable effort to foster honest academic conduct and to assure that the evaluation of students reflects their true merit . . . they avoid any exploitation of students for their private advantage and acknowledge significant assistance from them. They protect students' academic freedom.[8]

As an instructor one is then obligated to set up a situation in which students in classes work in an atmosphere promoting intellectual development. It thus follows that instructors have an obligation to do nothing which could be reasonably seen by students as an inhibition to their intellectual development. Hence, the instructor's intention alone is not the only concern.

Given this, I claim that the above example in the pub is one of involving negligence on the part of the instructor. Despite the fact that she did not intend to threaten the student with a lower grade if he did not engage in sexual actions with her, she *should have known* that her actions could reasonably be so construed given the circumstances. This is a situation in which her claim to ignorance is not an acceptable excuse.

In cases like this, even if the instructor, when questioned about his or her actions, claimed there was no intent to lower the grade if the student did not agree to sex, we would be justified in rejecting this excuse as irrelevant. Given the obligations of instructors to evaluate students fairly and to promote an atmosphere of intellectual freedom, such actions would be unpardonable. Given the obligations explicitly stated in the handbooks, an instructor should have known better. Ignorance is thus inexcusable.

We thus have a fifth type of sexual harassment involving coercion: implicit unintended threat, no intended harm. This category of harassment is the most difficult to deal with since it involves the additional problem of clarifying when it is reasonable to believe that one has been threatened. Still it does not enable us to reject as irrelevant pleas of ignorance in the clear cases such as the one in the pub.

Sexual harassment involving coercion of sexual activity by threat of punishment thus involves five classes:

- Explicit intended threat, intention to harm
- Explicit intended threat, no intention to harm
- Implicit intended threat, intention to harm
- Implicit intended threat, no intention to harm
- Implicit unintended threat, no intention to harm.

The moral and legal severity of the harassment will depend upon the nature of the action the student is coerced to do, whether harm is in fact intended if the student refuses to comply, the nature of such harm if it is intended, and so on. . . .

GENERAL SEXIST BEHAVIOR OR REMARKS

Last year I went to see a professor about signing up for an independent study project. When he invited me into his office, and in the presence of another professor, he greeted me at the door saying something to the effect of "Well, well, what can I do for you?" After I told him that I wanted to take an independent study, and after he told me that I could not have it, he tried to get me to sign up for a class that he was teaching. Throughout this time, he was looking me up and down while making stops between runs. His colleague was so embarrassed that he kept his eyes on the floor.[9]

One physics professor gave his students a lecture on the effects of outer space on humans. His example consisted of crude drawings of a shapely woman supine in a vessel; the effects of vacuum were demonstrated by changes in the size of her "boobs." This man—a "mature" adult—told the story with all of the sniggering, head-hanging, and red-facedness I might have expected from an adolescent.[10]

This final category is probably the most controversial case of academic sexual harassment. One might argue that such cases are sexist and involve stereotyping, but are not situations in which students are being sexually harassed. In opposition to this objection, I will argue that it is, in large part, the inherent sexual context of such cases which is damaging to the student. I will show that such statements and actions emphasize the sexuality of students, often in ways which are coercive, and thereby impair students' full enjoyment of educational benefits, climate, and opportunities. In other words, such cases involve sexual harassment.

If we consider the first described case, it should now be clear to the reader that in such a situation a student would be justified in perceiving an implicit threat. In ogling the student, the instructor sets up a situation charged with sexuality. The student will feel coerced into allowing the instructor to treat her in such a manner. She knows that a complaint in such a situation could result in the "fragile sexual ego" of her instructor being damaged and thus leading to retaliations on his part in the form of lowered grades, lost positions, damaging evaluations, and/or malicious gossip. Hence, the educational rights of the student are at stake.

Consider also the personal effect on the student in the independent study situation. She was, we can assume, interested in a particular area of study and was looking forward to a semester of work devoted to the topic. Once she became aware that the instructor she had hoped to work with was ogling her, her excitement about the project was diminished. She could pretend not to notice his stare, but she could not ignore it. It intruded upon her and made her see that the instructor perceived her as flesh. She realized that her ideas and creativity would not be appreciated. The stare turned her into a sexual object. She was once again subjected to the stereotype of women as sexual beings, a stereotype which is tied to women being in a subordinate and vulnerable position to men in our society. This instructor's action maintained this woman's position of subordination by adversely affecting her sense of self-worth.

Given this analysis, it should be clear that cases of sexist behavior or remarks similar to the independent study case do involve sexual harassment. Such a situation could reasonably be perceived by a student as involving an implicit threat of harm should they attempt to stop the instructor from, for example, visually undressing them. In the above case, the instructor used his authority to emphasize the sexuality of the student in a manner which was both annoying and coercive. Such actions do harm students by impairing their full enjoyment of educational benefits. I thus contend that these situations are similar to cases of sexual harassment involving implicit, and perhaps unintended, coercion.

Situations like that with the crude drawings of a woman are cases of sexual harassment which do not involve coercion. Although no student is coerced or compelled, the instructor in this case is emphasizing the sexual identity of the women students in that class in such a way as to cause them harm. The women in this class will feel self-conscious and uncomfortable. They are being belittled. The instructor is not talking to them, but to the men in the class. In such a case the instructor attempts to bond with the men through voyeuristic laughter which is at the expense of the women in the class. This causes the women to feel demeaned and excluded. They will feel "other."

Seen in this way, it should be clear that actions such as this are annoying to students and create [an] unacceptable classroom climate. Such attitudes and remarks tie into a whole social context about women, where a woman's rational abilities are inferior to those of men and where her merits are to be measured in terms of her sexual attactiveness and compliance and not upon her skills or class performance. It is a social context in which women are seen as being successful by sexually purchasing grades or positions.

All students have a right to study in an atmosphere free of such discriminatory intimidation, derogatory attitudes, and sexual objectification. They have a right to be treated as inquiring human beings. Understood within the current social context concerning sexuality, the dynamics of sexism, and the powerlessness of students to stop unwanted actions of their instructors, it should be clear that such actions cause students harm by emphasizing their sexual identity. Thus situations like this one must also be classified as involving sexual harassment.

GENERAL CONCLUSIONS

. . . • Sexual harassment can occur even in situations in which the instructor has no intention of threatening the student. Given an instructor's obligations to students, if it was reasonable for the student to perceive a threat, then the instructor is morally responsible for the sexual harassment even though he or she did not intend it.

• Sexual relationships between instructors and students in their classes or students they are academically evaluating are questionable at best. Given power dynamics and the complexity of sexual relations, I would advise instructors to refrain from developing a relationship beyond that of teacher/student until they no longer have an educational or supervisory responsibility for the student.

• Certain acts of sexual harassment are much less visible than others and because of this are more easily overlooked, even by a conscientious instructor. Because of this, it is important for educational institutions to inform both students and faculty of the various manifestations of academic sexual harassment. . . .

NOTES

1. [Frank J.] Till, *Sexual Harassment: A Report on the Sexual Harassment of Students* (Washington, D.C.: National Advisory Council on Women's Educational Programs, 1980). Since there had been few studies of sexual harassment in academia, the Council chose to structure its Call for Information without a definition of sexual harassment in order to allow victims to define the problem. It was believed that such an approach would allow for the development of a definition of sexual harassment not limited to any particular bias or ideology.

2. Ibid., p. 7. This study was directed at the sexual harassment of students by faculty. Given this, I shall limit my analysis to the dynamics of sexual harassment between students and faculty. Academic sexual harassment is, of course, not limited to such student/faculty relationships. It also occurs between senior faculty and junior faculty, faculty and administrators, etc. Although I will not discuss such cases, my analysis is applicable to them with only minor modification.

3. [Jane E.] Richards, p. 57. "An Assessment of Sexual Harassment of Female Students in a University Setting." Unpublished thesis, Southern Illinois University at Carbondale, 1979.

4. Phyllis Schlafly, Report to the Senate Labor and Human Resources Committee, 1980.

5. See Richards, "An Assessment of Sexual Harassment of Female Students in a University Setting," pp. 57–60. As one example consider the following response: "So far . . . I have not received any form of sexual harassment. I have although seen some female students trying to use their 'favors' in order to receive a better grade. The professors though seemed uninterested. I feel that if there are any forms of sexual harassment [at this campus], the female students ask for it," p. 57.

6. One might object that I am outlining the situation as if students have no power, that is, the students are powerless, the instructors powerful. I admit that the situation is not this simplistic. Students do have some institutional power with respect to instructors—but it is comparatively small. Students often write course evaluations. In such evaluations they do have the power to evaluate the instructor according to criteria of their own choice. However, evaluation procedures vary from school to school. At my institution, the evaluations are given to the instructor to read prior to being put on file, giving the instructor complete freedom to throw away negative evaluations. Poor evaluations are often dismissed as attempts to get back at an instructor from whom a student got a low grade. My position then is that although the student has some power in relation to an instructor, it is usually too small to be helpful. Remember that discussing academic sexual harassment, only institutional power (power coming from one's position within the university) is relevant. If someone is extremely good looking, in our society that gives them power. A very good looking instructor may employ their classical Greek profile to aid in the seduction of a student. But if that seduction employs no abuse of their authority, intended or unintended, and does not impair the student's intellectual development, then that action does not fall under the definition of academic sexual harassment. However, I will be arguing that situations in which an instructor can seduce a student without violating such conditions are very rare if that student is or has been in one of his or her classes.

7. Till, *Sexual Harassment*, p. 19.

8. *American Association of University Professors Bulletin* 55 (1969): 86–87.

9. Till, *Sexual Harassment*, p. 10.

10. Ibid.

4

Is Sexual Harassment Coercive?

Larry May and John C. Hughes

A number of recent lawsuits filed under Title VII of the 1964 Civil Rights Act have brought the problem of sexual harassment into the footlights of contemporary political and moral discussion.[1] Is sexual harassment a purely private matter between two individuals, or is it a social problem? If sexual harassment is to be treated as something more than a purely personal dispute, how do we distinguish the social problem from benevolent forms of social interaction between members of a work hierarchy? We will argue here that sexual harassment of women workers is a public issue because it is inherently coercive, regardless of whether it takes the form of a threat for noncompliance, or of a reward for compliance. We will further argue that the harm of harassment is felt beyond the individuals immediately involved because it contributes to a pervasive pattern of discrimination and exploitation based on sex.

The term *sexual harassment* refers to the intimidation of persons in subordinate positions by those holding power and authority over them in order to exact sexual favors that would ordinarily not have been granted. Sexual harassment of male subordinates by female superiors is conceivable, and probably occurs, albeit infrequently. Positions of authority are more likely to be occupied by males, while women are predominantly relegated to positions of subservience and dependency. Furthermore, strong

From *Moral Rights in the Workplace,* edited by Gertrude Ezorsky. Copyright © 1987. Reprinted by permission of the State University of New York Press.

cultural patterns induce female sexual passivity and acquiescence to male initiative.[2] These factors combine to produce a dominant pattern of male harassment of females. However, it might be reflecting that the poisoning of the work environment that may result from sexual intimidation may affect members of both sexes, so that sexual harassment should be viewed as more than merely a woman's issue.

Truly systematic empirical studies of the incidence of sexual harassment are yet to be done. Most of the studies by social scientists to date suffer from severe methodological flaws. Nevertheless, they reveal a pattern of sexual harassment of working women that is too strong to ignore. . . .

I

Like most interpersonal transactions, sexual advances may take many forms. There is of course the sincere proposal, motivated by genuine feeling for another, made in a context of mutual respect for the other's autonomy and dignity. Such offers are possible between members of a work hierarchy, but are of no concern here. Rather, we are interested in advances that take the following forms: (1) Sexual threat: "If you don't provide a sexual benefit, I will punish you by withholding a promotion or a raise that would otherwise be due, or ultimately fire you." (2) Sexual offer: "If you provide a sexual benefit, I will reward you with a promotion or a raise that would otherwise not be due." There are also sexual harassment situations that are merely annoying, but without demonstrable sanction or reward. It is worth noting at the outset that all three forms of sexual harassment have been proscribed under recently promulgated Equal Employment Opportunity Commission guidelines implementing Title VII.[3]

Sexual harassment in the form of threats is coercive behavior that forces the employee to accept a course of conduct she wouldn't otherwise accept. What is wrong with this? Why can't she simply resist the threats and remain as before? Viewed in this abstract, one can seemingly resist threats, for unlike physical restraint, threatening does not completely deny individual choice over her alternatives. A person who is physically restrained is literally no longer in control of her own life. The victim is no longer reaching decisions of her own and autonomously carrying them out. Threats do not have this dramatic effect on a person's autonomy. Rather, the effect of the threat is that the recipient of a threat is much less inclined to act as she would have absent the threat—generally out of fear. Fear is the calculation of expected harm and the decision to avoid it. Reasonably prudent individuals will not, without a sufficiently expected possibility of gain, risk harm. The first thing wrong with sexual threats then is that, for the reasonable person, it now takes a very good reason to resist the threat, whereas no such strength of reasoning was required before to resist a sexual advance.

Sexual threats are coercive because they worsen the objective situation the employee finds herself in. To examine this claim, consider her situation before and after the threat has been made (preproposition stage and postproposition stage).[4] In the preproposition stage, a secretary, for example, is judged by standards of efficiency to determine whether she should be allowed to retain her job. She would naturally view her employer as having power over her, but only in the rather limited domain concerning the job-related functions she performs. Her personal life would be her own. She could choose her own social relationships, without fear that these decisions might adversely affect her job. In the postproposition stage, she can no longer remain employed under the same conditions while not choosing to have relations with her employer. Further, the efficient performance of job-related functions is no longer sufficient for the retention of her job. She can no longer look to her supervisor as one who exercises power merely over the performance of her office duties. He now wields power over a part of her personal life. . . . [She] cannot simply go on as before, for [her] new situation is correctly perceived as worse than the old situation.

It is the worsening of the woman's situation after the threat has been made that contributes to the likelihood of her acquiescence to the threat. The perception of job insecurity created by the threat can only be alleviated by her acceptance of the sexual proposition. But what of the woman who prefers to have a sexual relationship with her employer than not to do so? Has this woman also been made objectively worse off then she was before the threat occurred? We contend that she has, for before the threat was made she could pursue her preference without feeling forced to do so. If the liaison developed and then turned sour, she could quit the relationship and not so clearly risk a worsening of her employment situation. Now, however, her continued job success might be held ransom to the continued sexual demands of her employer. This also may adversely affect other women in the business organization. What the employer has done is to establish a precedent for employment decisions based upon the stereotype that values women for their sexuality rather than for their job skills. This has a discriminatory impact on women individually and as a group. Focusing on this effect will shed some light on the harm of both sexual threats and sexual offers.

II

Consider the following case.[5] Barnes was hired as an administrative assistant by the director of a federal agency. In a preemployment interview, the director, a male, promised to promote Barnes, a female, within ninety days. Shortly after beginning her job, (1) the director repeatedly asked her for a date after work hours, even though she consistently refused; (2) made repeated remarks to her that were sexual in nature; and (3) repeatedly told her that if she did not cooperate with him by engaging in sexual relations, her employment status would be affected. After consistently rebuffing him, she finally told him she wished for their relationship to remain a strictly professional one. Therefore the director, sometimes in concert with others, began a campaign to belittle and demean her within the office. Subsequently she was stripped of most of her job duties, culminating in the eventual abolition of her job. Barnes filed suit, claiming that these actions would not have occurred but for the fact that she was a woman.

Under Title VII, it is now widely accepted that the kind of sexual threat illustrated by this case is an instance of sex discrimination in employment.[6] Such threats treat women differently than men in employment contexts even though gender is not a relevantly applicable category for making employment-related decisions. The underlying principle here is that like persons should be treated alike. Unless there are relevant differences among persons, it is harmful to disadvantage one particular class of persons. In the normal course of events, male employees are not threatened sexually by employers or supervisors. The threats disadvantage a woman in that an additional requirement is placed in her path for successful job retention, one not placed in the path of male employees. When persons who are otherwise similarly situated are distinguished on the basis of their sex, and rewards or burdens are apportioned according to these gender-based classifications, illegal sex discrimination has occurred. Applying this theory of discrimination to Barnes's complaint, the federal appellate court ruled:

> So it was, by her version, that retention of her job was conditioned upon submission to sexual relations—an exaction which the supervisor would not have made of any male. It is much too late in the day to contend that Title VII does not outlaw terms of employment for women which differ appreciably from those set for men and which are not genuinely and reasonably related to the performance on the job. . . . Put another way, she became the target of her superior's sexual desires because she

was a woman and was asked to bow to demands as the price for holding her job.[7]

There is a second way in which this behavior might be viewed as discriminatory. Sexual threats also contribute to a pervasive pattern of disadvantaged treatment of women as a group. Under this approach, the harm is not viewed as resulting from the arbitrary and unfair use of gender as a criterion for employment decisions. Rather, emphasis is on the effect the classification has of continuing the subordination of women as a group. The harm results regardless of whether the specific incident could be given an employment rationale or not. Sexual harassment perpetuates sex discrimination, and illustrates the harm that occurs for members of a group that have historically been disadvantaged. This theory was applied to sexual harassment in another federal lawsuit, *Tomkins* v. *Public Service Gas and Electric Co.*[8] The plaintiff's lawyers argued that employer tolerance of sexual harassment and its pattern of reprisals had a disparate impact upon women as an already disadvantaged group and was inherently degrading to all women.

Sexual threats are harmful to the individual woman because she is coerced and treated unfairly by her employer, disadvantaging her for no good reason. Beyond this, such practices further contribute to a pervasive pattern of disadvantaged status for her and all women in society. The sexual stereotyping makes it less likely, and sometimes impossible, that women will be treated on the basis of job efficiency, intelligence, or administrative skill. These women must now compete on a very different level, and in the case where sexual threats are common or at least accepted, this level is clearly inferior to that occupied by men. The few male employees who are harassed in the workplace suffer the first harm but not the second. We shall next show that there are also two harms of sexual offers in employment, only one of which can also be said to befall men.

III

The harm of sexual offers is much more difficult to identify and analyze. Indeed, some may even see sexual offers as contributing to a differentiation based on sex that advantages rather than disadvantages women, individually and as a group. After all, males cannot normally gain promotions by engaging in sexual relations with their employers. We shall argue, on the contrary, that a sexual offer disadvantages the woman employee by changing the work environment so that she is viewed by others, and may come to view herself, less in terms of her work productivity and more in terms of her sexual allure. This change, like the threat, makes it unlikely that she can return to the preproposition stage even though she might prefer to do so. Furthermore, to offset her diminished status and to protect against later retaliation, a prudent woman would feel that she must accept the offer. Here, sexual offers resemble the coercive threat. The specific harm to women becomes clearer when one looks at the group impact of sexual offers in employment. Women are already more economically vulnerable and socially passive than men. When sexual offers are tendered, exploitation of a woman employee is accomplished by taking advantage of a preexisting vulnerability males generally do not share.

Seduction accomplished through sexual offers and coercive threats blend together most clearly in the mixed case of the sexual offer of a promotion with the lurking threat of retaliation if the offer is turned down. Both combine together to compel the woman to engage in sexual relations with her employer. Gifts are so rare in economic matters that it is best to be suspicious of all offers and to look for their hidden costs. . . .

Why are the clearly mixed cases, where there is both an offer and a (sometimes only implied) threat, coercive rather than noncoercive? To return to our initial discussion, why is it that one is made worse off by the existence of these proposals? In one sense they enable women to do things they couldn't otherwise do, namely, get a promotion that they did not deserve, thus seeming to be noncoercive. On the other hand, if the woman prefers not having sexual relations with her employer (while retaining her job) to having sexual relations with him (with ensuing promotion), then it is predominantly a threat and more clearly coercive. The best reason for not preferring the postproposition stage is that she is then made worse off if she rejects the proposition, and if she accepts, she nonetheless risks further harm or retaliation. This latter condition is also true for more straightforward offers, as we shall now show.

A number of contemporary philosophers have argued that offers place people in truly advantageous positions, for they can always be turned down with the ensuing return to the preoffer stage.[9] In the case of sexual offers, however, the mere proposal of a promotion in exchange for sexual relations changes the work environment. Once sexual relations are seriously proposed as a sufficient condition for employment success, the woman realizes that this male employer sees her (and will probably continue to see her) as a sex object as well as an employee. A prudent woman will henceforth worry that she is not being regarded as an employee who simply happens to be a woman, but rather as a woman made more vulnerable by the fact that she happens to be an employee. If she accepts the offer, she lends credence to the stereotype, and because of this, it is more likely that she may experience future offers or even threats. She would thus worry about her ability to achieve on the basis of her work-related merits. If she rejects the offer, she would still worry about her employer's attitude toward her status as a worker. Furthermore, because of the volatility of sexual feelings, these offers cannot be turned down without the risk of offending or alienating one's employer, something any employee would wish to avoid. She may reasonably conclude from these two considerations that neither postoffer alternative is desirable. This is one of the hidden costs of sexual offers in the workplace.

It may be claimed that such environmental changes are no different for men who can also be the objects of sexual offers in the workplace. One needs to show that the changed environment is worse for those who are women. Sexual employment offers take advantage of unequal power relations that exist between employer and employee so as to force a particular outcome further benefitting those who are already in advantageous positions. But beyond this, sexual offers are doubly exploitative for female employees, because women already enter the employment arena from a position of vulnerability. As we have indicated, this is true because of the history of their economic powerlessness and because of their culturally ingrained passivity and acquiescence in the face of male initiatives. Women enter the employment arena much more ripe for coercion than their male colleagues. Thus, women are more likely to be harmed by these offers.

. . . Men are not similarly harmed by sexual offers because they do not have the same history of sexual exploitation. Men are likely to regard such seductive offers either humorously or as insults to be aggressively combatted, while women have been socialized to be passive rather than combative in such situations. The woman to whom the offer is made becomes less sure of her real abilities by virtue of the proposal itself. This self-denigrating response to an unwelcomed proposal is a vestige of women's history of subordination. Even without the veiled threat, sexual offers can cause women to act in ways they would not choose to act otherwise. To this extent, these sexual offers are coercive.

Most offers are not coercive because one would prefer to have the offer made. This is because one of the postoffer alternatives (rejecting the offer) is equivalent to the preoffer alternative (having no offer at all). Sexual offers made by male employers to female employees are different, however, because they more closely resemble threats than ordinary offers.[10] As we have shown, the preoffer alternative, being employed, unpromoted, yet able to obtain promotion according to one's merits—is different from, and preferable to, either of the postoffer alternatives—accepting the promotion, and having sexual relations with her employer, with all of its negative consequences, or rejecting the offer of promotion, but with the risk that the promotion may now prove unobtainable on the basis of merit. By blocking a return to the more preferable preoffer alternative, the male employer has acted similarly to the employer who uses sexual threats. The woman is forced to choose between two undesirable alternatives because she cannnot have what she would have chosen before the proposal was made. Stressing these hidden costs, which are much greater for women than for men, exposes the coercive element inherent in sexual offers as well as in sexual threats. We are thus led to conclude that both of these employment practices are harmful to women and recently were properly proscribed by the U.S. Equal Employment Opportunity Commission.

NOTES

1. For a careful analysis of these cases we recommend Catharine MacKinnon's book, *Sexual Harassment of Working Women* (New Haven, Conn.: Yale University Press, 1979).

2. For the historical evidence, see William Chaffe, *Women and Equality* (New York: Oxford University Press, 1977). For the sociological evidence, see J. R. Feagin and C. B. Feagin, *Discrimination American Style* (Englewood Cliffs, N.J.: Prentice-Hall, 1978).

3. 45 Fed. Reg. 74, 677 (1980); 29 C.F.R. 1604.11 (a).

4. We proceed from the general analysis developed by Robert Nozick, "Coercion," *Philosophy, Science and Method,* Morgenbesser, Suppes, and White, eds. (New York: St. Martin's Press, 1969). A very large literature has grown out of this analysis. We recommend the essays by Bernard Gert, Michael Bayles, and especially Virginia Held, collected in *NOMOS XIV: Coercion* (New York: Lieber Atherton, 1973).

5. Summary of the facts for *Barnes* v. *Costel,* 561 F.2d 984 (D.C. Cir. 1977).

6. For more elaboration, see Section II of our essay, "Sexual Harassment," *Social Theory and Practice* (1980), pp. 256–68.

7. 561 F.2d 989, 990, 992 n. 68 (D.C. Cir. 1977).

8. 568 F.2d 1044 (3rd Cir. 1977).

9. See Michael Bayles, "Coercive Offers and Public Benefits," *The Personalist* 55 (1974); Donald Vandeveer, "Coercion, Seduction and Rights," *The Personalist* 58 (1977); and Nozick, "Coercion," among others.

10. Some other employment offers have been seen as coercive also. See David Zimmerman, "Coercive Wage Offers," *Philosophy and Public Affairs* 10 (1981).

5

The Definition of Sexual Harassment

Edmund Wall

As important as current scientific, legal, and philosophical definitions of sexual harassment are, many of them omit the interpersonal features which define the concept. The view defended in Part I of this essay is that the mental states of the perpetrator and the victim are the essential defining elements. Sexual harassment is described as a form of communication that violates its victim's privacy rights. This interpersonal definition purports to capture the more subtle instances of sexual harassment while circumventing those sexual advances that are not sexually harassing. This proposed definition is contrasted with behavior descriptions of sexual harassment, an approach widely used by sociologists and psychologists. Part II of this essay criticizes definitions formulated in terms of the alleged discriminatory and coercive effects of a sexual advance, and the federal legal definition which omits reference to relevant mental states.

I

There are many types of behavior that may be classified as instances of sexual harassment, and some people, such as Kenneth Cooper, have proposed that managers explain the concept to their employees primarily

From *Public Affairs Quarterly* 5, no. 4 (1991): 371–85. Reprinted, with modifications, by permission of the publisher.

through descriptions of various behavior patterns. This is no surprise, as numerous sociological and psychological studies which survey people's attitudes toward sexual harassment and which attempt to gauge its frequency also explain sexual harassment primarily or entirely through behavior descriptions. Cooper addresses the sexual harassment of female employees by male managers in an essay that describes what he terms "six levels of sexual harassment." He seems to order these levels according to what he assumes to be two complementary considerations: a third party's ability to identify the perpetrator's behavior as sexually harassing and the severity of the infraction. The categories are presented in ascending order with the first category ostensibly representing the least flagrant type of behavior, the sixth category representing the most flagrant type of behavior. Cooper writes that "obvious and blatant harassment may be decreasing, but borderline harassment behavior has never let up."[1] He takes the first four categories to be accounts of "borderline" cases.

Cooper refers to the first type of behavior as "aesthetic appreciation." This refers to comments which "express a nonaggressive appreciation of physical or sexual features." For example, an alleged perpetrator says to a co-worker: "Gee . . . sigh . . . you're looking better every day!"[2] Cooper refers to such examples as the most "innocent" type of sexual harassment, but believes that these examples, nevertheless, constitute sexual harassment. In such cases the harassment is concealed.

Does managerial behavior, which falls under "aesthetic appreciation," necessarily constitute sexual harassment? Cooper argues that "regardless of how harmless these appreciative comments may seem, they are put-downs which lower the group stature of the target." The manager, he tells us, is in a "superior position" from which to judge the employee's physical attributes.[3]

Comments of "aesthetic appreciation" made by male managers to female employees may not be appropriate, but Cooper's argument does not show that all such comments are, as he suggests, instances of sexual harassment. Cooper argues that managerial comments of "aesthetic appreciation" made to employees are sexually harassing because they are "put-downs which lower the group stature of the target." There is a problem here. Cooper has not shown that such comments necessarily reflect a group differential.[4] Of course, the manager is in a "superior position" in relation to his employee, but only with respect to her corporate duties, not to judgments about her physical attributes. The manager may try to use his corporate authority in order to force his employee to listen to his assessment of her physical charms. Furthermore, the employee may feel as though she must submit to the manager's remarks, even if he does not openly attempt to coerce her. However, his sexually harassing behavior need not inherently be an exercise of corporate authority. It could simply be misguided human behavior which utilizes corporate authority.

The second type of behavior which, according to Cooper, constitutes sexual harassment is "active mental groping." Under this heading Cooper places "direct verbal harassment," which evidently includes sexual jokes about the employee, and also the type of staring that may leave employees feeling as though managers are "undressing them with their eyes."[5] This is followed by "social touching." Cooper maintains that, along with the first two categories of behavior, this type of behavior is "borderline," since the offender remains "within normal social touching conventions." In other words, such touching misleadingly appears "totally innocent" to a "third party."[6]

As far as "social touching" is concerned, Cooper distinguishes an innocent "friendly touch" from a "sensual touch." While not providing an example of a "friendly touch," Cooper gives as an example of a "sensual touch" "a caressing hand laid gently on the [employee]," or the movement of the manager's hand up and down his employee's back.[7] Unfortunately, Cooper offers no defense of his distinction between two types of touching. Neither does he clearly relate this distinction to his account of sexual harassment, although he seems to assume that a manager's "friendly touch" does not constitute sexual harassment, whereas his "sensual touch" would. He merely warns managers against any "social touching."

The reason why the distinction between an innocent "friendly touch" and a "sensual touch" makes sense is also the reason why behavior descriptions are not central to the definition of sexual harassment. The basis for the distinction lies in the manager's mental state, not in his behavior. A sincerely "friendly touch" would depend, among other things, upon the manager's motive for touching his employee. Sexual harassment refers to a defect in interpersonal relations. Depending upon the manager's and employee's mental states, it is possible that some examples of managerial behavior which satisfy Cooper's first, most "innocent" category (i.e., "aesthetic appreciation"), would actually be more objectionable than his second and third categories (i.e., "active mental groping" and "social touching," respectively). Indeed, depending upon the manager's and employee's mental states, cases that fall under any of Cooper's first three categories of sexual harassment could be characterized as "innocent."

Consider the case in which a manager finds that one of his employees strikingly resembles his mother. He has managed this employee for three years without incident, and one day in the corporate dining room they begin to discuss their parents. He may tell her of the resemblance between her and his mother. He may stare at her for a long time while (this would constitute "active mental groping" on Cooper's view). He may tell her that her cheekbones are as pretty as those of his mother (an example of "aesthetic appreciation," according to Cooper). Finally, he may put his hand on her shoulder (i.e., an example of friendly "social touching" on Cooper's view) and say "Oh well, I must be getting back to my desk." Given this scenario, it is obvious that at least some employees would take no offense at the manager's behavior. Such a case need not involve sexual harassment, even though mere behavior descriptions would lead us to the opposite conclusion.

Cooper refers to his fourth and final "borderline" category as "foreplay harassment." Unlike "social touching," the touching here is not "innocent in nature and location," although its inappropriateness is still concealed.[8] Examples of "foreplay harassment" include a manager noticing that a button on an employee's blouse is undone. Instead of telling her about it, he buttons it. Another example would be brushing up against her, "as if by accident."[9]

Cooper suggests that the "scope, frequency, and feel" of the touching "shows an obvious intent on the part of the offender to push the limits of decency. . . ."[10] In his description of sexual harassment Cooper alludes to the importance of the manager's motive, but does not make its importance explicit. He does not express it as one of the essential descriptions of sexual harassment. Accidental physical contact between a manager and his employee is not, of course, sexual harassment. When the manager deliberately makes contact with his employee from a certain motive or due to his negligence, then he becomes an offender. Whether or not he makes physical contact, he may still be an offender. Indeed, as Cooper recognizes, an employee could be sexually harassed without *any* physical contact between her and her manager.

Cooper overlooks the possibility that what appears to be "foreplay harassment" of an employee might not be. Even when a manager is sexually "petting" an employee in his office, he is not necessarily sexually harassing her, even though his behavior would be viewed as inappropriate. Consider the case in which a manager and an employee form an uncoerced agreement to engage in such inappropriate office behavior.[11] This is not sexual harassment. The general problem with behavior descriptions of sexual harassment can be seen when we attempt to construct examples of sexual harassment. The application of any of Cooper's four "borderline" categories to our examples may yield false determinations, depending upon the mental states involved.

Cooper's fifth and sixth categories are not "borderline," but involve flagrant sexual advances. They are "sexual abuse" and "ultimate threat," respectively. The latter, which refers to a manager's coercive threats for sexual favors, will be discussed in Part II of this essay. The other category, "sexual abuse," is usually limited to forced sexual contact, but, like "sexual harassment," it may be broader than this.

Probably any behavior which constitutes sexual harassment (i.e., which satisfies certain descriptions of the manager's and employee's mental states) would also constitute sexual abuse—whether physical or verbal. When an individual is maliciously or negligently responsible for unjustified harm to someone, it would seem that he or she has abused that person. Abuse can be subtle; it may include various ways of inflicting psychological harm. In fact, there is a more subtle form of sexual harassment accomplished through stares, gestures, and innuendo. For example, a manager may sexually harass his employee by staring at her and "undressing her with his eyes." *In light of this and the other limitations of behavior descriptions we need a definition of sexual harassment that is capable of capturing all subtle instances of sexual harassment while filtering out (even overt) sexual behavior which is not harassing.*

Where X is the sexual harasser and Y the victim, the following conditions are offered as the definition of sexual harassment:

(1) X does not attempt to obtain Y's consent to communicate to Y, X's or someone else's alleged sexual interest in Y.

(2) X communicates to Y, X's or someone else's alleged sexual interest in Y. X's motive for communicating this is some perceived benefit that he or she expects to obtain through the communication.

(3) Y does not consent to discuss with X, X's or someone else's alleged sexual interest in Y.

(4) Y feels emotionally distressed because X did not attempt to obtain Y's consent to this discussion and/or because Y objects to what Y takes to be the offensive content of X's sexual comments.

The first condition refers to X's failure to attempt to obtain Y's consent to discuss someone's sexual interest in Y. X's involvement in the sexual harassment is not defined by the type of sexual proposition that X may make to Y. If the first condition was formulated in terms of the content of X's sexual proposition, then the proposed definition would circumvent some of the more subtle cases of sexual harassment. After all, Y may actually agree to a sexual proposition made to her or him by X and still be sexually harassed by X's attempting to discuss it with Y. In some cases Y might not feel that it is the proper time or place to discuss such matters. In any event *sexual harassment primarily involves wrongful communication.* Whether or not X attempts to obtain Y's consent to a certain type of communication is crucial. What is inherently repulsive about sexual harassment is not the possible vulgarity of X's sexual comment or proposal, but X's failure to show respect for Y's rights. It is the obligation that stems from privacy rights that is ignored. Y's personal behavior and aspirations are protected by Y's privacy rights. The intrusion by X into this moral sphere is what is so objectionable about sexual harassment. If X does not attempt to obtain Y's approval to discuss such private matters, then he or she has not shown Y adequate respect.

X's lack of respect for Y's rights is not a sufficient description of sexual harassment, however. X's conduct must constitute a rights violation. Essentially, the second condition refers to the fact that X has acted without concern for Y's right to consent to the communication of sexual matters involving Y. Here X "communicates" to Y that X or someone else is sexually interested in Y. This term includes not only verbal remarks made by X, but any purposeful conveyance such as gestures, noises, stares, etc., that violate its recipient's privacy rights. Such behavior can be every bit as intrusive as verbal remarks.

We need to acknowledge that X can refer to some third party's alleged sexual interest in Y and still sexually harass Y. When X tells Y, without Y's consent, that some third party believes Y is physically desirable, this may be a case of sexual harassment. Y may not approve of X telling him or her this—even if Y and the third party happen to share a mutual sexual interest in each other. This is because X's impropriety lies in the invasive approach to Y. It does not hinge upon the content of what X says to Y. X may, for example, have absolutely no sexual interest in Y, but believes that such remarks would upset Y, thereby affording X perverse enjoyment. Likewise, X's report that some third party is sexually interested in Y may be inaccurate, but this does not absolve X from the duty to respect Y's privacy.

X's specific motive for communicating what he or she does to Y may vary, but it always includes some benefit X may obtain from this illegitimate communication. X might or might not plan to have sexual relations with Y. Indeed, as we have seen, X might not have a sexual interest in Y at all and still obtain what X perceives to be beneficial to himself or herself, perhaps the satisfaction of disturbing Y.[12] Perhaps, as some contemporary psychologists suggest, X's ultimate motive is to mollify his or her feelings of inferiority by controlling Y's feelings, actions, or environment. Yet another possibility is that, if X is male, he might want to conform to what he believes to be parental and/or peer standards for males. The proposed first and second conditions can account for these various motives. The point is that, whatever the perceived benefit, it is the utility of the approach as perceived by X, and not necessarily the content of X's message, that is important to the harasser. Furthermore, the "benefit" that moves X to action might not be obtainable or might not be a genuine benefit, but, nevertheless, in X's attempt to obtain it, X violates Y's rights.

The third condition refers to Y's not consenting to discuss with X, X's or someone else's alleged sexual interest in Y. Someone might argue that the first condition is now unnecessary, that X's failure to obtain Y's consent to the type of discussion outlined in the third condition will suffice; the first condition describing X's failure to *attempt* to obtain Y's consent is, therefore, unnecessary. This objection would be misguided, however. The first condition ensures that some sexual comments will not be unjustly labeled as "harassing." Consider the possibility that the second and third conditions are satisfied. For example, X makes a sexual remark about Y to Y without Y's consent. Now suppose that the first condition is not satisfied, that is, suppose that X *did attempt* to obtain Y's consent to make such remarks. Furthermore, suppose that somewhere the communication between X and Y breaks down and X honestly believes he or she has obtained Y's consent to this discussion, when, in fact, he or she has not. In this case, X's intentions and actions being what they are, X does not sexually harass Y. X has shown respect for Y's privacy. Y may certainly *feel* harassed in this case, but there is no offender here. However, after X sees Y's displeasure at the remarks, it is now X's duty to refrain from such remarks, unless, of course, Y later consents to such a discussion.

The case of the ignorant but well-intentioned X demonstrates the importance of distinguishing between accidents (and merely unfortunate circumstances) and sexual harassment. The remedy for avoiding the former is the encouragement of clear communication between people. Emphasis on clear communication would also facilitate the identification of some offenders, for some offenders would not refrain from making sexual remarks after their targets clearly expressed their objections to those remarks. The above case also reveals the need for people to clearly express their wishes to others. For example, when someone wishes not to discuss an individual's sexual interest in them, it would be foolish for them to make flirting glances at this individual. Such gestures may mislead the individual to conclude that they consent to this communication.

By themselves the first three conditions are not adequate descriptions of sexual harassment. What is missing is a description of the victim's mental state. In sexual harassment cases the wrongful communication must distress Y for a certain reason. Let us say that X has expressed sexual interest in Y without any attempt to obtain Y's consent to such a discussion. Y, in fact, does not consent to it. However, perhaps Y has decided against the discussion because Y finds X too refined and anticipates that X's sexual advances will not interest Y. Perhaps Y welcomes crass discussions about sexual matters. In this case Y might not be sexually harassed by X's remarks. As the fourth condition indicates, Y must be distressed because X did not attempt to ensure that it was permissible to make sexual comments to Y which involve Y, or because the content of X's sexual comments are offensive in Y's view. Yet another possibility is that both the invasiveness of X's approach and the content of what X says causes Y emotional distress. In this example, however, it would appear that Y would neither find the content of X's sexual remarks to be offensive nor would Y object to the fact that X did not attempt to obtain Y's consent to make these remarks to Y. Due to Y's views concerning sexual privacy this case is similar to one in which X does not attempt to obtain Y's consent to discuss with Y how well Y plays tennis, or some other mundane discussion about Y.

II

We have postponed a discussion of the relation of sexual harassment to coercion and discrimination against women. Let us now explore this relation.

The fact that male employers and managers represent the bulk of the reported offenders has caused some legal theorists and philosophers to conclude that sexual harassment necessarily involves discrimination against women as a class. This approach is unacceptable. Sexual harassment is not necessarily tied to discrimination or to coercion.

In an essay titled "Is Sexual Harassment Coercive?" Larry May and John C. Hughes argue that sexual harassment against women workers is "inherently coercive"—whether the harassment takes the form of a threat or an offer. They also maintain that the harm of sexual harassment against women "contributes to a pervasive pattern of discrimination and exploitation based upon sex."[13] May and Hughes begin by defining sexual harassment as "the intimidation of persons in subordinate positions by those holding power and authority over them in order to exact sexual favors that would ordinarily not have been granted."[14]

May and Hughes recognize that male employees might be sexually harassed, but choose to limit their discussion to the typical case in which a male employer or manager sexually harasses a female employee. They choose this paradigm because it represents the "dominant pattern" in society and because they believe that, as a class, women have been conditioned by society to acquiesce "to male initiative."[15] According to May and Hughes, women represent an injured class. The fact that men dominate positions of authority and status in our society renders women vulnerable to sexual harassment. Furthermore, the sexual harassment of female employees by male employers and managers sparks a general increase in the frequency of the crime, since such behavior reinforces male stereotypes of women as sexual objects.[16]

Even if May and Hughes's social assumptions are accepted, that would not entail that their definition of sexual harassment, which includes a power differential between the offender and the victim, is adequate. Unhappily, this circumvents the sexual harassment between employees with equal capabilities and corporate status. Suppose that X and Y are co-workers for some company. X makes frequent comments concerning Y's sexual appeal and repeatedly propositions Y despite Y's refusals. Authority and rank are superfluous here. Y may be sexually harassed regardless of X or Y's corporate status. As argued above in the critique of Cooper's article, the harassment at issue is not an extension of X's corporate authority, nor is the harassment essentially explained by the exercise of his authority. Rather, it is essentially explained by X's lack of respect for Y's right to refuse to discuss sexual matters pertaining to Y. If Y chooses not to enter X's discussion or is upset by X's refusal to recognize Y's privacy rights, then sexual harassment has occurred. The essential element is X and Y's mental state, not an alleged power differential between them.

Of course May and Hughes would also say that society has shaped the "mental states" of men and women in an unhealthy fashion. Women are conditioned to be passive and to expect treatment as sexual objects. According to May and Hughes, the difference in social status between women and men which affords men the opportunity and encouragement to dominate women reflects how sexual harassment is an issue of power. The problem here is that even if such sweeping social assumptions could be verified scientifically, the social conditions referred to in those assumptions would have to play essential roles in the sexual harassment cases in our society—if sexual harassment is to be *defined* in terms of these social conditions. May and Hughes would need to demonstrate that social inequities and issues of power are central to all sexual harassment cases before they could say without qualification that sexual harassment is a form of sex discrimination.

May and Hughes's inaccurate definition of sexual harassment skews their inquiry. Their main objective is to illustrate the coercive nature of sexual harassment; more specifically, the coercive nature of sexual threats and conditional offers made to women employees by male corporate authorities. They focus on the type of sexual advances that are tied to hiring, promotions, or raises.[17] May and Hughes briefly refer to a third type of sexual advance, one that is "merely annoying" and "without demonstrable sanction or reward."[18] However, after introducing this third category the authors circumvent it. This oversight is a serious one. The essence of sexual harassment lies not in the content of the offender's proposal, but in the inappropriateness of his approach to the victim. It lies in the way he violates the victim's privacy. This is the "annoying" aspect of the offender's approach which needs elucidating. May and Hughes could not pursue this third type of sexual advance because they had defined sexual harassment in terms of someone in authority acquiring some sexual favor from his employee. They set themselves the task of proving that sexual harassment is necessarily coercive. Their definition thereby hinged on the alleged coercive effects of the harasser's proposal, rather than on his mental state.

We still need to examine May and Hughes's position that all sexual threats and offers made by male employers or managers to female employees are sexually harassing as well as coercive. They describe a conditional sexual threat from the employer's position: "If you don't provide a sexual benefit, I will punish you by withholding a promotion or raise that would otherwise be due, or ultimately fire you."[19] According to their "baseline" approach to coercion, "sexual threats are coercive because they worsen the objective situation the employee finds herself in." Before the threat the retention of her job only depended upon "standards of efficiency," whereas, after the threat, the performance of sexual favors becomes a condition of employment.[20] Presumably, these same "baseline" considerations also render the threat sexually harassing.

May and Hughes acknowledge their debt to Robert Nozick's "baseline account" of coercive threats. Elsewhere, I have defended an interpersonal description of coercive threats against the "baseline accounts" of Nozick and others.[21] According to my description X issues Y a coercive threat (in his attempt to get Y to do action "A") when X intentionally attempts to create the belief in Y that X will be responsible for harm coming to Y should Y fail to do A. X's coercive threat is described primarily in terms of his intentions. His motive for attempting to create this belief in Y is his desire to bring about a state of affairs in which Y's recognition of this possible harm to himself influences Y to do A. May and Hughes are correct that every conditional sexual threat issued by a male superior to a female subordinate is a coercive threat. (Indeed, a conditional sexual threat issued against anyone is a coercive threat.) The male manager would be trying to create the belief in the female employee that he will be responsible for harm coming to her (i.e., her termination, demotion, etc.) should she fail to comply with his sexual request. He would do this because he wants the prospect of this harm to motivate her to comply. Nevertheless, it is not true that every conditional sexual threat *as May and Hughes describe these threats* would be coercive. If, for example, the employer and the employee are playfully engaging in "banter" when he tells her that without her compliance he will fire her, then she is not being threatened. He does not intend to create the belief in her that harm will come to her. In this scenario she would not be sexually harassed either because the employer has a good faith belief that she consents to this "banter." Therefore, May and Hughes need a more rigorous description of coercive threats which includes the intentions of the person making the threat.

May and Hughes argue that if the employee wants to provide sexual favors to her employer regardless of the employer's demand, she is still coerced. They maintain that her objective baseline situation is still made worse, for now it would be very difficult for her to cease a sexual relationship with her employer should she choose to do so.[22] May and Hughes do not tell us who or what would specifically be making the coercive proposal if the *employee* propositioned the employer. After all, on their view, her offer would worsen her objective situation for the same reason his threat would. Perhaps they would refer to this as a coercive situation, or would find the employer's consent to the sexual relationship to include some sort of a coercive stance, but, nevertheless, their external analysis overlooks the mental state of the individual who is supposedly victimized. Depending upon her values and personal outlook she may, without reservation, accept her employer's demand as a "career opportunity." By excluding the employee's mental state in their "baseline analysis," May and Hughes overlook the fact that her situation may improve after the demand and that, to her, the prospect of a permanent sexual relationship with her employer is no problem. According to this "baseline account" she would not be coerced or harassed. Unlike May and Hughes's analysis, the proposed interpersonal account of sexual harassment maintains that an employee who receives a sexual threat from her employer is not necessarily sexually harassed. Let us say that he told her she must have sex with him or else be demoted. Still, she may welcome his demand as a "career opportunity." If she is not offended by his demand, then she is not sexually harassed by the threat.

As we have seen, May and Hughes maintain that the sexual harassment of a female employee by a male corporate authority is coercive because it worsens the employee's employment situation. They say that sexual harassment by a male employer makes for an unfair employment condition against women as a class. May and Hughes therefore believe that the discriminatory nature of sexual harassment against female employees is tied to these "coercive" dimensions. They argue that men do not have to endure the maligned "job requirement" foisted upon women, and that when men make sexual threats to their female subordinates they "establish a precedent for employment decisions based upon the stereotype that values women for their sexuality. . . ."[23] Because the sexual harassment of female employees by male employers worsens the employment situation of women as a class, we supposedly have a necessary relation between ("coercive") sexual harassment and sex discrimination.

May and Hughes are not alone in their belief that sexual harassment and discrimination are necessarily related. When they describe their arguments for the coercive-discriminatory effects of a male employer's sexual threat on a female employee, they refer to such a threat as an "instance of discrimination in the workplace."[24] Here they follow federal law by claiming that sexual threats in the workplace fall under the rubric of Title VII of the Civil Rights Act of 1964. They are relying on the fact that in 1980, the Equal Employment Opportunity Commission (EEOC) set a precedent by finding that sexual harassment is a form of sex discrimination.[25]

The view that the sexual harassment of women is a form of sex discrimination is ill-founded. Even if we follow May and Hughes and limit our discussion to the sexual harassment of female employees by male employers—something that the EEOC cannot do—a male employer's sexual threat is not necessarily an "instance" of sex discrimination. For a given sexual harassment case, gender may not be a consideration at all. Picture the bisexual male employer who indiscriminately threatens or propositions the male and female employees in his company. The additional "job requirement" referred to by May and Hughes would, in this case, apply to all employees, male and female. Although the proposed interpersonal account is compatible with the assumptions that sexual harassment against women generally contributes to discrimination against women and that the negative effects of sexual harassment are generally more serious for women than for men, the proposed account does not take sex discrimination to be an essential feature of sexual harassment.

May and Hughes's position must have been influenced by Catharine MacKinnon's book *Sexual Harassment of Working Women: A Case of Sex Discrimination.*[26] MacKinnon has helped to persuade the legal establishment and many social theorists to view the sexual harassment of women as sex discrimination. It appears that May and Hughes's account coincides with that of MacKinnon, except on one major point—MacKinnon acknowledges that the case of the bisexual harasser does not involve sex discrimination (although she says that such cases are rare). At the end of her book she refers to a "bisexual superior who harasses subordinates in a way that shows no gender bias." MacKinnon leaves open the possibility that the bisexual harasser can construct a legal defense sufficient to "negate the claim of sex discrimination."[27]

However, MacKinnon's position on sex discrimination is not clear. Earlier on in her book she says that according to the U.S. Supreme Court's account of sexual harassment—an account she finds inadequate—the case of the bisexual employer is "probably not sex discrimination." In such a case, the Supreme Court would find that the employees are not (mis)treated differently due to gender considerations.[28] Yet, the account of sex discrimination that MacKinnon prefers is not the one offered by the Supreme Court. MacKinnon apparently suggests that one *could* find sex discrimination in the case of the bisexual harasser. This finding would hinge on MacKinnon's view that society has defined the female gender in terms of sexuality and "makes a woman's sexuality a badge of female servitude."[29] MacKinnon refers to the special vulnerability of women and to the "disparate impact" of sexual harassment on women. She argues that even "neutral" employment practices which involve equal *treatment* of female and male employees may still have a disparate *impact* on the employees. Unlike men, women can suffer special negative effects from ostensibly neutral employment practices.[30] Given that society values women primarily for their sexuality, even the harassment of the bisexual supervisor may be seen as reinforcing this type of discrimination.

Does MacKinnon want to say that the case of the bisexual harasser does not involve sex discrimination, thereby qualifying her claim that sexual harassment is sex discrimination, or does she want to say that discrimination is found even in this example because women are disadvantaged in a way that men are not? It seems that there must be at least a few cases involving no special disadvantages, but even if all sexual harassment cases impacted on women in an especially negative way, this would not prove that the special disadvantages render the harassment itself discriminatory. In order to prove this, one would have to overcome the objection that discrimination seems to be more closely tied to an offender's actions and motives rather than to the disadvantageous results of an offender's actions.

Of course, the possibility that federal authority was misdirected when the EEOC set policy for sexual harassment in the workplace, does not entail that the EEOC's definition is incorrect. They maintain that:

Unwelcome sexual advances, requests for sexual favors, and other verbal or physical conduct of a sexual nature constitute sexual harassment when (1) submission to such conduct is made either explicitly or implicitly a term or condition of an individual's employment, (2) submission to or rejection of such conduct by an individual is used as the basis for employment decisions affecting such an individual, or (3) such conduct has the purpose or effect of unreasonably interfering with an individual's work performance or creating an intimidating, hostile, or offensive working environment.

The EEOC's conditions of sexual harassment appear to include not only sexual threats and offers, but also "annoyances" and other more subtle violations. The EEOC's definition thereby avoids May and Hughes's mistake. Their third condition also allows for sexual harassment between employees, something also lacking in May and Hughes's account. Unfortunately, the EEOC's first two conditions seem to suggest that all sexual threats and offers made by employers to employees are sexually harassing. As argued above, not all sexual threats made by employers to employees need be harassing, their inappropriateness notwithstanding. The EEOC's definition of sexual harassment is too inclusive because it fails to capture precisely the victim's mental state and the way that the victim reacts to the threat. In omitting a description of the victim's mental state the EEOC's definition allows a severely paranoid "victim" to claim sexual harassment against a considerate employer who has merely made some innocent comment or gesture. Moreover, the EEOC makes no provision for the intentions of the employer.

Some states throughout the country maintain that sexually explicit materials which disturb employees are sexually harassing. This stance seems to be in line with the EEOC's definition. According to the EEOC the employer or employee who, for example, displays a sexually explicit poster may exhibit "physical conduct of a sexual nature" that creates an "offensive working environment." This is a difficult example, but it seems that an employee's mere disapproval of such materials does not entail that the employee is being sexually harassed. Even if the disgruntled employee disapproves of the poster's explicit sexual representations, this does not mean that the person displaying the poster is intending to communicate anything to the employee about the employee. Of course, in many cases the poster bearer may be making a subtle statement to the employee about the employee's sexual appeal. For example the individual may be using the poster in order to communicate a sexual interest in the employee. According to the interpersonal account these cases would involve sexual harassment. If the person is merely displaying the poster for the person's own benefit, however, then this behavior is rude, but not sexually harassing. There is a difference between the disrespect involved in rudeness, which indicates poor taste or a breach of etiquette, and the disrespect involved in sexual harassment. In the latter case the privacy of some specific individual has not been respected.

If May and Hughes's position that all conditional sexual threats by male employers to female employees are sexually harassing and discriminatory in nature has successfully been overturned, their contention that the same considerations also apply to sexual offers collapses. They describe a sexual offer from the male employer's position: "If you provide a sexual benefit, I will reward you with a promotion or a raise that would otherwise not be due."[31] Since the benefit would ostensibly improve the employee's baseline situation, she is made an offer by her employer. Without the offer, she would not get the promotion or raise.

Interestingly, May and Hughes argue that such offers actually worsen the employee's baseline situation and are, therefore, coercive offers. They do not explain how the employee's situation is simultaneously improved and worsened, but perhaps they have the following in mind: the employer's proposal is an offer because it may improve the employee's strategic status, whereas his offer is coercive because of certain social considerations. May and Hughes tell us that the employer's sexual offer changes the work environment so that the employee "is viewed by others, and may come to view herself, less in terms of her work productivity and more in terms of her sexual allure." Moreover, they say that, since women are more "economically vulnerable and socially passive than men," they are inclined to "offset [their] diminished status and to protect against later retaliation" by acquiescing to employer demands. Thus, according to May and Hughes, they are necessarily coerced by a male employer's sexual offer.[32]

May and Hughes argue that there is usually an implicit threat concealed in an employer's sexual offer and that this makes the offer coercive. Of course, here it may be the threat that is coercive and not the offer. What we are interested in is their argument that the employer's sexual offer itself is coercive because it reduces the female employee's self-esteem and also raises the specter of some future threat (should the employee fail to comply or otherwise fall victim to the employer's "bruised" ego). Even if May and Hughes are correct and these are the general social effects of these sexual offers, this does not entail that a sexual offer made by a male employer to a female employee is itself coercive. It would be unreasonable to suggest that every female employee would experience these hardships following a male employer's sexual offer. As mentioned in the discussion of sexual threats, the employee's values and personality contribute to the effects of an employer's presumably coercive proposal. Moreover, May and Hughes's claim about the coercive effects of these sexual offers hinges upon their "baseline account" of coercion (which has been criticized above).

There is a more plausible alternative to a "baseline account" of coercive offers. An interpersonal account is possible. X makes Y a coercive offer when X intends to create the belief in Y that X will not prevent harm from coming to Y unless Y complies with X's request. A genuine offer, on the other hand, would be limited to a mutual exchange of perceived benefits, or it may be a gift. This offer could become coercive if X attempts to cause Y to believe that Y's rejection of X's request will result in some harm to Y. Essentially, the coercive element is that X makes the proposed assistance in preventing this harm conditional upon Y's agreement to X's request. X tries to use Y's belief that harm will occur as a way of controlling Y. Not all offers by male employers to female employees are like this. Thus, on this interpersonal description of offers, a male employer's offer is not coercive by nature.

We still need to address May and Hughes's account of the implications of an employer's sexual offer to an employee. We are told that a noncompliant employee may worry that a disgruntled employer may threaten or harm her at some future date. This is certainly possible. However, such proposals are not coercive unless they involve the relevant intentions. The proposed account does acknowledge that an employer's noncoercive sexual offer might be sexually harassing. As argued above, this depends upon the legitimacy of his approach to the employee and on the employee's wishes. Moreover, the fact that, according to the proposed view, some of these sexual offers are not coercive or sexually harassing does not alter the fact that an employer who is both considerate and prudent would avoid any behavior that could be construed as sexually harassing.[33]

NOTES

1. Kenneth C. Cooper, "The Six Levels of Sexual Harassment," *Contemporary Moral Controversies in Business,* A. Pablo Iannone, ed. (New York: Oxford University Press, 1989), p. 190.

2. Ibid.

3. Ibid.

4. See Part II for a detailed discussion of sexual harassment and discrimination.

5. Cooper, "The Six Levels of Sexual Harassment," p. 191.

6. Ibid.

7. Ibid.

8. Ibid.

9. Ibid., pp. 191–92.

10. Ibid., p. 192.

11. See Part II for a discussion of coercion and sexual harassment.

12. Some sociologists would disagree with me. They believe that the offender must have set himself a "sexual goal" in order for sexual harassment to occur. See K. Wilson and L. Kraus, "Sexual Harassment in the University." This paper was presented at the annual meetings of the American Sociological Association (Toronto, 1981).

13. Larry May and John C. Hughes, "Is Sexual Harassment Coercive?" in *Moral Rights in the Workplace,* Gertrude Ezorsky, ed. (Albany, N.Y.: State University of New York Press, 1987), pp. 115–22.

14. Ibid., p. 115.

15. Ibid.

16. Ibid., p. 118.

17. Ibid., pp. 116–117.

18. Ibid., p. 117.

19. Ibid., pp. 116–117.

20. Ibid., pp. 117–118.

21. "Intention and Coercion," *Journal of Applied Philosophy* 5, no. 1 (1988): 75–85.

22. May and Hughes, "Is Sexual Harassment Coercive?" p. 118.

23. Ibid., pp. 118–119..

24. Ibid., p. 118.

25. Equal Employment Opportunity Commission, 45 *Federal Register,* 74, 677 (1980).

26. Catharine A. MacKinnon, *Sexual Harassment of Working Women: A Case of Sex Discrimination* (New Haven, Conn.: Yale University Press, 1979).

27. Ibid., pp. 236–37.

28. Ibid., p. 203.

29. Ibid., p. 189.

30. Ibid., p. 192.

31. May and Hughes, "Is Sexual Harassment Coercive?" p. 117.

32. Ibid., p. 120.

33. I am grateful to Burleigh Wilkins for helpful comments on this paper.

Part Two

Explanations and Causes

6

Sexual Harassment at Work: Three Explanatory Models

Sandra S. Tangri, Martha R. Burt,
and Leanor B. Johnson

Several major explanations of sexual harassment have been offered in legal briefs (see Goodman 1981, MacKinnon 1979), in feminist writings, and by the press. However, until recently there has not been a sufficiently large or reliable data base to test these alternative interpretations of this recently "discovered" but long buried phenomenon (Bularzik 1978). In this [essay] we will describe the three broad models that emerge out of our review of the literature on sexual harassment, and will offer some empirical tests of each. Each model suggests certain predictions regarding: (a) who should be likely victims of sexual harassment, (b) who should be likely harassers, (c) the kinds of acts or behaviors to be expected, (d) how victims should feel and react to those acts, (e) what outcomes and consequences are likely, and (f) what characteristics of the work situation should be associated with greater harassment. For each model, we will first present the general description with citations to the pertinent literature, and then extrapolate to make various predictions. The three models are: (1) the natural or biological model, (2) the organizational model, and (3) the sociocultural model.

From *The Journal of Social Issues* 38, no. 4 (1982): 33–54. Reprinted by permission of The Society for the Psychological Study of Social Issues.

Briefly, the first model asserts that sexual harassment is simply natural sexual attraction between people. This model has two versions. The first maintains that sexually harassing behavior is not meant as such, but is merely a natural expression of men's stronger sex drive; the second version posits no unequal sex drive, but stresses that any individual may be attracted to any other individual, and may pursue that attaction without intent to harass.

The second, or organizational, model argues that sexual harassment is the result of certain opportunity structures created by organizational climate, hierarchy, and specific authority relations. In various versions it may or may not take into account the differential distribution of men and women within the authority structure.

The third, or sociocultural, model argues that sexual harassment reflects the larger society's differential distribution of power and status between the sexes. It is also seen as a mechanism that functions specifically to maintain male dominance over women within the workplace and within the economy generally. Various versions posit the existence or absence of a conscious collaboration among men toward this end.

We use the term "model" for want of a better one; in many ways these are positions, or preferences for interpreting sexually harassing behavior in particular ways, in the service of particular ends. The "natural model" admits the behavior but denies that the intent is to harass, discriminate, or dominate. Lest anyone think we have only described the natural model in order to shoot it down, we must point out that this model or position has been most vehemently argued in court by corporations seeking to avoid charges of sex discrimination for allowing harassment to exist, and has been the primary interpretation in need of change in the effort to bring sexual harassment under the purview of sex discrimination statutes. The organizational model looks to fairly simple causes and remedies without assuming much in the way of motives or psychological processes contributing to continuing harassment. The cultural model or position views sexual harassment as only one manifestation of a pervasive cultural enforcement of gender inequality. The evidence we report in this [essay] can, at best, negate some premises of these models and support others, rather than "proving" that one or another model is the correct view of the world.

Note that the natural/biological theory is primarily a motivational model; the organizational approach stresses facilitating factors; and the sociocultural model focuses on power differentials of males and females, male motivation to maintain this differential, and female socialization to acquiescence. Thus, the first theory is most sharply differentiated from the second and third by positing positive (i.e., "natural") rather than negative motives for behavior that might appear to be sexual harassment. The organizational and sociocultural models are most similar when the former takes into account the typical differential distribution of women and men in the organizational structure. Therefore, to more clearly differentiate our predictions the organizational model will be treated without this refinement. Finally, we expect that none of these theories will be either totally supported or totally rejected. However, it may be possible to conclude which one yields the greater explanatory power, and which one(s) offers less potential.

THE NATURAL/BIOLOGICAL MODEL

The natural or biological model rests on a number of assumptions about sexual behavior in the workplace, all of which result in a denial that such sexual behavior should be considered illegitimate and discriminatory. One assumption of this model holds that the human sex drive is stronger in men, leading them by biological propensity to aggress sexually against women, but without discriminatory intent (see, e.g., *Bundy* v. *Jackson* 1981, *Dothard* v. *Rawlinson* 1977). That they do this in work settings as well as other situations is neither surprising nor grounds for court action. If this assumption is true, we would expect to see more harassers in the age groups with the highest biological sex drives, and would not expect harassing behavior to vary by organizational position or status.

A second assumption of the natural model maintains that men and women are naturally attracted to each other, that both sexes participate in sexually oriented behavior in the workplace, and that they like it that way (see, e.g., *Corne and DeVane* v. *Bausch and Lomb* 1975, *Miller* v. *Bank of America* 1979, *Vinson* v. *Taylor* 1980). If sexual harassment is simply normal mutual sexual attraction, we would expect it to follow well-established patterns for liking and romantic attraction (Berscheid and Walster 1969, Winch 1971). Male-female pairs should be similar in age, race, and other background characteristics, attitudes, and statuses. Further, if asked, both should express interest in and attraction to each other, and no one should want to file a complaint.

A third prong found in the literature by proponents of the natural model attributes sexually harassing behavior to the idiosyncratic ("sick") proclivities of a minority of men (see e.g., *Corne and DeVane* v. *Bausch and Lomb* 1975). While admitting that harassment isn't "nice," this assumption denies any systematic pattern of sexual harassment, or any motive deriving from sex-based discrimination. If this assumption is true, we should see sexually harassing behavior randomly distributed among males of all ages, statuses, and occupational positions (*and* a *low* base-rate of harassers).

The various assumptions of the natural model have the effect of both trivializing sexual harassment (it is normal, idiosyncratic, individual, harmless) and aggrandizing it until all remedies seem hopeless (if it's human nature, change efforts must be futile). All versions of the natural model deny that sexual behavior at work has the intention or the effect of discriminating against women and reducing women's chances to compete successfully in the workplace (see, e.g., *Bundy* v. *Jackson* 1981, *Neely* v. *American Fidelity Assurance Co.* 1978, *Smith* v. *Amoco Chemical Corp.* 1979). This is its critical characteristic. A failure to find any systematic pattern of harassment, or any evidence of harmful effects on women, would support the natural model of sexual harassment.

Predictions Derived from the Natural/Biological Model

Expected Victims

Expected victims should be women or both sexes, and should be similar to their harasser in age, race, and occupational status. If they are truly objects of romantic interest, they should also be unmarried or otherwise "eligible" as continuing partners, and the only person to whom the harasser directs his attention.

Expected Harassers

Harassers should be men or both sexes. If men, they should be young, and if women, middle-aged, to correspond to the times of highest sex drive for males and females, respectively. They should tend to be unmarried, and thus have fewer regular sexual outlets. Harassers should be found in all organizational settings and climates, distributed generally or randomly among the population. Further, incidents should involve only one harasser, since multiple harassers would suggest the sociocultural model rather than the natural one.

Expected Acts

Acts should resemble courtship behavior, and should stop if and when one party indicates disinterest.

Expected Victim Reactions and Behavior

"Victims" should be flattered by the behaviors, or at least not be offended by them. Harassing behaviors should have positive effect or no effect on victims' feelings or work performance or working conditions. Victims would not file any formal complaints or take any other actions to bring the behavior to an end.

Expected Outcomes and Consequences

No negative consequences will happen to the victim.

Work Characteristics

Harassment incidents should not vary by work characteristics or atmosphere, according to the natural model.

THE ORGANIZATIONAL MODEL

The organizational model holds that institutions may provide an opportunity structure that makes sexual harassment possible. Since work organizations are characterized by vertical stratification, individuals can use their power and position to extort sexual gratification from their subordinates. Although typically males harass females, in principle it is possible for females to sexually harass males. It is less likely only because women tend to be employed in occupations subordinate to men (Evans 1978). Minority women, because they usually have the least organizational power, face the greatest economic disadvantage. This asymmetrical relation between superordinate (male) and subordinate (female) deprives subordinates of the material independence and security necessary to resist sexual harassment, and leaves them vulnerable to its economic, psychological, physical, and social consequences (MacKinnon 1979). Economic consequences can be more severe, for all recourses have the potential to affect the subordinate's immediate job and long-term career adversely. When faced with objectionable sexual advances, subordinates' options are to: (a) quit, (b) request a transfer, (c) tolerate, (d) acquiesce, or (e) file a complaint to a superior (Farley 1978, MacKinnon 1979).

Differential power is only one of several organizational characteristics which set the stage for sexual harassment. Martin and Fein[1] and Martin (1978) cite other principal factors: visibility and contact in sex-integrated jobs, the sex ratio, occupational norms, one's job function, and availability of grievance procedures and job alternatives. In *sex-integrated* jobs some employees may work alone, in pairs, or in groups. Some have a work area which is exclusively theirs and others do not. Each working condition allows varying opportunities for sexual harassment. It is possible that the *ratio of males to females* can facilitate or inhibit sexual harassment. The greater visibility of tokens, and "newcomer" status, may make them scapegoats for the dominant group's frustration. If they have colleagues or subordinates who resent their presence, harassment could serve to keep them isolated, humiliated, and uncomfortable enough to resign. *Organizational norms* vary from one occupation to another. As indicated by revealing waitress costumes and the terms "casting couch" and "sexcretary," sexual harassment receives strong informative support in some occupations. Within occupations there may also exist workplace norms that inhibit or facilitate sexual harassment. *Job tasks and requirements,* such as overtime work and business trips, may call into play leisure norms that conflict with work norms. Thus, "kidding around" with the opposite sex may lead to a more "sexy" atmosphere than found during normal working hours. It is possible that subordinates who have access to *informal or formal grievance procedures* and/or alternative jobs are less likely to tolerate or encounter sexual harassment. In sum, the organizational model relates sexual harassment to aspects of the workplace infrastructure that provide opportunities for sexual aggression.

Predictions Derived from the Organizational Model

Expected Victims

The most likely victims are those low in organization power: trainees; temporary or part-time workers; those in low grade or income levels; workers on probation, or newcomers such as token women or men, and low-status workers who are highly dependent on their job.

Expected Harassers

Conversely, the most likely harassers are those higher in organizational power than the victim or those co-workers who, by banding together, can present a powerful front to the victim. Persons who report that they have been accused of sexual harassing others are likely to have a more secure position in the organization.

Expected Acts

The greater the differential power in the organization or the higher the status of the harasser, the more severe and frequent the acts of sexual harassment.

Expected Victim Reactions and Behavior

Negative victim reactions should be greater for (a) the lowest status workers (see *Expected Victims*) and (b) those who do not see themselves as having any formal or informal recourse.

Expected Outcomes and Consequences

The organizational model says that sexual harassment is a way to intimidate and control subordinates by using organizational authority to extort sexual favors. The use of such organizational authority should be seen in the loss of occupational mobility as the price of resisting such demands. It would therefore predict that various negative economic consequences for the victim should be part of the sexual harassment experience.

Work Characteristics

Sexual harassment is more likely in work organizations that (a) are highly structured and stratified, (b) discourage redress on work-related concerns, (c) have options or requirements for weekend or overtime work, (d) have skewed sex ratios, and (e) have expectations for "sexy" behavior within the workplace. Furthermore, the severity of sexual harassment should be a function of both the degree of privacy in the work space and the work group size: (f) more severe forms of sexual harassment are most likely in organizations with large work groups and private or semi-private offices, and (g) less severe forms of harassment are most likely when semi- or private work space is *not* provided and the work groups are small.

THE SOCIOCULTURAL MODEL

According to the sociocultural model, sexual harassment is one manifestation of the larger patriarchal system in which men rule and social beliefs legitimize their rule (Farley 1978, MacKinnon 1979, 1981). According to this model, male dominance is maintained by cultural patterns of male-female interaction as well as by economic and political superordinancy. Society rewards males for aggressive and domineering sexual behaviors and females for passivity and acquiescence. Members of each sex are socialized to play their respective and complementary roles. Because women, more than men, are taught to seek their self-worth in the evaluation of others, particularly of men (Bardwick 1971), they are predisposed to try to interpret male attention as flattery, making them less likely to define unwanted attention as harassment. Their training to be sexually attractive, to be social facilitators and avoid conflict, to not trust their own judgment about what happens to them, and to feel responsible for their own victimization contributes to their vulnerability to sexual harassment. According to this model, the function of sexual harassment is to manage ongoing male-female interactions according to accepted sex status norms, and to maintain male dominance occupationally and therefore economically, by intimidating, discouraging, or precipitating removal of women from work.

Predictions Derived from the Sociocultural Model

Expected Victims

The sociocultural model would predict that gender is a better predictor of who is victimized than organizational position and that women are more often victims than men. It would also predict that a given harasser is likely to bother several victims. Women who are breaking into traditional male turf occupationally are also more likely to be harassed than other women.

Expected Harassers

As was the case for expected victims, the model predicts that gender is a better predictor of who will harass than organizational position, and that men are more often harassers than are women.

Expected Acts

The model does not suggest that certain forms of sexual harassment will be more common than others since all forms serve the same purpose. However, we would expect that women more than men would experience the "do it, or else" types of sexual harassment.

Expected Victim Reactions and Behavior

The sociocultural model predicts that female victims would react as power-less persons do, with damaged feelings about themselves and their work. It would also predict that it would have similar effects on other women, and that the emotional consequences would be worse for those victims with fewer options and a greater need for the job.

Because of their relative powerlessness and sex role socialization, women victims are not likely, according to this model, to take interpersonally as-sertive action or to act on an expectation that the organization will help them solve their problem. The theory would also predict that women are correct in not expecting management to help them.

Expected Outcomes and Consequences

The sociocultural model says that the function of sexual harassment is to keep women economically dependent and generally subordinate. It would therefore predict that various negative economic consequences for the victim would be a part of the harassment experience.

Work Characteristics

Sexual harassment should occur more frequently, according to this model, when the sex-ratio in the work group is highly skewed either way, al-though for different reasons. The singular or heavily outnumbered women would be targeted as intruders invading male territory and without suf-ficient numbers to support each other. The female-dominated workplace is likely to be a traditionally feminine job with low status, several rungs below a male supervisor. These women are likely to have little job se-curity, and traditional sex-role socialization.

A SURVEY OF FEDERAL EMPLOYEES

The data presented here were collected by the U.S. Merit Systems Protec-tion Board, to which the authors served as consultants on the design of the study. The U.S. Merit Systems Protection Board (USMSPB) is a fed-eral agency headquartered in Washington whose mission is to protect the merit system in federal employment practices. Data were collected in May 1980 from a stratified random sample of federal employees listed in the Central Personnel Data File of the Office of Personnel Management. The sample excluded: a) persons working outside the continental U.S., Alaska, or Hawaii; b) military personnel; c) persons employed by the FBI, CIA, Federal Election Commission, U.S. Postal Service and Postal Rate Commission, National Security Agency, Federal Reserve Board, White House Office, and Tennessee Valley Authority Agency; and d) persons whose file lacked legitimate values for any of the stratification variables. The sample was stratified by sex (male, female), minority status (minority, nonminority), salary (five ordered categories), and organization (Department of Defense, Veteran's Administration, all others) in order to assure adequate representation from all parts of the federal work force, and particularly those segments which, though small in number, might be disproportionately subject to harassment. For instance, low-income minority women constitute a very small portion of the federal work force, but might on theoretical grounds be expected to experience a disproportionate amount of harassment. An equal number of cases were drawn from each of the 60 cells ($2 \times 2 \times 5 \times 3$). All data presented here have been weighted by the appropriate sampling ratios. Anonymous, confidential, and usable questionnaries were returned from 83.8 percent of the 23,964 persons who received the questionnaire. The response rates from the various cells ranged from a low of 67.6 percent for low income minority men in the Veteran's Administration, to a high of 93.6 percent for medium-low income minority women in the Defense Department. The final sample size is 20,083 (10,644 women and 9,439 men).

"Victims" are persons who indicated that they had experienced one or more forms of sexual harassment on the job during the previous twenty-four months. All others are termed "nonvictims." Most of the figures presented here are contained in the MSPB's final report (USMSPB 1981) to the President and Congress.

PARTIAL TESTS OF THE MODELS USING SURVEY RESULTS

We cannot test all derivations from the three models with the data available, but even though incomplete, the tests we can make are instructive. Some conclusions are very clear. Models Two and Three receive more support than Model One. Male and female victims have different experiences, and men and women have different views about sexual behavior at work. The survey results are presented in relation to the questions asked of each model in the first part of the paper.

Who Are the Victims?

Men and women are not equally likely to experience sexual harassment. Forty-two percent of the women and only 15 percent of the men report having been sexually harassed at work within the preceding twenty-four months. Also, a higher percentage of female victims than of male victims experienced the most severe form of sexual harassment (3.1 percent vs. 1.7 percent). The "normal sexual attraction" version of Model One would suggest attention focused on only one person at a time, rather than indiscriminately spread over whoever is an easy target. Yet only a small minority (3 percent of the women and 8 percent of the men) report that they are unique in suffering the attentions of their harasser (a majority of each sex doesn't know whether there are other victims, but 43 percent of the women and 31 percent of the men report that there are other victims).

Single and divorced women are more likely to be victims (53 percent and 49 percent, respectively) than married women (37 percent). The incidence rate for widows is somewhat lower (31 percent) than for married women, but this may be associated with age as well. The same pattern holds for men even more strongly.

Neither the findings on sex of victim nor multiplicity of victims per harasser unequivocally support Model One's interpretation of sexual harassment. However, the relationship to marital status certainly does.

The evidence for more victimization of organizationally vulnerable workers is mixed. Women trainees report more harassment (51 percent) than other workers, but otherwise there is no relationship between job categories (Blue Collar, Clerical, Professional, Administration/Management) and harassment for either women or men. For men there is a clear negative relationship between GS level and incidence of harassment, which ranges from 9 percent of the GS 16's and above to 19 percent for GS 1 to GS 4. But for women, only being in the very highest GS levels somewhat reduces the probability of harassment (36 percent vs. 41–43 percent), while being in an ungraded or "Other" slot increases it somewhat. For both sexes, being a supervisor and not being on probation somewhat reduces one's risk of being harassed (46 percent and 54 percent, respectively). There is no clear relationship between income and incidence of sexual harassment, and education is *positively* related to incidence of harassment. Persons with less than a high school diploma report the least harassment while those with some graduate education report the most. This may reflect differences in awareness, differences in work situation (sex-ratio of one's work group, nontraditionally of one's job), or other factors.

Two measures of *personal* vulnerability, on the other hand, are strongly related to sexual harassment for both sexes. Younger workers report more harassment than older workers, and dependence on the job ("at the time of this experience, how much did you need this job?") dramatically increases the incidence of harassment (over 60 percent of the victims report "great" dependence on that job), a result that correlates with frequency of harassment and with duration of harassment for women.

We also find that women pioneers are more likely to be victims (53 percent) than nonpioneers (41 percent). But the same is true of men pioneers (20 percent) vs. nonpioneers (14 percent). The findings on education fit Model Three better than they fit Model Two, but the findings on GS level and income (which are highly correlated) support neither. Perhaps any single monotonic relationship is wiped out because both—opposite— forces are at work.

Who Are the Harassers?

The preponderance of harassers are male (78 percent of the victims were harassed by males only; 95 percent of female victims and 22 percent of male victims). Most victims (about 80 percent) were harassed by only one person but about a fifth were harassed by more than one person. While most women were harassed by married persons (67 percent), men were somewhat more likely to be harassed by single persons than by married persons.

It is difficult to test the similarity of victim and harasser on demographic variables because the data are imprecise or absent. With respect to age we only know whether the harasser was younger, older, or the same age, but we do not know how much older or younger. We do not know the harasser's level of education, income, or religion. With respect to ethnicity, we do know whether it is the same as or different from the victim's. Most victims were harassed by a person of the same ethnicity as themselves (63 percent of female victims, 68 pecent of male victims), although women were more likely to be victimized by someone of a different ethnicity (26 percent) than men were (17 percent). But most women's harassers are older than themselves (68 percent) while men's harassers, in contrast, are most likely to be younger (38 percent), less than half as likely as women's harassers to be older (29 percent), and somewhat more likely to be the same age (18 percent). These findings provide some support for Model One in the similarity of ethnicity, but not for age or marital status.

The pattern of organizational relationships is also somewhat different for male and female victims. Although co-workers are the most common harassers for both sexes (65 percent for female victims, 76 percent for male victims), supervisors are two and a half times more common as harassers of women (37 percent) than as harassers of men (14 percent). For female but not male victims, subordinates are the least common harassers (4 percent and 16 percent, respectively). Thus the power differential component of sexual harassment, though not typical, is more common for women victims than men victims. Co-worker harassment, although not usually a direct abuse of organizational power, still may be a power move by one or more co-workers trying to invoke the victim's sexual rather than work status in a work setting. Also, when organizational hierarchies fail to prohibit co-worker harassment, the situation becomes one in which official power implicitly condones and supports harassment.

Thus, women's harassers are most likely to be older married men, while men's harassers are most likely to be younger, single women. While both sexes are most likely to be harassed by a co-worker, more women than men are harassed by a superior and more men than women are harassed by subordinates. These differences suggest that the male's harasser might be more attractive to him than the female's harasser would be to her.

This pattern of difference, together with findings presented later on attitudinal differences and with other findings on the nature and outcome of the harassment, suggests that sexual harassment of women conforms more to a model suggesting intimidation while that of men conforms more to a model suggesting attraction (whether or not this is reciprocated).

What Took Place?

One percent of the female work force reported actual or attempted rape or sexual assault, as did .03 percent of the male workforce. This corresponds to 3 percent of the female victims and almost 2 percent of the male victims reporting on the USMSPB survey. Almost three times as many men as women report that this happened to them more than once (56 percent vs. 20 percent). Less serious forms of harassment (sexual remarks, suggestive looks, deliberate touching) occurred more frequently than more serious forms of harassment (pressure for dates or sexual favors, letters or phone calls, rape or assault).

The *quid pro quo* type of harassment (in which victims fear retaliation if they do not cooperate) was somewhat more common among female victims than male victims, and was even reported by victims harassed by co-workers as well as superiors. For each type of penalty (worse assignments, unable to get promotions, losing one's job, etc.), a slightly higher proportion of women than men victims thought this would happen if they did not go along with the harasser. However, the differences are only a few percentage points. Oddly enough, men victims were equally or more likely than women victims to think there would be benefits if they *did* go along. Again, however, most of the differences are very small.

How Did the Victim Respond?

The data on female victims' response to sexual harassment [are] perhaps the most damaging to the view that harassment is an expression of attraction which the perpetrator presumably expects or would like to have reciprocated. Only a very small number of female victims go along with the overtures of the harasser (8 percent). But fully one-fourth of male victims do report "going along." Even these figures may overrepresent the number of true romance among these incidents, since some of these individuals may have gone along out of fear of retaliation as Models Two and Three would predict. Furthermore, 23 percent of these female victims and 21 percent of the male victims also said that doing so made things worse.

As shown before, a majority of victims harassed by their immediate supervisor did think something bad would happen if they did not go along with the supervisor (56 percent of both sexes); and a substantial minority of victims of other harassers also expected negative consequences (20 to 60 percent). Yet less than five percent of male and female victims took any formal action against the harasser, and most but not all of these did not see any need to report the behavior (61 percent females, 71 percent males).

Rather than it making victims feel good, the harassment worsened their emotional or physical condition (33 percent of the women and 21 percent of the men), worsened their ability to work with others on the job (15 percent and 15 percent), and worsened their feelings about work (36 percent and 19 percent).

The evidence for feelings of powerlessness among these victims is also mixed. Less than 10 percent of the victims felt that there is very little that either employees or management can do to reduce sexual harassment. At the same time, however, only slightly more than 10 percent felt that any formal action they took would be effective in stopping sexual harassment. Almost half the women and two-fifths of the men responded by avoiding the person who was harassing them. Another sixty-plus percent ignored the behavior or did nothing. Such indirect and nonthreatening behavioral responses may reflect feelings of powerlessness or may reflect victim's feelings that the behavior is not a problem for them. Supportive of the latter interpretation is the finding that 61 percent of the women and 71 percent of the men said they "saw no need to report it."

More women than men did nothing because they were embarrassed (15 percent and 10 percent), because they did not think anything would be done (33 percent and 17 percent), because they thought it would be held against them (23 percent and 11 percent), or because they didn't know what action to take (15 percent and 7 percent).

What Outcomes or Consequences Ensued?

The vast majority of victims reported no actual changes in their job situation (81 percent of the women and 87 percent of the men) with respect to assignments, promotions, etc. One percent or fewer reported that some aspect of their work situation became better. Less than 10 percent reported that their working conditions or assignments worsened or that they experienced other negative job changes (denial of promotion, step increase, good performance rating, or reference; being reassigned or fired; quitting without another job; transferring or quitting to another job). Although the differences are small (1–4 percentage points), more female than male victims did experience negative job consequences.

Other kinds of negative consequences were more common. Over a third of the female victims (36 percent) and almost a fifth of the male victims (19 percent) reported that their "feelings about work became worse"; similar numbers reported that their "emotional or physical condition became worse" (33 percent women, 21 percent men); and eight to fifteen percent reported deterioration in their ability to work with others on the job, in their time and attendance at work, and in the quantity or quality of their work. These kinds of consequences are likely to have negative effects of some magnitude on one's ability to and likelihood of advancing in the job market. One should also remember that even though the percentages of each sex reporting a given outcome are similar, the actual numbers of women and men being affected are very different since there are three-fourths again as many women victims as men victims (294,000 to 168,000 in the federal workforce as a whole, extrapolating from survey data).

Part of Model Three is the assumption that the maintenance of dominance relations does not require that every woman be a victim, nor that every victim suffer all possible consequences. As with rape, the widespread knowledge that such things can and do happen serves to keep many women in the psychological condition of being wary—of being potential victims. Thus data on what victims *expected* to happen are also important in evaluating this model. Many more victims expected negative consequences than actually experienced such outcomes, especially when the harasser was a supervisor. More than half expected some kind of negative job-related consequences if they did not go along with their immediate boss. The figures are somewhat lower for the perceived penalty of not going along with a superior above their immediate boss. Moreover, 30 percent of the female victims (and 26 percent of the male victims) expected penalties if they did not go along with a co-worker who was harassing them. On the other hand, 12 to 29 percent of the women (and 20 to 35 percent of the men) thought they would obtain some job advantage if they did go along with a supervisor. Even going along with a co-worker or some other nonsupervisory worker was perceived as having some potential pay-offs by some workers (2 to 9 percent of the victims of each sex).

Model Three would also predict that, beyond the abuse of power by an individual as predicted by Model Two, the organizations them-selves—as male-dominated entities—would tacitly tolerate (or even en-courage) sexual harassment of women as a way of perpetuating that dominance. This prediction is not generally supported: Only 4 percent of the women but 16 percent of the men victims reported that their organization was hostile or took action against them while 6 percent of the women and less than one-tenth of 1 percent of the men report that their organization did nothing. In fact, taking some kind of formal action was more effective in remedying the situation than was generally expected by the sample as a whole, and was generally more effective than informal actions. Of the organizational variables, only sex ratio, climate, and management respon-siveness show a relationship to incidence of sexual harassment. For both sexes, likelihood of experiencing sexual harassment is associated with working in a group where the opposite sex predominates. This finding is most consistent with Models Two and Three. Victims of both sexes are more likely to report working in a sexy climate than nonvictims, and less likely to report working under a management that is responsive to their concerns. Neither size of work group, privacy of work space, nor work schedule show any relationship to incidence of sexual harassment.

Attitudes: How Do Men and Women View Sexually Harassing Behaviors?

Although the models as presented do not include predictions about peo-ple's *consciousness* regarding sexual harassment, it is instructive to exam-ine the data available to us on this question. The first section of the questionnaire presented a series of attitudinal items . . . regarding various aspects of sexual behavior at work, and the second section asked respond-ents to indicate which specific sexual behaviors (by a supervisor or a co-worker) would bother them and which they would consider sexual harassment. The attitudinal items contained statements representing each of the three models, i.e., some items reflect a view of sexual harassment as natural and nonserious, some reflect the perspective that it is based on organizational power rather than gender, and some that it is a part of a large power structure based on gender.

Of the six attitudinal items that reflect a view of sexual behavior at work as natural, nonthreatening, and even legitimately useful, only one receives the support of a majority of respondents: "People can usually stop unwanted sexual attention by telling the offender to stop." There is least agreement with using sex to get ahead: Less than 5 percent of both men and women felt this was all right for either sex to do. Greater differences between the male and female respondents are found on the remaining three items, and in each case more men than women agreed. Less than one-fourth of the women, but over 40 percent of the men, agreed that, "The issue of sexual harassment has been exaggerated—most incidents are simply normal sexual attraction between people." More than a third of the women (36 percent) agreed with the statement, "People shouldn't be so quick to take offense when someone expresses a sexual interest in them," but this is still fewer than the percentage of men agreeing with it (48 percent). And finally, 17 percent of the women and 26 percent of the men think that "It's all right for people to have sexual affairs with people they work with." Thus most of the respondents do not endorse items consistent with a natural/biological view of sexual harassment, although more men than women do so. However, while they do not strongly endorse this view, many respondents (more men than women) downplay the seriousness of the behavior and exaggerate the ease with which victims are expected to handle it.

Only one item directly reflects the organizational view of sexual harassment, namely that it is simply one expression of the abuse of power that comes with a hierarchical structure, and persons of either sex having that power are equally likely to abuse it. Half of the men and two-fifths of the women agreed that, "Women in positions of power are just as likely as men in such positions to sexually bother the people who work for them."

Only one item directly expresses the view that sexual harassment is essentially a power play which is not necessarily dependent on, or related to, organizational position: "Those who sexually bother others are usually seeking power over those they bother." Interestingly, while women endorsed this item at about the same rate as they did the "organizational" item (43 percent and 41 percent, respectively), men were less likely to endorse this item than the previous one (33 percent vs. 50 percent). In fact, this is the only attitude item which women endorsed at a higher rate than men did.

Two other items discredit the concept of sexual harassment as "uninvited and unwanted sexual attention" by either blaming the victim or discrediting the victim's claims. Endorsement of either item reflects a view which is contrary to both Models Two and Three. Only a minority of either sex endorsed these items, although again more men than women did so. Less than a third of the men and a fourth of the women agreed that, "People who receive annoying sexual attention have usually asked for it." Thirteen percent of the men and 7 percent of the women agreed that "When people say they've been sexually harassed, they're usually trying to get the person they accuse into trouble."

In sum, most respondents strongly reject the attitudinal derivatives of Model One, but do not strongly reject those of Models Two and Three. More men than women hold views consistent with the biological/natural model, while more women than men hold views consistent with the cultural model.

For all of the specific sexual behaviors presented, a majority of men and women say they would be bothered if a co-worker or supervisor did these, and would call it sexual harassment in either case. There was one exception. Fewer than half the men said that they would consider sexual teasing, jokes, remarks, or questions from a co-worker to be sexual harassment. Consistent with the sex differences on attitudes, more women than men said that each kind of behavior from each source (supervisor or co-worker) would bother them, and would be sexual harassment. Both sexes consider such behaviors from supervisors more serious than from co-workers (more persons would be bothered by these behaviors and call it sexual harassment); and both sexes rank the behaviors similarly.

Thus, although women and men appear to apply the same criteria for using the term "sexual harassment," women's threshold is lower, and they are more bothered by it.

CONCLUSIONS

The most striking thing about these findings is not some clear-cut support for one model or the other, but rather that no clear pattern emerges. Certainly one conclusion to be drawn from these data is that sexual harassment is not a unitary phenomenon, especially across the sexes, but even within those incidents reported by women. Some sexual harassment may indeed be clumsy or insensitive expressions of attraction, while some is the classic abuse of organizational power. Our data suggest that men are more likely than women to be victims of the former, while women are more likely than men to be victims of the latter. Most clear is that the victim experiences the most adverse effect in the latter case, and in almost no case does sexual harassment have beneficial outcomes. Women, who are four times as likely to be victims as men, also view sexual harassment more negatively, and in general are more likely to feel that sexual behavior and work don't mix.

These are actually important findings to document, since the data set on which they rest is the first random sample available for analysis in which nonself-selected individuals were asked about sexual harassment, with that specific label attached to behaviors many people experience. In the past, self-selected samples (all female) have reported much more homogeneous harassment experiences which more directly fit the *quid pro quo* ("do it or else") type of harassment. The three theoretical models posited in this [essay] were derived from the literature, court cases, and legal defenses describing these more homogeneous situations. Now that we have data reflecting a broader range of experience among a valid sample of respondents, what conclusions can we draw?

The consistent negative reactions of female victims to incidents they consider harassing, plus the tendency of individuals with greater degrees of personal vulnerability and dependence on their job to experience more harassment constitute the strongest evidence available in these data against the natural model. Nevertheless, given the relatively simple hypotheses with which we began, each model receives some support from these data. An important area for further analysis would be to separate co-worker harassment from superior-subordinate harassment, with further splits by sex of victim and seriousness of harassment, and look for differential patterns of causes and consequences within the different types thus created. This would best be done not as tests of three models, but rather as a multivatiate analysis exploring the interactive role of demographic, organizational, and cultural factors on incidence and consequences.

Even with the type of analysis just described, however, we now have some doubt about the predictability of harassment incidents themselves. If sexual harassment is as widespread as the results of the MSPB survey indicate, it may approximate a random event in women's working lives—something which is highly likely to happen at some time, with just when, where, and how being so multi-determined that prediction is difficult. This very fact supports the cultural model in some ways, but it also implies that finding empirical support for the cultural model will not be easy, if only because few, if any, circumstances exist where the dominant culture does not exert its influence. Even within the minds of the survey respondents, what they call sexual harassment and how they respond to it will already be determined by the cultural context. For instance, most respondents who experienced sexual harassment did not report it to anyone, and did not see reporting it as an appropriate response. As researchers, we must interpret this finding, but have little basis in the survey results for doing so. Do respondents believe any appeal to organizational authority would be ineffective? Since most of the incidents involve co-workers, do respondents view these as not organizationally threatening enough to warrant formal action? Are respondents caught up in the cultural mandate, based on the natural model, that they should be able to handle such incidents themselves? If thinking about the acceptability of sexual harassment changes, would we be likely to see more formal action and more anger at employers for permitting harassment to continue? We cannot answer these questions, and therefore cannot finally decide which model best reflects what "is." In no small part, this inability arises because what "is" is changing, respondents are themselves at different points along an ideological continuum, and thus what they report and how they see it will be full of contradictions for some time to come.

A survey of the USMSPB type is useful for documenting incidence and prevalence, and certain general patterns of sexual harassment at single points in time. As such, it provides an invaluable snapshot not heretofore available. Nevertheless, such data, on such a large sample, can only scratch the surface of understanding the intrapersonal and interpersonal dynamics of sexual harassment. If at all possible, future research should use these data and the types of harassment derivable from them to structure more in-depth explorations of how victims see sexual harassment and their options when confronted with it. In particular, creative thought must be given to ways to explore the cultural assumptions underlying harassment, since survey methods may not be able to discover enough variance to make that particular mode of analysis meaningful. A similar in-depth analysis of consequences would need to explore victims' reduced expectations and aspirations for a satisfying work environment, changed perceptions of self, changes in self-confidence, and productivity factors which are easily denied in a survey research format.

NOTE

1. S. Martin and S. Fein. *Sexual Harassment in the Workplace: A Problem Whose Time Has Come,* Paper presented at the annual meeting of the Society for the study of Social Problems, September 2, 1978.

REFERENCES

Bardwick, J. *The Psychology of Women.* New York: Harper and Row, 1971.
Berscheid, E., and Walster, E. *Interpersonal Attraction.* Reading, Mass.: Addison-Wesley, 1969.
Bularzik, M. "Sexual Harassment at the Workplace: Historical Notes." In F. Brodhead et al., eds., *Radical America* 12, no. 4 (1978).
Bundy v. *Jackson.* D.C. Action No. 77-1359 (D.C. Cir., January 12, 1981).
Corne and DeVane v. *Bausch and Lomb, Inc.* 390 F. Suppl. 161 (D. Ariz. 1975). Reversed and remanded on other grounds, 562 F. 2n 55 (9th Cir. 1977).
Dothard v. *Rawlinson,* 433 U.S. 321 (1977).
Evans, L. J. "Sexual Harassment: Women's Hidden Occupational Hazard." In J. Roberts Chapman and M. Gates, eds., *The Victimization of Women.* Beverly Hills, Calif.: Sage Publications, 1978, pp. 203–23.
Farley, L. *Sexual Shakedown: The Sexual Harassment of Women on the Job.* New York: McGraw Hill, 1978.
Goodman, J. "Sexual Harassment: Some Observations of the Distance Traveled and the Distance Yet to Go." *Capital Universal Law Review* 10, no. 3 (1978): 445–70.
MacKinnon, C. A. Introduction. *Capital University Law Review,* 1981, 10(3), i–viii.
―――. *Sexual Harassment of Working Women.* New Haven, Conn.: Yale University Press, 1979.
Martin, S. "Sexual Politics in the Workplace: The Interactional World of Policewomen." *Symbolic Interaction* 1, no. 2 (1978): 44–60.
Miller v. *Bank of America.* 418 F. Supp. 233 (N.D. Cal. 1976), (Rev'd 600 F. 2d 211 C.D.C. Cir. 1979) Appeal Pending.
Neely v. *American Fidelity Assurance Co.,* 17 F.E.P. 482 (W.D. Okla. 1978).
Smith v. *Amoco Chemical Corp.,* 20 F.E.P. 724 (S.D. Texas 1979).
U.S. Merit Systems Protection Board. *Sexual Harassment in the Federal Workplace: Is It a Problem?* Washington, D.C. US GPO., 1981.
Vinson v. *Taylor,* 23 F.E.P. 37 (D.D.C. 1980).
Winch, R. F. *The Modern Family* 3rd. ed. New York: Holt, Rinehart and Winston, 1971.

7

Sexual Aggression and Nature

Camille Paglia

In the beginning was nature. The background from which and against which our ideas of God were formed, nature remains the supreme moral problem. We cannot hope to understand sex and gender until we clarify our attitude toward nature. Sex is a subset to nature. Sex is the natural in man.

Society is an artificial construction, a defense against nature's power. Without society, we would be storm-tossed on the barbarous sea that is nature. Society is a system of inherited forms reducing our humiliating passivity to nature. We may alter these forms, slowly or suddenly, but no change in society will change nature. Human beings are not nature's favorites. We are merely one of a multitude of species on which nature indiscriminately exerts its force. Nature has a master agenda we can only dimly know.

Human life began in flight and fear. Religion rose from rituals of propitiation, spells to lull the punishing elements. To this day, communities are few in regions scorched by heat or shackled by ice. Civilized man conceals from himself the extent of his subordination to nature. The grandeur of culture, the consolation of religion absorb his attention and win his faith. But let nature shrug, and all is in ruin. Fire, flood, lightning, tornado, hurricane, volcano, earthquake—anywhere at any time. Disaster

From *Sexual Personae: Art and Decadence from Nefertiti to Emily Dickinson* (New Haven, Conn.: Yale University Press, 1990), pp. 1-5, 7-10, 19, 20, 30-33. Copyright © 1990 by Camille Paglia. Reprinted by permission of the publisher.

falls upon the good and bad. Civilized life requires a state of illusion. The idea of the ultimate benevolence of nature and God is the most potent of man's survival mechanisms. Without it, culture would revert to fear and despair.

Sexuality and eroticism are the intricate intersection of nature and culture. Feminists grossly oversimplify the problem of sex when they reduce it to a matter of social convention: readjust society, eliminate sexual inequality, purify sex roles, and happiness and harmony will reign. Here feminism, like all liberal movements of the past two hundred years, is heir to Rousseau. *The Social Contract* (1762) begins: "Man is born free, and everywhere he is in chains." Pitting benign Romantic nature against corrupt society, Rousseau produced the progressivist strain in nineteenth-century culture, for which social reform was the means to achieve paradise on earth. The bubble of these hopes was burst by the catastrophes of two world wars. But Rousseauism was reborn in the postwar generation of the sixties, from which contemporary feminism developed.

Rousseau rejects original sin, Christianity's pessimistic view of man born unclean, with a propensity for evil. Rousseau's idea, derived from Locke, of man's innate goodness led to social environmentalism, now the dominant ethic of American human services, penal codes, and behaviorist therapies. It assumes that aggression, violence, and crime come from social deprivation—a poor neighborhood, a bad home. Thus feminism blames rape on pornography. . . . But rape . . . [has] been evident throughout history and, at some moment, in all cultures.

This. . . [selection] takes the point of view of Sade, the most unread major writer in Western literature. Sade's work is a comprehensive satiric critique of Rousseau, written in the decade after the first failed Rousseauist experiment, the French Revolution, which ended not in political paradise but in the hell of the Reign of Terror. Sade follows Hobbes rather than Locke. Aggression comes from nature; it is what Nietzsche is to call the will-to-power. For Sade, getting back to nature (the Romantic imperative that still permeates our culture from sex counseling to cereal commercials) would be to give free reign to violence and lust. I agree. Society is not the criminal but the force which keeps crime in check. When social controls weaken, man's innate cruelty bursts forth. The rapist is created not by bad social influences but by a failure of social conditioning. Feminists, seeking to drive power relations out of sex, have set themselves against nature. Sex *is* power. Identity is power. In western culture, there are no nonexploitative relationships. Everyone has killed in order to live. Nature's universal law of creation from destruction operates in mind as in matter. As Freud, Nietzsche's heir, asserts, identity is conflict. Each generation drives its plow over the bones of the dead.

Modern liberalism suffers unresolved contradictions. It exalts individualism and freedom and, on its radical wing, condemns social orders as oppressive. On the other hand, it expects government to provide materially for all, a feat manageable only by an expansion of authority and a swollen bureaucracy. In other words, liberalism defines government as tyrant father but demands it behave as nurturant mother. Feminism has inherited these contradictions. It sees every hierarchy as repressive, a social fiction; every negative about woman is a male lie designed to keep her in her place. Feminism has exceeded its proper mission of seeking political equality for women and has ended by rejecting contingency, that is, human limitation by nature or fate.

Sexual freedom, sexual liberation. A modern delusion. We are hierarchical animals. Sweep one hierarchy away, and another will take its place, perhaps less palatable than the first. There are hierarchies in nature and alternate hierarchies in society. In nature, brute force is the law, a survival of the fittest. In society, there are protections for the weak. Society is our frail barrier against nature. When the prestige of state and religion is low, men are free, but they find freedom intolerable and seek new ways to enslave themselves, through drugs or depression. My theory is that whenever sexual freedom is sought or achieved, sadomasochism will not be far behind. Romanticism always turns into decadence. Nature is a hard taskmaster. It is the hammer and the anvil, crushing individuality. Perfect freedom would be to die by earth, air, water, and fire.

Sex is a far darker power than feminism has admitted. Behaviorist sex therapies believe guiltless, no-fault sex is possible. But sex has always been girt around with taboo, irrespective of culture. Sex is the point of contact between man and nature, where morality and good intentions fall to primitive urges. I called it an intersection. This intersection is the uncanny crossroads of Hecate, where all things return in the night. Eroticism is a realm stalked by ghosts. It is the place beyond the pale, both cursed and enchanted.

. . . Integration of man's body and mind is a profound problem that is not about to be solved by recreational sex or an expansion of women's civil rights. Incarnation, the limitation of mind by matter, is an outrage to imagination. Equally outrageous is gender, which we have not chosen but which nature has imposed upon us. Our physicality is torment, our body the tree of nature on which Blake sees us crucified.

Sex is daemonic. This term, current in Romantic studies of the past twenty-five years, derived from the Greek *daimon,* meaning a spirit of lower divinity than the Olympian gods (hence my pronunciation "daimonic"). The outcast Oedipus becomes a daemon at Colonus. The word came to mean a man's guardian shadow. Christianity turned the daemonic into the demonic. The Great daemons were not evil—or rather they were both good and evil, like nature itself, in which they dwelled. Freud's unconscious is a daemonic realm. In the day we are social creatures, but at night we descend to the dream world where nature reigns, where there is no law but sex, cruelty, and metamorphosis. Day itself is invaded by daemonic night. Moment by moment, night flickers in the imagination, in eroticism, subverting our strivings for virtue and order, giving an uncanny aura to objects and persons revealed to us through the eyes of the artist.

The ghost-ridden character of sex is implicit in Freud's brilliant theory of "family romance." We each have an incestuous constellation of sexual personae that we carry from childhood to the grave and that determines whom and how we love or hate. Every encounter with friend or foe, every clash with or submission to authority bears the perverse traces of family romance. Love is a crowded theater, for as Harold Bloom remarks, "We can never embrace (sexually or otherwise) a single person, but embrace the whole of her or his family romance."[1] We still know next to nothing of the mystery of cathexis, the investment of libido in certain people or things. The element of free will in sex and emotion is slight. As poets know, falling in love is irrational.

Like art, sex is fraught with symbols. Family romance means that adult sex is always representation, ritualistic acting out of vanished realities. A perfectly humane eroticism may be impossible. Somewhere in every family romance is hostility and aggression, the homicidal wishes of the unconscious. Children are monsters of unbridled egotism and will, for they spring directly from nature, hostile limitations of immorality. We carry that daemonic will within us forever. Most people conceal it with acquired ethical precepts and meet it only in their dreams, which they hastily forget upon waking. The will-to-power is innate, but the sexual scripts of family romance are learned. Human beings are the only creatures in whom consciousness is so entangled with animal instinct. In Western culture,there can never be a purely physical or anxiety-free sexual encounter. Every attaction, every pattern of touch, every orgasm is shaped by psychic shadows. . . .

Sex cannot be understood because nature cannot be understood. Science is a method of logical analysis of nature's operations. It has lessened human anxiety about the cosmos by demonstrating the materiality of nature's forces, and their frequent predictability. But science is always playing catch-up ball. Nature breaks its own rules whenever it wants. Sci-

ence cannot avert a single thunderbolt. Western science is a product of
the Apollonian mind: its hope is that by naming and classification, by
the cold light of intellect, archaic night can be pushed back and defeated. . . .

The westerner knows by seeing. Perceptual relations are at the heart
of our culture, and they have produced our titanic contributions to art.
Walking in nature, we see, identify, name, *recognize*. This recognition is
our apotropaion, that is, our warding off of fear. Recognition is ritual cog-
nition, a repetition-compulsion. We say that nature is beautiful. But this
esthetic judgment, which not all peoples have shared, is another defense
formation, woefully inadequate for encompassing nature's totality. What is
pretty in nature is confined to the thin skin of the globe upon which we
huddle. Scratch that skin, and nature's daemonic ugliness will erupt. . . .

. . . The identification of woman with nature was universal in prehis-
tory. In hunting or agrarian societies dependent upon nature, femaleness
was honored as an immanent principle of fertility. As culture progressed,
crafts and commerce supplied a concentration of resources freeing men
from the caprices of weather or the handicap of geography. With nature
at one remove, femaleness receded in importance.

Buddhist cultures retained the ancient meanings of femaleness long
after the West renounced them. Male and female, the Chinese yang and
yin, are balanced and interpenetrating powers in man and nature, to which
society is subordinate. This code of passive acceptance has its roots in
India, a land of sudden extremes where a monsoon can wipe out 50,000
people overnight. The femaleness of fertility religions is always double-
edged. The Indian nature-goddess Kali is creator *and* destroyer, grant-
ing boons with one set of arms while cutting throats with the other. She
is the lady ringed with skulls. The moral ambivalence of the great mother
goddesses has been conveniently forgotten by those American feminists
who have resurrected them. We cannot grasp nature's bare blade without
shedding our own blood.

Western culture from the start has swerved from femaleness. The last
major Western society to worship female powers was Minoan Crete. And
significantly, that fell and did not rise again. The immediate cause of its
collapse—quake, plague, or invasion—is beside the point. The lesson is
that cultic femaleness is no guarantee of cultural strength or viability. What
did survive, what did vanquish circumstance and stamp its mindset on
Europe was Mycenaean warrior culture, descending to us through Homer.
The male will-to-power: Mycenaeans from the south and Dorians from
the north would fuse to form Apollonian Athens, from which came the
Greco-Roman line of Western history.

Both the Apollonian and Judeo-Christian traditions are transcendental. That is, they seek to surmount or transcend nature. . . . Judeo-Christianity, like Greek worship of the Olympian gods, is a sky-cult. It is an advanced stage in the history of religion, which everywhere began as earth-cult, veneration of fruitful nature.

The evolution from earth-cult to sky-cult shifts woman into the nether realm. Her mysterious procreative powers and the resemblance of her rounded breasts, belly, and hips to earth's contours put her at the center of early symbolism. . . .

. . . From the beginning of time, woman has seemed an uncanny being. Man honored but feared her. She was the black maw that had spat him forth and would devour him anew. Men, bonding together, invented culture as a defense against female nature. Sky-cult was the most sophisticated step in this process, for its switch of the creative locus from earth to sky is a shift from belly-magic to head-magic. And from this defensive head-magic has come the spectacular glory of male civilization, which has lifted woman with it. The very language and logic modern woman uses to assail patriarchal culture were the invention of men.

Hence the sexes are caught in a comedy of historical indebtedness. Man, repelled by his debt to a physical mother, created an alternate reality, a heterocosm to give him the illusion of freedom. Woman, at first content to accept man's protections but now inflamed with desire for her own illusory freedom, invades man's systems and suppresses her indebtedness to him as she steals them. By head-magic she will deny there ever was a problem of sex and nature. He has inherited the anxiety of influence.

The identification of woman with nature is the most troubled and troubling term in this historical argument. Was it ever true? Can it still be true? Many feminist readers will disagree, but I think this identification not myth but reality. All the genres of philosophy, science, high art, athletics, and politics were invented by men. But by the Promethean law of conflict and capture, woman has a right to seize what she will and to vie with man on his own terms. Yet there is a limit to what she can alter in herself and in man's relation to her. Every human being must wrestle with nature. But nature's burden falls more heavily on one sex. With luck, this will not limit woman's achievement, that is, her action in male-created social space. But it must limit eroticism, that is, our imaginative lives in sexual space, which may overlap social space but is not identical with it.

Nature's cycles are woman's cycles. Biologic femaleness is a sequence of circular returns, beginning and ending at the same point. Woman's centrality gives her a stability of identity. She does not have to become but only to be. Her centrality is a great obstacle to man, whose quest for identity she blocks. He must transform himself into an independent being, that is, a being free of her. If he does not, he will simply fall back into her. Reunion with the mother is a siren call haunting our imagination. Once there was bliss, and now there is struggle. Dim memories of life before the traumatic separation of birth may be the source of Arcadian fantasies of a lost golden age. The Western idea of history as a propulsive movement into the future, a progressive or Providential design climaxing in the revelation of a Second Coming, is a male formulation. No woman, I submit, could have coined such an idea, since it is a strategy of evasion of woman's own cyclic nature, in which man dreads being caught. Evolutionary or apocalyptic history is a male wish list with a happy ending, a phallic peak. . . .

What has nature given man to defend himself against woman? Here we come to the source of man's cultural achievements, which follow so directly from his singular anatomy. Our lives as physical beings give rise to basic metaphors of apprehension, which vary greatly between the sexes. Here there can be no equality. Man is sexually compartmentalized. Genitally, he is condemned to a perpetual pattern of linearity, focus, aim, directedness. He must learn to aim. Without aim, urination and ejaculation end in infantile soiling of self or surroundings. Woman's eroticism is diffused throughout her body. Her desire for foreplay remains a notorious area of miscommunication between the sexes. Man's genital concentration is a reduction but also an intensification. He is a victim of unruly ups and downs. Male sexuality is inherently manic-depressive. Estrogen [i.e., the female hormone] tranquilizes, but androgen [i.e., the male hormone] agitates. Men are in a constant state of sexual anxiety, living on the pins and needles of their hormones. In sex as in life they are driven *beyond*—beyond the self, beyond the body. Even in the womb this rule applies. Every fetus becomes female unless it is steeped in male hormones, produced by a signal from the testes. Before birth, therefore, a male is already beyond the female. But to be beyond is to be exiled from the center of life. Men know they are sexual exiles. They wander the earth seeking satisfaction, craving and despising, never content. There is nothing in that anguished motion for women to envy.

The male genital metaphor is concentration and projection. Nature gives concentration to man to help him overcome his fear. Man approaches woman in bursts of spasmodic concentration. This gives him the delusion of temporary control of the archetypal mysteries that brought him forth. It gives him the courage to return. Sex is metaphysical for men, as it is not for women. Women have no problem to solve by sex. Physically and psychologically, they are serenely self-contained. They may choose to achieve, but they do not need it. They are not thrust into the beyond by their own fractious bodies. But men are out of balance. They must quest, pursue, court, or seize. Pigeons on the grass, alas: in such parkside rituals we may savor the comic pathos of sex. How often one spots a male pigeon making desperate, self-inflating sallies toward the female, as again and again she turns her back on him and nonchalantly marches away. But by concentration and insistence he may carry the day. Nature has blessed him with obviousness to his own absurdity. His purposiveness is both a gift and a burden. In human beings, sexual concentration is the male's instrument for gathering together and forcibly fixing the dangerous chthonian* superflux of emotion and energy that I identify with woman and nature. In sex, man is driven into the very abyss which he flees. He makes a voyage to nonbeing and back.

Through concentration to projection into the beyond. The male projection of erection and ejaculation is the paradigm for all cultural projection and conceptualization—from art and philosophy to fantasy, hallucination, and obsession. Women have conceptualized less in history not because men have kept them from doing so but because women do not need to conceptualize in order to exist. I leave open the question of brain differences. Conceptualization and sexual mania may issue from the same part of the male brain. Fetishism, for instance, a practice which like most of the sex perversions is confined to men, is clearly a conceptualizing or symbol-making activity. Man's vastly greater commercial patronage of pornography is analogous.

An erection is *a thought* and the orgasm an act of imagination. The male has to will his sexual authority before the woman who is a shadow of his mother and of all women. Failure and humiliation constantly wait in the wings. No woman has to prove herself a woman in the grim way a man has to prove himself a man. He must perform, or the show does not go on. Social convention is irrelevant. A flop is a flop. Ironically, sexual success always ends in sagging fortunes anyhow. Every male projection is transient and must be anxiously, endlessly renewed. Men enter in triumph but withdraw in decrepitude. The sex act cruelly mimics history's decline and fall. Male bonding is a self-preservation society, collegial reaffirmation through larger, fabricated frames of reference. Culture is man's iron reinforcement of his ever-imperiled private projections. . . .

. . . Man's focus, directedness, concentration, and projection, which I identified with urination and ejaculation, are his tools of sexual survival, but they have never given him a final victory. The anxiety in sex-

---

*Paglia defines "chthonian" as " 'of the earth'—but earth's bowels, not its surface." (Ed.)

ual experience remains as strong as ever. This man attempts to correct by the cult of female beauty. He is erotically fixated on woman's "shapeliness," those spongy material fat deposits of breast, hip, and buttock which are ironically the wateriest and least stable parts of her anatomy. Woman's billowy body reflects the surging sea of chthonian nature. By focusing on the shapely, by making woman a sex-object, man has struggled to fix and stabilize nature's dreadful flux. Objectification is conceptualization, the highest human faculty. Turning people into sex objects is one of the specialties of our species. It will never disappear, since it is intertwined with the art-impulse and may be identical to it. A sex object is ritual form imposed on nature. It is a totem of our perverse imagination. . . .

Man, the sexual conceptualizer and projector, has ruled art because art is his Apollonian response toward and away from woman. A sex object is something to aim at. The eye is Apollo's arrow following the arc of transcendance I saw in male urination and ejaculation. The Western eye is a projectile into the *beyond,* that wilderness of the male condition. . . .

Western culture has a roving eye. Male sex is hunting and scanning: boys hang yelping from honking cars, acting like jerks over strolling girls; men lunching on girders go through the primitive book of wolf whistles and animal clucks. Everywhere, the beautiful woman is scrutinized and harassed. She is the ultimate symbol of human desire. The feminine is that-which-is-sought; it recedes beyond our grasp. Hence there is always a feminine element in the beautiful young man of male homosexuality. The feminine is ever-elusive, a silver shimmer on the horizon. We follow this image with longing eyes: maybe this one, maybe this time. The pursuit of sex may conceal a dream of being freed from sex. Sex, knowledge, and power are deeply tangled; we cannot get one without the other. Islam is wise to drape women in black, for the eye is the avenue of eros. Western culture's hard, defined personalities suffer from inflammation of the eye. They are so numerous that they have never been catalogued, except in our magnificent portrait art. Western sexual personae are nodes of power, but they have made a torment of eroticism. From this torment has come our grand tradition of literature and art. Unfortunately, there is no way to separate the whistling ass on his girder from the rapt visionary at his easel. In accepting the gifts of culture, women may have to take the worm with the apple. . . .

NOTE

1. *The Anxiety of Influence: A Theory of Poetry* (New York, 1973), p. 94.

8

The Social Causes of Sexual Harassment

Catharine A. MacKinnon

According to Catharine MacKinnon, society believes that being male or female is a biological given when, in fact, the meaning and consequences of such categories are primarily determined by society itself. Society has attributed submission and sexuality to the female role, thereby defining women as sexual objects. Women are therefore subordinated, or treated as if they are not equal to men in dignity and worth.

MacKinnon believes that society's discrimination against women manifests itself in various ways. One way is through unwanted sexual advances in contexts of unequal power (i.e., sexual harassment). But women are also subordinated to men in many other ways—through acts of violence as well as through social mechanisms that deny women the social and economic opportunities and resources available to men. Thus, MacKinnon views sexual harassment against the background of a society systematically shaped by beliefs, attitudes, and practices which devalue, degrade, and disadvantage women on the basis of their sex. Although she takes sexual harassment to be one of the products of a society that discriminates against women, MacKinnon recognizes that "discrimination based upon sex" is often not a simple notion.

Much is riding on the view that sexual harassment is sex discrimination.

Legal actions in sexual harassment law are usually brought under Title VII of the Civil Rights Act of 1964. This outlaws discriminatory employment practices, whether these practices are based upon race, color, religion, national origin—or sex. Among other things, this legislation enables the Equal Employment Opportunity Commission to initiate action on behalf of plaintiffs in sexual harassment cases. [Ed.]

NATURAL/BIOLOGICAL

With a tone of "you can't change *that,*" the cases rejecting sexual harassment claims repeatedly excuse the incidents as "biological" or "natural." In the *Miller* case, Judge Williams, denying relief, stated with astonishing equanimity and/or candor: "The attraction of males to females and females to males is a natural sex phenomenon and it is probable that this attraction plays at least a subtle part in most personnel decisions."[1] One wonders what this factor has to do with merit and whether subtle racial revulsion is equally permissible. The brief for Bausch and Lomb was similarly explicit in its appeal to nature to exonerate the perpetrator: "Obviously, certain biological differences exist between male and female. . . . [I]t would appear that in the foreseeable future that the attraction of males to females and females to males will not soon disappear."[2] The *Tomkins* district court also referred to "this natural sex attraction," stating, in a breathtaking but indecisive mid-sentence reversal, "while sexual desire animated the parties, or at least one of them. . . ."[3]

    . . . In the biological view, sexual expression seems presumed to derive from a biological need or genital drive or to be deeply rooted in a natural order that connects biological differences with expressions of mutual attraction. The idea is that biology cannot be questioned or changed, and is legitimate, while society can be, and may be "artificial." Perhaps this presumption underlies the clear doctrinal necessity, if sexual harassment is to be considered sex discrimination under existing conceptions, to establish sexual harassment as less a question of "sexuality" than of gender status: an implicit legal presupposition that sexuality is buried in nature, while gender status is at least in part a social construct. In the above quotations, in an attempt to justify legal nonintervention, sexual harassment is implicitly argued to be an inevitable and integral part of the naturally given, not socially contingent or potentially changeable, sexual relations between women and men.

    Upon closer scrutiny, these presumptions about sex have little to do with the occurrence of sexual harassment. Women possess a physical sex drive equal to or greater than that of men,[4] yet do not systematically harass men sexually. Some men, who have nothing wrong with them sexually, seem able to control their behavior. Not all women experience sexual attraction to all men, nor all men to all women. These factors suggest that something beyond pure biology is implicated. Usually, the last thing wanted in these incidents is species reproduction, which removes any connection with a natural drive in that direction. Moreover, not everything deemed natural by defining all sexual behavior as biological is thereby made socially acceptable. If economically coerced intercourse is biological, rape must be also, but it is not legally allowed for that reason.

The image of codetermination in sexual matters by men and women is scrupulously maintained in these cases. But for the unwilling woman, no "attraction" is involved, and little power. Even if the "attractiveness of the sexes for one another" were inevitable, that would not make its expression indiscriminate. Calling sex "natural" means here, in effect, that women are to be allowed no choice of with whom and under what conditions to have sexual relations. In these cases, we are dealing with a male who is allegedly exercising his power as an employer, his power over a woman's material survival, and his sexual prerogatives as a man, to subject a woman sexually. One would have to argue that sexual power is by nature asymmetrical, and hence that it is biological for males to threaten, force, blackmail, coerce, subject, exploit, and oppress women sexually, to conclude that sexual harassment is natural. . . .

WHAT IS SEX?

The legal interpretation of the term *sex,* as illustrated by the foregoing, has centered upon the gender difference between women and men, which the law views as a biological given. "Gender per se" is considered to refer to an obvious biological fact with a fixed content. Factors "other than gender per se," but correlated with it, may also ground a discrimination claim. These factors are treated in legal discourse accretions—some biological, some social—upon the biological foundation. These presuppositions about sex and gender have been so widely assumed that it has seldom been considered whether they are appropriate foundations for a social policy directed toward women's equality, or even whether they are, to the best of our current knowledge, true.

One major contradiction within the legal conception of sex as gender was posed by the *Gilbert* analysis.* The plaintiff argued that pregnancy was a gender distinction per se because only women become pregnant. The majority of the Supreme Court argued that pregnancy was other than gender per se, in part because it is voluntary, while gender is not; in part because not all women become pregnant, so it is not a characteristic of the sex; and in part because no men become pregnant, so women and men were not being *treated* discriminatorily, they merely *are* different. Defining sex with reference to gender was inadequate to resolve the issue of whether, in order for a classification such as pregnancy to be considered sex-based, all women must be actually or potentially so classified, or whether it is sufficient that all those so classified are women, with no men even potentially included, or whether the fact that no men can be so affected means that the exclusion *cannot* discriminate against women.

To generalize beyond the explicit terms of the Supreme Court's holding, its resolution of this issue could be stated as follows: for differential treatment of the sexes to be considered sex-based, it must occur, or potentially occur, to all members of a group defined by biological gender, but not for reasons unique to that biology. That is, to be sex-based, a treatment (or classification or factor) must be universal to women but not unique to women. It must affect all women and, in some sense, not only women. Pregnancy was considered both not universal to women and unique to women, thus not a gender classification. . . .

Several empirical presumptions are implicit in this approach. It is assumed that a solid physical underpinning exists for the sex difference and that sex is dimorphic. The sexes are understood in terms of their differences and these differences are considered physical and bipolar. It is assumed that a clear, known line can be drawn between those attributes of gender which are biological and those which are other than biological. The relevant referent for the legal meaning of sex is supposed to be primarily in biology rather than society.

The particular place of "sexuality" as one index to maleness or femaleness has never been firmly located in this legal scheme of sex as gender and gender as biology. Other than in the few sexual harassment cases, the question has rarely been posed. One recent EEOC [Equal Employment Opportunity Commission] case, justifying the lack of protection for homosexuals under Title VII, distinguished "sexual practice" from "gender as such," the latter defined as "an immutable characteristic with which a person is born."[5] Sexuality, or at least homosexuality, seemed to mean something one does, gender something one is. Similarly, the *Har-*

Gilbert v. *General Electric,* 429 U.S. (1976) [*Ed.*]

vard Law Review implicitly distinguished between sexuality and sex as gender under Title VII as follows: "Although jobs which require sex appeal may exploit their occupants as sex objects, [Title VII] was not designed to change *other* views that society holds about sexuality"[6] (emphasis added). A series of interconnected propositions emerges: "sex" in the legal sense is primarily a matter of gender status; gender status is a matter of innate biological differences; homosexuality is a "practice," not a matter of gender status, hence not within the ambit of sex discrimination. But what exactly is heterosexuality? What is its relationship to the gender difference? How do gender and heterosexuality interrelate in what discrimination law means by "sex"?

The relationship of sexuality to gender is the critical link in the argument that sexual harassment is sex discrimination. Empirically, gender is not monolithic. Three dimensions can be distinguished: physical characteristics, gender identification, and sex role behavior. Contrary to legal presumptions, current research shows that none of these dimensions is perfectly intercorrelated with, nor strictly predetermines, any other. Gender, then, is not as simple as the biological difference between women and men, nor is that difference itself purely or even substantially a biological one. Sexuality as a complex interaction of (at least) all three is even less simply biologically determinate. It is neither simply a matter of gender status nor a practice without reference to biological differences. Perhaps most significantly, social and cultural factors, including attitudes, beliefs, and traditional practices—quite proper targets for legal change, compared with biological facts—are found to have a substantially broader and more powerful impact upon gender, even upon its biological aspects, than legal thinking on the sex difference has recognized.

Physical characteristics which provide indices of gender include internal and external reproductive organs and genitalia, gonads, hormone balance, and genetic and chromosomal makeup.[7] Strictly speaking, in several of these physical senses gender is not immutable, merely highly tenacious. A transsexual operation, with hormone therapy, can largely transform gender on the physical level, with the major exception of reproductive capacity. But then many born males and females do not possess reproductive capacity for a variety of biological and social reasons. Aside from these characteristics, some evidence of physical differences between the sexes in the aggregate exists in the following areas: body shape, height and weight, muscularity, physical endurance, possibly metabolic rate, possibly some forms of sensory sensitivity, rate of maturation, longevity, susceptibility to certain physical disorders, and some behaviors at birth (irritability, type of movement, and responsiveness to touch).[8] The scientific research stresses the wide, if not complete, mutability of even these differences by social factors such as psychological reinforcements, type of customary physical activity, and career patterns.[9] Moreover, on the biological level, the sex difference is not a polar opposition, but a continuum of characteristics with different averages by sex grouping. . . .

Most sexual behaviors which differ by sex or within sex groupings have been found to lack any known biological basis. Choice of sexual object in terms of sex preference for the same or opposite sex is one; intensity of sexual desires and needs is another. Masters and Johnson's research has decisively established that women's sexual requirements are no less potent or urgent than those of men.[10] "There is little factual basis for the belief that males need sex more than do females. It is more likely that men do not exercise [as] much control over sexual behavior. Male sexual behavior is condoned, even encouraged, whereas females are taught restraint in sexual expression."[11] Social factors rather than biological differences are seen to shape observed differences in sexual needs and patterns of their expression.[12] For example, in spite of physiological differences between women and men, there is no physiological basis for male aggressiveness and female passivity in sexual initiation. Without changing biology, "a woman can be aggressively receptive and a man be motivationally passive in the sexual act."[13] Some scholars locate sexual excitement itself more in society than in nature. "The very experience of sexual excitement that seems to originate from hidden internal sources is in fact a learned process and it is only our insistence on the myths of naturalness that hides these social components from us."[14] Sexual feeling and expression are seen as a form of "scripted" behavior[15] which is as powerfully determined by sexism as by sex.[16] Gagnon and Simon note that "many women's . . . participation in sexual activity, has often—historically, possibly more often than not—had little to do with their own sense of the erotic."[17] The social facts of sexual inequality increasingly appear to define this fact of the meaning of sex, rather than the facts of sex differences providing an irrefutable argument against their existence.

Nor is gender *identity* primarily determined by physical attributes, according to current thought and research. Gender identification, defined as the sense one has of being a man or a woman and the presentation of self and acceptance by others as such, is neither a fact nor a sense "with which one is born." Rather, it is assigned and learned. John Money's innovative experiments on hermaphrodites[18] show that gender identity need not correspond to internal organs, external genitalia, hormones, or chromosomes. In cases where, because of external genital ambiguity or deformity, a child's sex is misidentified (in the sense of later proving to be at odds with the body), children after age six persist immovably in the gender identity originally assigned; resistance to change survives even surgical conformity of external genitalia with internal sex organs. Sexual behavior in such cases is socially appropriate to the learned gender rather than to the physical one. Irrespective of sexual biology, the sex socially assigned a child, through deep and early psychological imprinting, becomes the gender identification of the adult. "One is confronted with the conclusion, perhaps surprising to some, that there is no primary genetic or other innate mechanism to preordain the masculinity or femininity of psychosexual differentiation." Money concludes that his research shows "a complete overriding of the sex-chromosomal constitution and of gonadal status in the establishment of gender role and identity."[19]

The importance of Money's research is not that one cannot tell a man from a woman, although there are difficulties at times; rather, it is that the element of sex that is made up of a basic gender identification as a man or a woman is not primarily determined by physiological factors. It is secondarily determined by the body, of course, in the social sense. Genital anatomy tends under usual circumstances to determine which gender parents assign a baby, to shape gender-specific social responses, and to elicit reinforcing behavior considered appropriate to each sex. But social factors aside, a female sexual identity does not feel intrinsically out of place in a biologically male body and vice versa. To the extent that one "is" a man or a woman because one takes oneself to be so, sexual biology does not predetermine gender.

The effect of biology on the behavior of the sexes, so often accepted as primary, has been found to be largely secondary. In its place, a vast body of research documents the powerful and pervasive impact of social sex roles on attitudes and behavior, including sexual ones. A "sex role" is a widely held, learned, acted upon, and socially enforced definition of behaviors, attitudes, or pursuits as intrinsically more appropriate or seemly for one sex than for the other. It refers to the cultural practice of allocating social roles according to gender. Socialization is the process by which men and women are socially created to correspond to each society's definition of its "masculine" and "feminine" sex roles. Although scholars differ in their views and evaluations of the origins, social functions, exact transmission processes, contents, and impact upon individual personality of sex roles, the existence of strongly sex-typed social patterns within most cultures is barely disputed.

Choice of occupation, activities, goals, and feelings are strongly associated with masculine or feminine roles in virtually all cultures. The content of these categories varies sufficiently across cultures to suggest that the institutionalization of specific sex role conceptions derives from the specific history and development of each society, rather than from anything intrinsic to the sex difference—even including dimorphism itself.[20] Some societies, for example, have more than two genders.[21] On the whole, sex roles reproduce themselves and tend to describe sex groups in the aggregate, which is not surprising, since people have been modeled in their image. As with biology, however, individual characteristics vary as much within sex groups as between them, and sex groups overlap to a considerable extent.[22]

What hermaphrodism does to the concept of biological gender, transsexuality does to the concept of sex roles. The rigid exclusivity of each sex of the other is undercut in the clear presence of some of both. Transsexuals experience a sense of sex identity cruelly trapped in a nonconforming body. Whatever the cause of this sense, it cannot be biological gender, since sex identity stands opposed to the body; nor can it be the sex role conditioning alone, since sex identity is also opposed to that. The source of such a thorough rejection of standard sex role conditioning as well as physiology is obscure. But it is testimony to the power of the social correlation of sexual identity with physiology that, in order to pursue the desired behavior patterns fully, transsexuals consider it necessary to alter their *bodies* to accord with their gender identity. A final observation captures both meanings: first, gender identification may be better understood as a social definition of biology than as a biological definition of society, and, second, the power of that definition. Commenting upon the justice of a proposed chromosome test for determining the femaleness of the transsexual tennis player Dr. Renee Richards, one woman observed: "I think nature is not always correct. . . . She looks like a woman, plays like a woman. She *is* a woman. Chromosomes make things scientific, but nature is not always a hundred percent correct."[23]

Socially as well as biologically, gender is not as rigidly dimorphic as it is commonly supposed to be in legal discussions of equality. It is, instead, a range of overlapping distributions with different median points. The majority of men and women are located in the area of overlap. If for most characteristics the majority of women and men fall in the area where the sexes overlap, to premise legal approaches to the sexes on their differences requires the exclusion of those persons whose characteristics overlap with the other sex—that is, most people. The extremes, the tails of both curves, which apply only to exceptional women and men, are implicitly used as guidelines for sex specificity. They become norms, ideals for emulation, and standards for judgment when they are not even statistically representative.

There is a real question whether it makes sense of the evidence to conceptualize the reality of sex in terms of differences at all, except in the socially constructed sense—which social construction is what the law is attempting to address as the *problem*. To require that a given characteristic, in order to be considered a sex characteristic, be universal to the sex grouping is to require something that is not uniformly true even of most of the primary indices of gender. To then require (as the *Gilbert* approach does) that that same characteristic be comparable to, while remaining different from, the corresponding characteristic of the opposite sex, tends to exclude those few characteristics that approach being truly generic to a sex group.

While the biological sex difference has been both exaggerated and used to justify different treatment, sex inequality as a social force has been reflected in the substantive content of sex roles. Sex roles shape the behavior and express the relative position of the sexes. Although social differences between the sexes are far more pronounced than biological differences, to the extent they have been seen as differences they have not been seen as inequalities. It is not at all a distortion of the evidence to characterize the *social* situation of the sexes as largely dimorphic. In fact, the sexes are, and have been, far more dimorphic socially than they are, or have been, biologically. Much of the specific content of sex roles in American culture are those stereotypes that the law prohibits as overt job qualifications: women are weak, good with their fingers, bad at numbers, unable to stand long hours, too emotional for high seriousness. Male sex roles encourage men to be strong, aggressive, tough, dominant, and competitive. These values, which come to be considered "male," do describe conforming and common male behavior in many spheres, including the sexual.[24] Interpreting sexual behavior in sex role terms, Diana Russell argues that rape should be viewed not as deviance but as overconformity to the male sex role.[25] In support, one recent study found that convicted rapists were "sexually and psychologically normal" according to male social norms.[26] Another study quotes a parole officer who worked with rapists in prison facilities: "Those men were the most normal men there. They had a lot of hang-ups, but they were the same hang-ups as men walking out on the street."[27] Although intending to exonerate men as a sex rather than to criticize male sex roles as socially defined, Lionel Tiger makes a corroborative observation that implicitly links rape findings to sexual harassment: "[It] is relatively 'normal' for males to seek sexual access to females who are their subordinates."[28]

As the examples suggest, such behaviors are almost never observed in women. Powerful social conditioning of women to passivity, gentleness, submissiveness, and receptivity to male initiation, particularly in sexual contact, tends effectively to constrain women from expressing aggression (or even assertion) sexually, or sexuality assertively, although there probably is no biological barrier to either. The constraints appear linked to women's relative social position.

[It is] males who are supposed to initiate sexual activity with females. Females who make "advances" are considered improper, forward, aggressive, brassy, or otherwise "unladylike." By initiating intimacy they have stepped out of their place and usurped a status prerogative.[29]

Women are considered synonymous with sex, yet female sexuality is seen as valid only under certain conditions, such as marriage. Even in more permissive ages like our own, there are still limits. One of these is the point where a female can be labeled promiscuous. Another is the point where she attempts to exercise any power: women who initiate and direct sexual activity with male partners find that they have gone too far and are feared and rejected as "castrators."[30]

Implicit in these observations is the view that sexual expression shaped by sex roles prescribes appropriate male and female conduct, defines normalcy, designs sexual rituals, and allocates power in the interest of men and to the detriment of women. In this respect, there definitely is a "difference" between the sexes:

The value of such a prerogative [to initiate intimacy] is that it is a form of power. Between the sexes, as in other human interaction, the one who has the right to initiate greater intimacy has more control over the relationship. Superior status brings with it not only greater prestige and greater privileges, but greater power.[31]

[The] fantasy world that veils [women's] experience is the world of sex as seen through male eyes. It is a world where eroticism is defined in terms of female powerlessness, dependency and submission.[32]

The substance of the meaning of sex roles, in sexuality as in other areas, just as with the social roles allocated to the races, is not symmetrical between women and men. Rather, male and female sex roles complement each other in the sense that one function of the female sex role is to reinforce the impression, and create the social actuality, of male dominance and female subordination. Ellen Morgan describes this asymmetry in sexual relationships as one means through which gender in equality is expressed and maintained in American society:

We have a sexual situation in which the humanity and personhood of the woman, which make her seek autonomy and action and expression and self-respect, are at odds with her socially organized sexuality. We have a situation in which the dominant male sexual culture aggrandizes the male ego whereas the subordinate female style damages the female ego. Sex means different things to women and men by this time.[33]

. . . The implications of these roles for interpersonal behavior on the one hand and systemic powerlessness on the other are drawn in the following quotation:

The "trivia" of everyday life—using "sir" or first name, touching others, dropping the eyes, smiling, interrupting and so on . . . are commonly understood as facilitators of social intercourse but are not recognized as defenders of the status quo—of the state, the wealthy, of authority, of those whose power may not be challenged. Nevertheless, these minutiae find their place on a continuum of social control which extends from internalized socialization (the colonization of the mind) . . . to sheer physical force (guns, clubs, incarceration).[34]

This examination suggests that the legally relevant content of the term *sex,* understood as gender difference, should focus upon its *social meaning* more than upon any biological givens. The most salient determinants of sexuality, much like those of work, are organized in society, not fixed in "nature." As might be expected, sex role learning, inseparably conjoined with economic necessity when the sexual aggressor is both a man and an employer, tends to inhibit women's effective resistance to "normal" male intrusions and claims upon women's sexuality, whether they come as a look or a rape. In this perspective, sexual harassment expresses one social meaning that sex roles create in the sex difference: gender distributes power as it divides labor, enforcing that division by sexual means. . . .

SEXUALITY

. . . The behaviors to which women are subjected in sexual harassment are behaviors specifically defined and directed toward the characteristics which define women's sexuality: Secondary sex characteristics and sex-role behavior. It is no accident that the English language uses the term *sex* ambiguously to refer both to gender status (as in "the female sex") and to the activity of intercourse (as in "to have sex"). The term *sexual* is used in both senses. Further study of the language reveals that references to sexuality have a pejorative connotation for woman as a gender that is not comparable for men.

> Words indicating the station, relationship or occupation of men have remained untainted over the years. Those identifying women have repeatedly suffered the indignity of degeneration, many of them becoming sexually abusive. It is clearly not the women themselves who have coined and used these terms as epithets for each other. One sees today that it is men who describe women in sexual terms and insult them with sexual slurs, and the wealth of derogatory terms for women reveals something of their hostility. . . . [T]he largest category of words designating humans in sexual terms are those for women—especially for loose women. I have located roughly a thousand words and phrases describing women in sexually derogatory ways. Theres is nothing approaching this multitude for describing men.[35]

As a critical convergence of the physiological, psychological, social, economic, cultural and aesthetic, and political forces, sexuality is overburdened with determinants. Gender itself is largely defined in terms of sexuality in that heterosexuality is closely bound up with the social conceptions of maleness and femaleness.

Woman's sexuality is a major medium through which gender identity and gender status are socially expressed and experienced. An attack upon sexuality is an attack upon womanhood. A deprivation in employment worked through women's sexuality is a deprivation in employment because one is a woman, through one of the closest referents by which women are socially identified as such, by themselves and by men. Only women, and (as is not the case with pregnancy) all women possess female sexuality,* the focus, occasion, and vehicle for this form of employment deprivation. Few men would maintain that they would have found a given woman just as ready or appropriate a target for sexual advances if she had been sexually male. Indeed, the close association between sexuality and gender identity makes it hard to imagine that a woman would be sexually the same if male. If any practice could be said to happen to a woman because she is a woman, sexual harassment should be one of the more straightforward examples of it. . . .

---

*Transsexuals and transvestites would probably be considered legally female for this purpose.

NOTES

1. [Miller v. Bank of America] 418 F. Supp. 233, 236 (N.D. Cal. 1976).

2. Answering Brief for Defendants—Appellees, at 32–33.

3. 422 F. Supp 553, 556 (D.N.J. 1976).

4. "It can hardly be claimed any longer that men have greater 'sex drives' and therefore, a lesser expression of sex must be attributed to an inhibition on the part of women to display sexual interest in this manner." Nancy Henley, "Power, Sex and Nonverbal Communication," in Thorne and Henley, eds., *Language and Sex: Difference and Dominance* (Rowley, Mass.: Newbury House, Publishers, 1975), p. 193. G. Schmidt and V. Sigusch in a study entitled "Women's Sexual Arousal" reported little gender difference in physiological or self-ratings of sexual arousal in response to erotic stimuli, in J. Zubin and J. Money, *Contemporary Sexual Behavior: Critical Issues in the 1970s* (Baltimore: Johns Hopkins University Press, 1973), pp. 117–43. Such differences are widely attributed to cultural factors. See, for example, W. J. Gadpaille, "Innate Masculine-Feminine Differences." *Med. Asp. Hum. Sexuality* (1973): 141–57.

5. 2 Empl. Prac. Guide (CCH) Par. 6493 (1976).

6. 84 *Harvard Law Review* (1971); 1109, 1184 (emphasis added). . . .

7. John Money, "Developmental Differentiation of Femininity and Masculinity Compared," in Farber and Wilson, eds., *The Potential of Woman* (New York: McGraw-Hill, 1963), p. 56; John Money and Patricia Tucker, *Sexual Signatures: On Being A Man or A Woman* (Boston: Little, Brown, 1975); R. Stoller, *Sex and Gender: On the Development of Masculinity and Femininity* (London: Hogarth, 1968); R. Green and J. Money, *Transsexualism and Sex Reassignment* (Baltimore: Johns Hopkins University Press, 1969); Edward S. David, "The Law and Transsexualism: A Faltering Response to a Conceptual Dilemma," *Connecticut Law Review* 7 (1975): 288; J. Money and A. Erhardt, *Man and Woman, Boy and Girl* (Baltimore: Johns Hopkins University Press, 1972); J. Money, *Sex Errors of the Body* (Baltimore: Johns Hopkins University Press, 1968); Note, *Transsexuals in Limbo, Maryland Law Review* 31 (1971): 236.

8. Ashton Barfield, "Biological Influences on Sex Differences in Behavior," in M. Tietelbaum, ed., *Sex Differences: Social and Biological Perspectives* (Garden City, N.Y.: Anchor Press, Doubleday, 1976), 107. Bibliography of research supporting this summary, ibid., p. 110–21.

9. Eleanor F. Maccoby, ed., *The Development of Sex Differences* (Stanford: Stanford University Press, 1966).

10. Robert Masters and Virginia Johnson, *Human Sexual Response* (Boston: Little, Brown, 1966).

11. R. Staples, "Male-Female Sexual Variations: Functions of Biology or Culture," *Journal of Sexual Response* 9 (1973): 11–20.

12. A. C. Kinsey et al., *Sexual Behavior in the Human Male* (Philadelphia: W. B. Saunders Co., 1948). Kinsey's famous studies of sexual arousal in women and men in the 1930s and 1940s seemed to confirm that the sexes differed sub-

stantially in this respect. Culturally, his results were used to endow men with animal lust, women with demure passionlessness. (Demonstrating that obscure ability of racism to 'survive evidence, the stereotype of the black woman as sex-crazed was never apparently confronted by these findings purporting to represent the sexuality of all: biological females.) A recent replication of Kinsey's studies suggests that cultural repression of women's sexuality largely accounts for his findings. Sigusch and Schmidt conclude that sexual arousability "is as strongly and quite similarly structured for both women and men." They explain the difference between their results and Kinsey's as follows:

> His findings cannot serve as evidence for a lesser capacity for women to become sexually aroused by pictoral and narrative stimuli. They reflect one aspect of the cultural desexualization of women in western societies which 20 to 30 years ago, when Kinsey collected his data, was more extensive than today.

V. Sigusch and G. Schmidt, "Women's Sexual Arousal," in Zubin and Money, *Contemporary Sexual Behavior: Critical Issues in the 1970s* (Baltimore: Johns Hopkins University Press, 1973), pp. 118–19.

13. J. Marmor, "Women in Medicine: The Importance of the Formative Years," *Journal of American Medical Women's Association* (July 1968), 621.

14. John H. Gagnon and William Simon, *Sexual Conduct: The Social Sources of Human Sexuality* (Chicago: Aldine Publishing Company, 1973), p. 9.

15. Ibid.,pp. 19–26.

16. See Judith Long Laws and Pepper Schwartz, *Sexual Scripts: The Social Construction of Female Sexuality* (Hinsdale, Ill.: The Dryden Press, 1977), who apply Gagnon and Simon's concept to women's sexuality specifically.

17. John H. Gagnon and William Simon, eds., *The Sexual Scene* (Chicago: Aldine Publishing Company, 1970), p. 4.

18. See above note 6.

19. Money, in Farber and Wilson, *The Potential of Woman,* p. 56.

20. Margaret Mead, *Sex and Temperament in Three Primitive Societies* (New York: Dell, 1935); Margaret Mead, *Male and Female: A Study of the Sexes in A Changing World* (New York: William Morrow & Co., 1975, pp. 7–8; Michele Rosaldo and Louise Lamphere, eds., *Woman, Culture and Society* (Palo Alto, Calif.: Stanford University Press, 1974); Rayna R. Reiter, ed., *Toward an Anthropology of Women* (New York: Monthly Review Press, 1975).

21. See Anna S. Meigs, "Male Pregnancy and the Reduction of Sexual Opposition in A New Guinea Highlands Society," *Ethnology: An International Journal of Cultural and Social Anthropology* 15, no. 4 (October 1976): 393–407; C. S. Ford and F. Beach, *Patterns of Sexual Behavior* (New York: Harper, 1951) provides background and several illustrative examples.

22. There are numerous excellent reviews and collections of sex role research. A classic in the field is Eleanor E. Maccoby, ed., *The Development of Sex Differences* (Stanford, Calif.: Stanford University Press, 1966). A bibliography

of research conducted from 1973 to 1974 can be found in *Women's Work and Women's Studies, 1973–4, A Bibliography* (The Barnard College Women's Center, 1975), pp. 285–302, and a list of bibliographies on the subject at ibid., pp. 321–22. Recent books on varying levels include Carol Tavris and Carole Offir, *The Longest War: Sex Differences in Perspective* (New York: Harcourt, Brace Jovanovich, 1977); Nancy Reeves, *Womankind: Beyond the Stereotypes* (Chicago: Aldine Publishing Company, 1977); Shirley Weitz, *Sex Roles: Biological, Psychological and Social Foundation* (Oxford University Press, 1977). For a political perspective on sex roles in terms of power, see, e.g., Nancy Hartsock, "Political Change: Two Perspectives on Power," *Quest: A Feminist Quarterly* (Summer 1974): 10–25. An application to the law is Barbara Kirk Cavanagh, "A Little Dearer Than His Horse: Legal Stereotypes and the Feminine Personality," 6 *Harv. C.R.C.L. Review* (1970): 260–87.

23. *New York Times,* August 22, 1976, (Sports Section), p. 3. See also the discussion by Germaine Greer of transsexual April Ashley, *The Female Eunuch* (New York: McGraw Hill, 1970), pp. 54–55, *but cf.* the legal decision in the same case, *Corbett* v. *Çorbett,* [1971], p. 83 (P. P. Div'l Ct.) (England).

24. A very different approach to analyzing sexuality for legal purposes can be found in the psychoanalytic interpretations collected in Ralph Slovenko, *Sexual Behavior and the Law* (Springfield, Ill.: Charles C. Thomas, 1965).

25. Diana E. H. Russell, *The Politics of Rape* (New York: Stein & Day, 1975), p. 260.

26. Andrea Medea and Kathleen Thompson, *Against Rape* (New York: Farrar, Straus & Giroux, 1974), pp. 29–30.

27. Susan Griffin, "Rape: The All-American Crime," *Ramparts,* 10 (September 1971): 25–35, reprint in Jo Freeman, ed., *Women: A Feminist Perspective* (Palo Alto, Calif.: Mayfield Publishing Co., 1975), p. 26.

28. Lionel Tiger, *Men in Groups* (New York: Random House, 1969), p. 271. Lynn Wehrli, "Sexual Harassment at the Workplace: A Feminist Analysis and Strategy for Social Change," (M.A. Thesis, Massachusetts Institute of Technology, December 1976) makes the same connection, p. 86.

29. Nancy Henley and Jo Freeman, "The Sexual Politics of Interpersonal Behavior," in Freeman, ed., *Women: A Feminist Perspective* (Palo Alto, Calif.; Mayfield Publishing Co., 1975), pp. 393–94.

30. Linda Phelps, "Female Sexual Alienation," in Freeman, *Women: A Feminist Perspective,* p. 20.

31. Henley and Freeman, in Freeman, *Women: A Feminist Perspective,* pp. 393–94.

32. Phelps, in Freeman, *Women: A Feminist Perspective,* p. 19.

33. Ellen Morgan, "The Erotization of Male Dominance/Female Subordination," University of Michigan, Papers in Women's Studies 2 (1975): 112–45, reprint by Know, Inc., p. 20. See also Nancy M. Henley, *Body Politics: Power, Sex and Nonverbal Communication* (Englewood Cliffs, N.J.: Prentice-Hall, 1977), pp. 94–123.

34. Henley, "Power, Sex and Nonverbal Communication," in Barrie Thorne and Nancy Henley, eds., *Language and Sex: Difference and Dominance* (Rowley, Mass.: Newbury House, Publishers, 1975), p. 184.

35. D. Schulz, "The Semantic Derogation of Women," in Thorne and Henley, *supra,* pp. 67, 71.

Part Three

Legal Responses

9

Sexual Harassment as Sex Discrimination

Catharine A. MacKinnon

TORT LAW

Women's bodies, particularly the conditions and consequences of men's sexual access to them, are not a novel subject for the law. . . . The law of torts, or private harms, historically provided civil redress for sexual invasions at a time when social morality was less ambiguous in defining a woman's sexuality as intrinsic to her virtue, and her virtue as partially constitutive of her value, hence as capable of compensable damage. Perhaps with this tradition in mind, several recent sexual harassment cases have suggested—usually as a reason for holding sexual harassment not to be sex discrimination—that sexual harassment should be considered tortious. The federal court in *Tomkins,* implicitly finding that since sexual harassment is a tort it is not discrimination, stated that Title VII "is not intended to provide a federal tort remedy for what amounts to physical attack motivated by sexual desire on the part of a supervisor and which happened to occur in a corporate corridor rather than a back alley."[1] One appellate judge, concurring in the judgment in *Barnes* that sexual harassment is sex discrimination, observed, "An act of sexual harassment which caused the victim, because of her rejection of such advances, to be damaged in her job, would constitute a tort."[2] Which tort is not specified, although "[t]here is no necessity whatever that a tort must have a name."[3] It is, however, necessary that the definition of the legal wrong fit the

From *Sexual Harassment of Working Women: A Case of Sex Discrimination* by Catharine A. MacKinnon (New Haven, Conn.: Yale University Press, 1979). Copyright © 1979. Reprinted by permission of the publisher and the author.

conceptual framework of tort law. Brief examination of traditional tort views of sexual wrongs against women illustrates that tort law is not simply wrong, and is partially helpful, but is fundamentally insufficient as a legal approach to sexual harassment.

Sexual touching that women do not want has historically been considered tortious under a variety of doctrines, usually battery, assault, or, if exclusively emotional damage is done, as the intentional infliction of emotional distress. A battery is a harmful or offensive contact which is intentionally caused. While contact must be intentional, hostile intent, or intent to cause all the damages that resulted from the contact, is not necessary. Variously formulated, "taking indecent liberties with a woman without her consent,"[4] "putting hands upon a female with a view to violate her person,"[5] or "intentional touching of a woman by a man without excuse or justification"[6] have been considered battery. Battery is said to include instances in which a compliment is intended, "as where an unappreciative woman is kissed without her consent."[7]

Battery, the actual touching, is often combined with assault, the fear of such a touching. The tort of assault consists in placing a person in *fear* of an immediate harmful or offensive contact. It is "a touching of the mind, if not of the body."[8] The invasion is mental. The defendant must have intended at least to arouse apprehension, and actually have done so. The fear-producing event must be more than words alone, but words can clarify an otherwise equivocal act. Defenses include consent, but only to those acts consented to; consent to a kiss, for example, does not extend to anything further. Nor are provocative words a defense.

Kissing a woman without her consent has been considered actionable under a combination (or confusion) of assault and battery doctrines. In 1899, a husband and wife recovered $700 for assault on the wife for forcibly hugging and kissing "against her wish and by force."[9] In 1921, a railroad was found responsible for the embarrassment and humiliation of a woman passenger caused when a drunken man, of whose boisterous conduct and inebriated condition the railroad was aware, fell down on top of her and kissed her on the cheek.[10] In 1895 in Wisconsin, a twenty-year-old schoolteacher recovered $1,000 from the employer of a railroad conductor who grabbed and kissed her several times despite her clear attempts to discourage and repel him.[11]

Other early cases finding sexual incursions actionable reveal that little has changed in men's sexual behavior, although something seems to have changed in the social and legal standards by which it is evaluated. In a case in 1915, a woman recovered damages for assault and battery against a man who squeezed her breast and laid his hand on her face. The defendant denied the whole incident, then characterized the touching as "nothing more than a harmless caress."[12] In a similar case in 1921, a woman recovered for the mental anguish arising from an indecent assault, defined as "the act of a male person taking indecent liberties with the person of a female, or fondling her in a lewd and lascivious manner without her consent and against her will." The judge found it unnecessary for the assault to be made in an angry or insolent manner: "Indecent assaults are not made in that way."[13] Sexual assault—whether or not it was done with bad feeling—is still assault.

Contemporary sexual mores make it difficult to imagine such cases in court. Women are, it seems, supposed to consider acts in this tradition harmless, and litigation in this area is now relatively uncommon. . . .

One common rejoinder to charges of sexual harassment is that the individual woman is unduly and overly sensitive to these advances, raising the question of the standards by which an at least partly subjective injury is to be evaluated. Unless the defendant has reason to believe that the individual would permit more or less contact, the tort standard in battery cases prohibits contact that would be "offensive to an ordinary person not unduly sensitive as to his dignity."[14] However, even "innocuous and generally permitted contacts may become tortious if they are inflicted with knowledge that the individual plaintiff objects to them and refuses to permit them."[15] For assault, in which the fear of contact constitutes the injury, the test is what the defendant's conduct "denote[d] at the time to the party assaulted."[16] The standard treatment of the hypersensitive individual is to find liability if the conduct would have been offensive to the person of ordinary sensibilities. If it would have been, the perpetrator is liable for all the damages caused *this* individual, whether she is unduly sensitive or not.

The standard of recovery in the stricty emotional area is particularly instructive. The tort of intentional infliction of emotional distress, codified by the second Restatement of Torts, allows recovery for purely emotional disturbance.[17] The conduct must be extreme and outrageous to a person of ordinary sensibilities. The departure here is that the perpetrator is liable for the emotional distress alone, and for the bodily harm that results from it, without requiring a physical act or invasion. The tort conception of "parasitic damages," in which a tortfeasor is liable for all the consequences of his acts (for example, loss of employment) once he is liable for the tort, raises the possibility of covering the entire range of consequences of sexual harassment in sufficiently aggravated circumstances.

Sexual propositions in themselves have not generally been considered torts where there is no physical incursion upon or trespass against the person, or no physical injury. In Magruder's famous formulation: "Women have occasionally sought damages for mental distress and humiliation on account of being addressed by a proposal of illicit intercourse. This is peculiarly a situation where circumstances alter cases. If there has been no incidental assault or battery, or perhaps trespass to land, recovery is generally denied, the view being apparently, that there is no harm in asking."[18] Expressing attitudes toward women's assertions of sexual injury which have remained largely unchanged to the present day, the court in one case of solicitation of sexual intercourse found the injury of a sexual proposition "generally considered more sentimental than substantial . . . vague and shadowy" and "easily simulated and impossible to disprove." Without physical "impact," the injury of a sexual proposition is considered "remote" and to have a "metaphysical character."[19] It is not an injury *in itself.*[20]

Sexual harassment that consisted solely in propositions as a condition of work apparently would not be tortious unless it became outrageous enough to constitute intentional infliction of emotional distress. One recently filed tort case, *Fuller* v. *Williames,*[21] makes just such allegations, pleading as intentional infliction of emotional distress a "condition of work" type situation of sexual harassment. The plaintiff complained that the defendants on several occasions, in the presence of others, "unlawfully, wilfully, maliciously, outrageously and contemptuously [did] insult, demean and humiliate plaintiff by making crude remarks of an explicit sexual nature including remarks deprecating to women in general," knowing that this conduct was likely to cause severe emotional distress. She allegedly

> became upset, embarrassed, humiliated, nervous and depressed; suffered frequent tension headaches, had difficulty sleeping, suffered stress in her marriage, and was unable to concentrate on her photographic work and public school and photographic teaching; suffered mental anguish and humiliation and damage to her reputation as a dignified self-respecting woman and impairment of her earning capacity.[22]

Damages included "unpaid wages due." In another case which also pled sexual harassment as sex discrimination, one count complained of intentional infliction of emotional stress through acts of sexual harassment wherein the defendant "disturbed and disquieted the plaintiff by soliciting her to be his sex object if she wished to continue to be employed." The plaintiff "regarded such proposals . . . [as] repugnant, abhorrent, and a shock to her moral sensitivities and ideals of decency and propriety," took steps to end his sexual advances, but they continued until her discharge.[23] The results in these cases may help to clarify the potential of this approach.

Torts prohibiting interference with family relations by sexual means—seduction, enticement, criminal conversation, alienation of affections, loss of consortium, and the like—have blended the enforcement of moral standards with protections for men's possessory interests, whether by design or pattern of administration. Civil recovery usually went to men for loss of consortium, a "relational injury" which included loss of "conjugal affection." Blackstone explains why husbands have recovered for this loss far more often than wives:

> We may observe that in these relative injuries notice is only taken of the wrong done to the superior of the parties related . . . while the loss of the inferior by such injuries is totally unregarded. One reason for which may be this; that the inferior hath no kind of property in the company, care or assistance of the superior, as the superior is held to have in those of the inferior, and therefore the inferior can suffer no loss or injury.[24]

.   .   .

Most actions for interference with domestic relations "which carry an accusation of sexual misbehavior" have been abolished by statute. The reasons, as summarized by William Prosser, are instructive on social attitudes toward women's accusations of sexual injury as these attitudes have been reflected in tort law:

> It is notorious that [such actions] have afforded a fertile field for blackmail and extortion by means of manufactured suits in which the threat of publicity is used to force a settlement. There is good reason to believe that even genuine actions of this type are brought more frequently than not with purely mercenary or vindictive motives; that it is impossible to compensate for such damage with what has derisively been called "heart balm"; and that no preventive purpose is served, since such torts seldom are committed with deliberate plan. Added to this is perhaps an increasing notion of personal or even sexual freedom on the part of women.[25]

The essence of the first objection is that women lie about sex for money. As to the second, one wonders why bad motives for bringing good suits is not a more common reason for eliminating many other causes of action. Further, money does not adequately compensate for most injuries (for example, wrongful death), yet the cause of action is not eliminated. Then, the sophisticated calculus so basic to tort that distinguishes negligent from intentional harm is abandoned in favor of the proposition that a tort committed without "deliberate plan" is not a tort at all. Money damages are required to serve a deterrent function in these cases, while it suffices for other torts that deterrence is merely a desirable by-product of the point of damages: to help make the victim whole for the injury. These inconsistencies lend themselves to the interpretation that society has increasingly come to view such incidents as not very damaging.

. . . This reference to women's increasing "personal or even sexual freedom" inadequately criticizes the premise common to all these causes of action: that a man's wife's sexuality belonged to him, in the sense that another man was liable to him in damages for sexual acts with her, even with her consent. This attitude may be no less prevalent although it is no longer legally enforceable in this way. The point is not that these common law* torts should be revived, but that their statutory abolition for these reasons reveals attitudes toward women's sexuality which can be expected to arise in connection with attempts to impose sanctions upon men's sexual violation of women in employment as well. . . .

Most broadly considered, tort is conceptually inadequate to the problem of sexual harassment to the extent that it rips injuries to women's sexuality out of the context of women's social circumstances as a whole. In particular, short of developing a new tort for sexual harassment as such, the tort approach misses the nexus between women's sexuality and women's employment, the system of reciprocal sanctions which, to women as a gender, become cumulative. In tort perspective, the injury of sexual harassment would be seen as an injury to the individual person, to personal sexual integrity, with damages extending to the job. Alternatively, sexual harassment could be seen as an injury to an individual interest in employment, with damages extending to the emotional harm attendant to the sexual invasion as well as to the loss of employment. The approach tends to pose the necessity to decide whether sexual harassment is essentially an injury to the person, to sexual integrity and feelings, with pendent damages to the job, or whether it is essentially an injury to the job, with damages extending to the person. Since it is both, either one omits the social dynamics that systematically place women in these positions, that may coerce consent, that interpenetrate sexuality and employment to women's detriment because they are women.

Unsituated in a recognition of the context that keeps women secondary and powerless, sexual injuries appear as incidental or deviant aber-

---

*The "common law" refers to legal principles, not necessarily mentioned in written laws or statutes, that evolved over time through judicial opinions. (Ed.)

rations which arise in one-to-one relationships gone wrong. The essential purpose of tort law, although it has policy assumptions and implications, is to compensate individuals one at a time for mischief which befalls them as a consequence of the one-time ineptitude or nastiness of other individuals. The occurrence of such events is viewed more or less with resignation, as an inevitability of social proximity, a fallout of order which can be confronted only probabilistically. Sexual harassment as [it should be] understood is not merely a parade of interconnected consequences with the potential for discrete repetition by other individuals, so that a precedent will suffice. Rather, it is a group-defined injury which occurs to many different individuals regardless of unique qualities or circumstances, in ways that connect with other deprivations of the same individuals, among all of whom a single characteristic—female sex—is shared. Such an injury is *in essence* a group injury. The context which makes the impact of gender cumulative—in fact, the context that makes it injurious—is lost when sexual harassment is approached as an individual injury, however wide the net of damages is cast. Tort law compensates individuals for injuries while spreading their costs and perhaps setting examples for foresightful perpetrators; the purpose of discrimination law is to change the society so that this kind of injury need not and does not recur. Tort law considers individual and compensable something which is fundamentally social and should be eliminated.

A related defect in the vision underlying the sexual tort cases, from the standpoint of their usefulness as a solution to sexual harassment, is their disabling (and cloying) moralism. The aura of the pedestal, more rightly understood as the foundation of the cage, permeates them. In one case, the judge opined, "Every woman has a right to assume that a passenger car is not a brothel and that when she travels in it, she will meet nothing, see nothing, hear nothing, to wound her delicacy or insult her womanhood."[26] Another case reveals an underlying reason for age limits on women's capacity to consent to sex. The ability fully to appreciate the consequences of sex outside of marriage is essential for an act which "when discovered ostracizes her from good society."[27] When it becomes clear that such protections of delicacy and purity have worked women's exclusion from the decisive arenas of social life, while the same society that morally approves economically punishes the sexually independent (that is, noncompliant) woman, more moralism looks like more of the problem. Just as women are tired of being commended rather than paid, they are tired of being considered sexually virtuous rather than hired or promoted—a choice men must seldom confront and a currency of compensation men must seldom settle for. Prohibitions on sexual harassment as acts conceived as moral violations emerge as repressive impositions of state morality. Inventing special rules of morality for the workplace would institutionalize new taboos rather than confront the fact that it is *women* who are systematically disadvantaged by the old ones. Resistance to sexual harassment can be misconstrued as a revival of moral delicacy only until it is grasped that sexual harassment is less an issue of right and wrong than an issue of power. Women are in no *position* to refuse, which is what makes refusal so moral an act and surrenders so unfairly the price of survival.

All of this is not to say that sexual harassment is not both wrong and a personal injury, merely that it is a social wrong and a social injury that occurs on a personal level. To treat it as a tort is less simply incorrect than inadequate. The law recognizes that individual acts of racism could be torts in recognizing that the dignitary harm of racist insults can be compensated like any other personal injury.[28] This does not preclude a finding that the same acts of racial invective on the job are race discrimination.[29] Although racial insults impact upon blacks on a personal level, they are systematically connected to the "living insult" of segregation.[30] Although reparations may be due,[31] the stigma is not eradicable by money damages to one black person at a time. As with sexual harassment, the reason these acts can occur and recur, and the source of their sting, is not the breaking of a code of good conduct, but the relegation to inferiority for which they stand.

To see sexual harassment as an injury to morality is to turn it into an extreme case of bad manners, when the point is that it is the kind of bad manners almost exclusively visited upon women by men with the power to get away with it. One can see the social invisibility of blacks as white rudeness, but it makes more sense to see it as racism. The major difference between the tort approach and the discrimination approach, then, is that tort sees sexual harassment as an illicit act, a moral infraction, an outrage to the individual's sensibilities and the society's cherished but unlived values. Discrimination law casts the same acts as economic coercion, in which material survival is held hostage to sexual submission. . . .

NOTES

1. *Tomkins* v. *Public Service Electric & Gas Co.,* 422 F. Supp. 553, 556 (D.N.J. 1976), rev'd, 568 F.2d 1044 (3d Cir. 1977).
2. *Barnes* v. *Costle,* 561 F.2d 983, 995 (D.C. Cir. 1977) (MacKinnon, J., concurring).

3. W. Prosser, *The Law of Torts,* 3.

4. Ibid., p. 36.

5. *Hough* v. *Iderhoff,* 69 Or. 568, 139 P. 931, 932 (1914).

6. *Gates* v. *State,* 110 Ga. App. 303, 138 So.2d 473, 474 (1964). This was a criminal battery, the quotation taken from another criminal battery case, *Goodrum* v. *State,* 60 Ga. 509 (1878). "If to put the arm, though tenderly, about the neck of another man's wife, against her will, is not an assault and battery, what is it? . . . There was nothing to excite rapture or provoke enthusiasm. Why should he embrace her? Why persist in caressing her? . . . He took the risk of not meeting with a responsive feeling in her, and must abide all the consequences of disappointment" ibid., at 510, 511. On the question of what is and is not a sexual touching, see *People* v. *Thomas,* 91 Misc. 2d 724 (1977).

7. Prosser, *The Law of Torts, supra,* note 62, at 36, n. 85.

8. *Kline* v. *Kline,* 158 Ind. 602, 64 N.E. 9, 10 (1902), cited in Prosser, *The Law of Torts, supra,* note 62, at 38.

9. *Ragsdale* v. *Ezell,* 20 Ky. 1567, 49 S.W. 775, 776 (1899).

10. *Liljegren* v. *United Rys. Co. of St. Louis,* 227 S.W. 925 (Mo. Ct. App. 1921). She was awarded $500, which corrected for inflation is $1,684 in 1977. Similarly corrected for inflation to 1977, the damage awards for sexual harassment tort cases, *infra,* are as follows. The actual awards are in parentheses. *Skousen* (1961), $7,350 ($3,500) actual, $3,015 ($1,500) punitive, for $10,065 ($5,000) total damages; *Hatchett* (1915), $2,969 ($500); *Martin* (1920), $1,354 ($450); *Kurpgeweit* (1910), $9,670 ($1,500); *Ragsdale* (1899), $5,051 ($700); *Craker* (1895), $7,220 ($1,000); *Davis* (1905), $26,740 ($4,000) (note that the *Davis* jury award was overruled).

11. In a situation familiar to sexually harassed women, the perpetrator simply did not believe her when she told him she wanted him to leave her alone. Their dialogue reportedly ended as follows: " 'Look me in the eye, and tell me if you are mad.' I said, 'I am mad.' " *Craker* v. *The Chicago and Northwestern Railway Company,* 36 Wis. 657, 659, 17 Am. Rep. 504 (1895). She apparently was. Her report precipitated his immediate firing; she proceeded criminally (for criminal assault and battery) and won, and then sued the employer for civil damages. The *Craker* decision is notable in several respects. The treatment of the size of the damage awarded—which amounts to an inquiry into how much this woman's bodily integrity and sexual feelings are worth—is incisive and sympathetic: "who can be found to say that such an amount would be in excess of compensation to his own or his neighbor's wife or sister or daughter?" 36 Wis., at 679. The judge's refusal to separate the woman's sense of wrong at the injustice done her from her mental suffering and pain, holding both proper objects of *compensatory* damages, would be considered pathbreaking had it been more widely followed:

And it is difficult to see how these are to be distinguished from the sense of wrong and insult arising from injustice and intention to vex and degrade. The appearance of malicious intent may indeed add to the sense of wrong; and equally, whether such intent be really there or not. But that goes to mental suffering, and mental suffering to compensation. . . . What human creature can penetrate the mysteries of his own sensations, and parcel out separately his mental suffering and his sense of wrong—so much for compensatory, so much for vindictive damages? 36 Wis., at 678.

The decision further held the employer responsible for this intentional tort by the employee, an unusual departure. The standard view is that employers are only responsible for employee negligence.

One employing another . . . would be as little likely to authorize negligence as malice. . . . [T]he true distinction ought to rest . . . on the condition whether or not the act of the servant be in the course of his employment. . . . If we owe bread to another and appoint an agent to furnish it, and the agent of malice furnish a stone instead, the principal is responsible for the stone and its consequences. In such cases, negligence is malice. 36 Wis., at 688–69.

12. *Hatchett* v. *Blacketer,* 162 Ky. 266, 172 S.W. 533 (1915).

13. *Martin* v. *Jensen,* 113 Wash. 290, 193 P. 674 (1920). By analogy with the law of trespass to property, recovery for mental anguish alone was allowed where suffering "is the result of a wanton or intentional trepass on the person of a woman." 193 P., at 676.

14. Prosser, *The Law of Torts, supra,* note 62, at 37.

15. Ibid., p. 37.

16. Ibid., p. 41.

17. Restatement (Second) of Torts § 46 (1965).

18. Magruder, "Mental and Emotional Disturbance in the Law of Torts," 49 *Harvard Law Review* (1936): 1033, 1055. It is interesting that the cases commonly cited in support of Magruder's proposition do not squarely support it. Some hold that the facts were improperly pleaded. *Prince* v. *Ridge* states that an attempt by words of persuasion to induce a female to have sexual intercourse does not constitute an assault, but finds that the instant case presents sufficient acts for a battery, an assault, or both. 32 Misc. 666, 66 N.Y.S. 454, 455 (Sup. Ct. 1900). It would seem usual that more than simply asking would be involved.

Other cases referenced to support the formulation require that a physical *injury,* not merely an *act,* must be alleged to make out an assault. As is often the case where sex is involved, this requirement confuses the basic doctrine. The doctrine of assault requires only an act, not an injury. An example of a correct application of assault doctrine requiring physical acts, not physical injuries, is one 1880 Vermont case, in which a blind traveling music teacher, sleeping overnight in the defendant's house, was propositioned. "During the night he stealthily entered her room, sat on her bed, leaned over her person, and made repeated solicitation to her for sexual intimacy, which she repelled." *Newell* v. *Witcher,* 53 Vt. 589 (1880), quoted in *Reed* v. *Maley,* 115 Ky. 816, 74 S.W. 1079, 1081

(1903). The defendant was found liable for trespass and assault on the person for sitting on the bed and leaning over her. (Although it was the defendant's property, the sleeping room was considered exclusively the plaintiff's for the night.) The assault finding meant that the plaintiff was found in fear of sexual touching from the proposition; the cited physical acts were sufficient to ground actionable assault, while the proposition alone would not.

Davis v. *Richardson,* 76 Ark. 348, 89 S.W. 318 (1905), by contrast, required physical *injury.* In this case, a fifteen-year-old girl was seized and embraced "in a rude and indecent manner" by a man who kissed her with "violent and indecent familiarity" and "acted like he was going to do something else." The damage award of $4,000 ($26,740 in 1977) was overturned because an instruction allowed the jury to conclude that the mere proposal was actionable, although acts sufficient for both assault and battery were evidenced. *Bennett* v. *McIntire,* 121 Ind. 231, 23 N.E. 78 (1889) similarly took the approach of requiring some physical invasion of itself actionable before any recovery could be allowed for sexual propositions. In a case for seduction and debauching of his wife, the plaintiff pleaded a cause of action in trespass. Defendant was argued to have gained permission to come upon plaintiff's property by fraud, then seducing his wife. It was held that since he was on the property by permission, albeit fraudulent, no damages were recoverable. Trespass was the only cause of action apparently considered, with seduction as aggravation of damages.

Similarly, in *Reed* v. *Maley,* 115 Ky. 818, 74 S.W. 1079 (1903), in which a man solicited a woman to have sexual intercourse, no cause of action was held to exist.

19. 74 S.W., at 1080 (referring to several other cases).

20. The judge posed a reverse familiar to readers of the early sexual harassment cases:

> Suppose a bawd should solicit a man upon a public street to have sexual intimacy with her; he certainly could not maintain a civil action against her. If an action could be maintained by a woman against a man for such solicitation, the same right to maintain one would exist in his favor. Whilst he might not suffer the same anguish and humiliation on account of such solicitation as the woman, yet the right of recovery would be the same. The amount of it would only be determined by reason of the difference in effect such a solicitation would have upon one or the other. 74 S.W. at 1081.

Although a proposition would have a different impact upon the sexes, it is nevertheless argued that because a man "certainly could not maintain a civil action" for a proposition by a woman (why not is not considered), a woman should be similarly precluded.

The dissenting judge in this case urged that a sexual proposition should be actionable as solicitation to commit adultery. It should be prohibited not because it preys upon women, but because "if unsuccessful, it is liable to lead to violence and bloodshed at the hands of the [one supposes male] relatives of the woman; and if successful it defeats the end for which marriage is intended, and destroys the woman." 74 S.W. 1079, 1083. He thought punitive damages appropriate for reasons that combined solicitude for the woman's shattered virtue with an eye toward her undone housework: "The purity of woman and the sanctity of the marriage relation lie at the basis of our whole social fabric. . . . The natural effect of an indecent proposal of this character to a virtuous woman would be to upset her nerves and unfit her for discharging for the time her domestic duties." 74 S.W. 1074, 1083–1084.

21. No. A7703–04001 (Or. Cir. Ct. 1977).

22. First Amended Complaint, *Fuller* v. *Williames et al.*

23. Complaint, *Morgenheim* v. *Hiber and Midnight Sun Broadcasters* (Alaska Superior Court, filed December 29, 1975).

24. 3 *W. Blackstone Commentaries,* pp. 142–43, quoted and discussed by Leo Kanowitz, *Women and the Law: The Unfinished Revolution* (Albuquerque: University of New Mexico Press, 1969), p. 82.

25. Prosser, *The Law of Torts,* note 3, at 887.

26. *Craker* v. *The Chicago and Northwestern Railway Co.,* 36 Wis. 657, 674, 17 Am. Rep. 504 (1895).

27. *Hough* v. *Iderhoff,* 69 Or. 568, 139 P. 931 (1914).

28. See, for example, *Alcorn* v. *Ambro Engineering, Inc.,* 468 P. 2d 216, 36 Cal. Rptr. 216 (Sup. Ct. 1970); *Wiggs* v. *Coursin,* 355 F. Supp. 206 (S.D. Fla. 1973); *Gray* v. *Serruto Builders,* 110 N.J. Sup. 297, 265 A. 2d 404 (1970).

29. See EEOC cases discussed at 210, *infra.*

30. *Brunson* v. *Board of Trustees,* 429 F. 2d 820, 826 (1970).

31. See Boris Bittker, *The Case for Black Reparations* (New York: Random House, 1973).

10

Bared Buttocks and Federal Cases

Ellen Frankel Paul

Women in American society are victims of sexual harassment in alarming proportions. Sexual harassment is an inevitable corollary to class exploitation; as capitalists exploit workers, so do males in positions of authority exploit their female subordinates. Male professors, supervisors, and apartment managers in ever increasing numbers take advantage of the financial dependence and vulnerability of women to extract sexual concessions.

These are the assertions that commonly begin discussions of sexual harassment. For reasons that will be adumbrated below, dissent from the prevailing view is long overdue. Three recent episodes will serve to frame this disagreement.

Valerie Craig, an employee of Y & Y Snacks, Inc., joined several co-workers and her supervisor for drinks after work one day in July of 1978. Her supervisor drove her home and proposed that they become more intimately acquainted. She refused his invitation for sexual relations, whereupon he said that he would "get even" with her. Ten days after the incident she was fired from her job. She soon filed a complaint of sexual harassment with the Equal Employment Opportunity Commission (EEOC), and the case wound its way through the courts. Craig prevailed, the company was held liable for damages, and she received back pay, reinstatement, and an order prohibiting Y & Y from taking reprisals against her in the future.

Carol Zabowicz, one of only two female forklift operators in a West

From *Society* 28, no. 4 (1991): 4–7. Reprinted by permission of Transaction.

Bend Co. warehouse, charged that her co-workers over a four year period from 1978–1982 sexually harassed her by such acts as: asking her whether she was wearing a bra; two of the men exposing their buttocks between ten and twenty times; a male co-worker grabbing his crotch and making obscene suggestions of growling; subjecting her to offensive and abusive language; and exhibiting obscene drawings with her initials on them. Zabowicz began to show symptoms of physical and psychological stress, necessitating several medical leaves, and she filed a sexual harassment complaint with the EEOC. The district court judge remarked that "The sustained, malicious, and brutal harassment meted out . . . was more than merely unreasonable; it was malevolent and outrageous." The company knew of the harassment and took corrective action only after the employee filed a complaint with the EEOC. The company was, therefore, held liable, and Zabowicz was awarded back pay for the period of her medical absence, and a judgment that her rights were violated under the Civil Rights Act of 1964.

On September 17, 1990, Lisa Olson, a sports reporter for the *Boston Herald,* charged five football players of the just-defeated New England Patriots with sexual harassment for making sexually suggestive and offensive remarks to her when she entered their locker room to conduct a post-game interview. The incident amounted to nothing short of "mind rape," according to Olson. After vociferous lamentations in the media, the National Football League fined the team and its players $25,000 each. The National Organization of Women called for a boycott of Remington electric shavers because the owner of the company, Victor Kiam, also owns the Patriots and who allegedly displayed insufficient sensitivity at the time when the episode occurred.

All these incidents are indisputably disturbing. In an ideal world— one needless to say far different from the one that we inhabit or are ever likely to inhabit—women would not be subjected to such treatment in the course of their work. Women, and men as well, would be accorded respect by co-workers and supervisors, their feelings would be taken into account, and their dignity would be left intact. For women to expect reverential treatment in the workplace is utopian, yet they should not have to tolerate outrageous, offensive sexual overtures and threats as they go about earning a living.

One question that needs to be pondered is: What kinds of undesired sexual behavior women should be protected against by law? That is, what kind of actions are deemed so outrageous and violate a woman's rights to such [an] extent that the law should intervene, and what actions should be considered inconveniences of life, to be morally condemned but not adjudicated? A subsidiary question concerns the type of legal remedy appropriate for the wrongs that do require redress. Before directly addressing these questions, it might be useful to diffuse some of the hyperbole adhering to the sexual harassment issue.

Surveys are one source of this hyperbole. If their results are accepted at face value, they lead to the conclusion that women are disproportionately victims of legions of sexual harassers. A poll by the Albuquerque *Tribune* found that nearly 80 percent of the respondents reported that they or someone they knew had been victims of sexual harassment. The Merit Systems Protection Board determined that 42 percent of the women (and 14 percent of men) working for the federal government had experienced some form of unwanted sexual attention between 1985 and 1987, with unwanted "sexual teasing" identified as the most prevalent form. A Defense Department survey found that 64 percent of women in the military (and 17 percent of the men) suffered "uninvited and unwanted sexual attention" within the previous year. The United Methodist Church established that 7 percent of its clergywomen experienced incidents of sexual harassment, with 41 percent of these naming a pastor or colleague as the perpetrator, and 31 percent mentioning church social functions as the setting.

A few caveats concerning polls in general, and these sorts of polls in particular, are worth considering. Pollsters looking for a particular social ill tend to find it, usually in gargantuan proportions. (What fate would lie in store for a pollster who concluded that child abuse, or wife beating, or mistreatment of the elderly had dwindled to the point of negligibility!) Sexual harassment is a notoriously ill-defined and almost infinitely expandable concept, including everything from rape to unwelcome neck massaging, discomfiture upon witnessing sexual overtures directed at others, yelling at and blowing smoke in the ears of female subordinates, and displays of pornographic pictures in the workplace. Defining sexual harassment, as the United Methodists did, as "any sexually related behavior that is unwelcome, offensive or which fails to respect the rights of others," the concept is broad enough to include everything from "unsolicited suggestive looks or leers [or] pressures for dates" to "actual sexual assaults or rapes." Categorizing everything from rape to "looks" as sexual harassment makes us all victims, a state of affairs satisfying to radical feminists, but not very useful for distinguishing serious injuries from the merely trivial.

Yet, even if the surveys exaggerate the extent of sexual harassment, however defined, what they do reflect is a great deal of tension between the sexes. As women in ever increasing numbers entered the workplace in the last two decades, as the women's movement challenged alleged male hegemony and exploitation with ever greater intemperance, and as women entered previously all-male preserves from the board rooms to the coal pits, it is lamentable, but should not be surprising, that this tension sometimes takes sexual form. Not that sexual harassment on the job, in the university, and in other settings is a trivial or insignificant matter, but a sense of proportion needs to be restored and, even more importantly, distinctions need to be made. In other words, sexual harassment must be de-ideologized. Statements that paint nearly all women as victims and all men and their patriarchal, capitalist system as perpetrators, are ideological fantasy. Ideology blurs the distinction between being injured—being a genuine victim—and merely being offended. An example is this statement by Catharine A. MacKinnon, a law professor and feminist activist:

> Sexual harassment perpetuates the interlocked structure by which women have been kept sexually in thrall to men and at the bottom of the labor market. Two forces of American society converge: men's control over women's sexuality and capital control over employees' work lives. Women historically have been required to exchange sexual services for material survival, in one form or another. Prostitution and marriage as well as sexual harassment in different ways institutionalize this arrangement.

Such hyperbole needs to be diffused and distinctions need to be drawn. Rape, a nonconsensual invasion of a person's body, is a crime clear and simple. It is a violation of the right to the physical integrity of the body (the right to life, as John Locke or Thomas Jefferson would have put it). Criminal law should and does prohibit rape. Whether it is useful to call rape "sexual harassment" is doubtful, for it makes the latter concept overly broad while trivializing the former.

Intimidation in the workplace of the kind that befell Valerie Craig— that is, extortion of sexual favors by a supervisor from a subordinate by threatening to penalize, fire, or fail to reward—is what the courts term *quid pro quo* sexual harassment. Since the mid-1970s, the federal courts have treated this type of sexual harassment as a form of sex discrimination in employment proscribed under Title VII of the Civil Rights Act of 1964. A plaintiff who prevails against an employer may receive such equitable remedies as reinstatement and back pay, and the court can order the company to prepare and disseminate a policy against sexual harassment. Current law places principal liability on the company, not the harassing supervisor, even when higher management is unaware of the harassment and, thus, cannot take any steps to prevent it.

Quid pro quo sexual harassment is morally objectionable and analogous to extortion: the harasser extorts property (i.e., use of the woman's body) through the leverage of fear for her job. The victim of such behavior should have legal recourse, but serious reservations can be held about rectifying these injustices through the blunt instrument of Title VII. In [outrageous] cases the victim is left less than whole (for back pay will not compensate for her ancillary losses), and no prospect for punitive damages are offered to deter would-be harassers. Even more distressing about Title VII is the fact that the primary target of litigation is not the actual harasser, but rather the employer. This places a double burden on a company. The employer is swindled by the supervisor because he spent his time pursuing sexual gratification and thereby impairing the efficiency of the workplace by mismanaging his subordinates, and the employer must endure lengthy and expensive litigation, pay damages, and suffer loss to its reputation. It would be fairer to both the company and the victim to treat sexual harassment as a tort—that is, as a private wrong or injury for which the court can assess damages. Employers should be held vicariously liable only when they know of an employee's behavior and do not try to redress it.

As for the workplace harassment endured by Carol Zabowicz—the bared buttocks, obscene portraits, etc.—that too should be legally redressable. Presently, such incidents also fall under the umbrella of Title VII, and are termed hostile environment sexual harassment, a category accepted later than *quid pro quo* and with some judicial reluctance. The main problem with this category is that it has proven too elastic: cases have reached the courts based on everything from off-color jokes to unwanted, persistent sexual advances by co-workers. A new tort of sexual harassment would handle these cases better. Only instances above a certain threshold of egregiousness or outrageousness would be actionable. In other words, the behavior that the plaintiff found offensive would also have to be offensive to the proverbial "reasonable man" of the tort law. That is, the behavior would have to be objectively injurious rather than merely subjectively offensive. The defendant would be the actual harasser not the company, unless it knew about the problem and failed to act. Victims of scatological jokes, leers, unwanted offers of dates, and other sexual annoyances would no longer have their day in court.

A distinction must be restored between morally offensive behavior and behavior that causes serious harm. Only the latter should fall under the jurisdiction of criminal or tort law. Do we really want legislators and judges delving into our most intimate private lives, deciding when a look is a leer, and when a leer is a Civil Rights Act offense? Do we really want courts deciding, as one recently did, whether a school principal's disparaging remarks about a female school district administrator was sexual harassment and, hence, a breach of Title VII, or merely the act of a spurned and vengeful lover? Do we want judges settling disputes such as the one that arose at a car dealership after a female employee turned down a male co-worker's offer of a date and his colleagues retaliated by calling her offensive names and embarrassing her in front of customers? Or another case in which a female shipyard worker complained of an "offensive working environment" because of the prevalence of pornographic material on the docks? Do we want the state to prevent or compensate us for any behavior that someone might find offensive? Should people have a legally enforceable right not to be offended by others? At some point, the price for such protection is the loss of both liberty and privacy rights.

Workplaces are breeding grounds of envy, personal grudges, infatuation, and jilted loves, and beneath a fairly high threshold of outrageousness, these travails should be either suffered in silence, complained of to higher management, or left behind as one seeks other employment. No one, female or male, can expect to enjoy a working environment that is perfectly stress-free, or to be treated always and by everyone with kindness and respect. To the extent that sympathetic judges have encouraged women to seek monetary compensation for slights and annoyances, they have not done them a great service. Women need to develop a thick skin in order to survive and prosper in the work force. It is patronizing to think that they need to be recompensed by male judges for seeing a few pornographic pictures on a wall. By their efforts to extend sexual harassment charges to even the most trivial behavior, the radical feminists send a message that women are not resilient enough to ignore the run-of-the-mill, churlish provocation from male co-workers. It is difficult to imagine a suit by a longshoreman complaining of mental stress due to the display of nude male centerfolds by female co-workers. Women cannot expect to have it both ways: equality where convenient, but special dispensations when the going gets rough. Equality has its price and that price may include unwelcome sexual advances, irritating and even intimidating sexual jests, and lewd and obnoxious colleagues.

[Outrageous] acts—sexual harassment per se—must be legally redressable. Lesser but not trivial offenses, whether at the workplace or in other more social settings, should be considered moral lapses for which the offending party receives opprobrium, disciplinary warnings, or penalties, depending on the setting and the severity. Trivial offenses, dirty jokes, sexual overtures, and sexual innuendoes do make many women feel intensely discomfited, but, unless they become outrageous through persistence or content, these too should be taken as part of life's annoyances.

The perpetrators should be either endured, ignored, rebuked, or avoided, as circumstances and personal inclination dictate. Whether Lisa Olson's experience in the locker room of the Boston Patriots falls into the second or third category is debatable. The media circus triggered by the incident was certainly out of proportion to the event.

As the presence of women on road gangs, construction crews, and oil rigs becomes a fact of life, the animosities and tensions of this transition period are likely to abate gradually. Meanwhile, women should "lighten up," and even dispense a few risqué barbs of their own, a sure way of taking the fun out of it for offensive male bores.

11

Social Theory and Legal Argument: Catharine MacKinnon on Sexual Harassment

J. P. Minson

.   .   .

TORT AND TABOO

. . . [MacKinnon's] attack on tort law is mainly directed against its "underlying" patriarchal vision of women.[1] In taking issue with MacKinnon's view of the place of tort law in justiciating sexual harassment I do not dispute her contention that sex-discrimination law offers a better pathway to legal redress for women. But in MacKinnon's eyes, tort remedies are not merely a second-best resort. The values, purposes, and the very language of these torts are subject to a far-reaching critique which, as we shall see, has implications for not only legal but also nonlegal measures.

In all this, MacKinnon displays an instructive consistency. Law, she maintains, is generally given over to enhancing male supremacy. One notorious way of achieving this end is manifest in the common law's paternalistic-protective attitude vis-à-vis concern to *protect* women's sexual integrity. By contrast, Anti-Discrimination Law acknowledged, for the first time in legal history, the principle of equality between the sexes *qua*

From the *International Journal of the Sociology of Law* 19 (1991): 365-74, 376, 377. Reprinted by permission of the publisher. The full version of this essay will appear in *Questions of Conduct: Sexual Harassment, Citizenship, and Government* (New York: St. Martins Press; London: Macmillan, 1992).

persons.[2] So, between anti-discrimination law, pointing forward to women's equal personhood, and sexual torts, pointing backwards to patriarchy and its pseudo-protections of women's bodily integrity, there *can* only be a radical discontinuity.[3] However, this argument that sexual torts are essentially patriarchal and radically discontinuous in respect to sex-discrimination remedies breaks down for a number of reasons.

To begin with, it is a statistical fact that the great majority of "Title VII" sexual harassment claims are *supplemented* by tort claims for punitive, exemplary, or emotionally consequential damages, over and above compensation for lost wages and other tangible job-opportunities.[4] Even more damaging to the assumptions of antipathy and discontinuity, however, is MacKinnon's own mindfulness of the contemporary value of these torts as precedents in legal argument. The first and broadest positive lesson of the case law pertaining to "torts of sexual invasion" is that

> Women's bodies, particularly the conditions and consequences of men's sexual access to them, are not a novel subject for the law. The law of torts historically provided civil redress for sexual invasions at a time when social morality was less ambiguous in defining a woman's sexuality as . . . capable of compensable damage . . . the examination of tort shows that the law is quite unaccustomed to treating cloudy issues of motive and intent, the meaning of ambiguous acts, the effects of words on liability for acts and the role of excessive sensitivity in determining liability and damages, all in a sexual context. These issues have arisen before. They have not been thought so subtle as to preclude a judicial resolution once a real injury was perceived to exist.[5]

Sexual touching, for example, including kissing without consent, has been considered under the torts of assault and battery (extending to "a touching of the mind" by placing the person in a state of fear) "along with corollary dignitary harm of the tort of intentional infliction of emotional distress." Much of what is now captured by the designation sexual harassment could even figure as criminal acts under such "antiquated" headings as *criminal conversation, loss of consortium, insult, lewdness, fornication,* and so on. In *Craker* v. *The Chicago and Northwestern Railway Co.* (36 Wis. 657, 17 Am. Rep. 504, 1895), the employer of a railway conductor who repeatedly grabbed and kissed a Wisconsin school teacher was successfully sued for $1,000. A further feature of this judgment which argues in favor of tort analogies is its incorporation of a distinction between "negligent" and "intentional" harms and its insistence that the former, no less than the latter, amounts to injustice, vexation, and degradation and is therefore compensable. . . . These are just as capable, in some circumstances, as anti-discrimination law of discounting (men's) "experience" where appropriate. Relatedly, the criteria of emotional distress do much to meet the standard defense that the victim of sexual harassment reacted "oversensitively."[6] MacKinnon also points out an instructive affinity between the tort of inflicting emotional distress and the modern concept of "stress" in health-and-safety regulation.

In general, therefore, it cannot be said that MacKinnon fails to appreciate any of the advantages of these torts. What does not seem to be appreciated is the extent to which these advantages redound to the discredit of her overall critique of tort law and of her overall conception of how and to what extent sexual harassment should be regulated (by law). One problem in this critique can be traced to her reliance on an extremely crude conception of "liberal" distinctions between private and public domains and their bearing on women's subordination. MacKinnon's main caveats against tort law remedies, it will be recalled, went to the difficulty of registering sexual harassment as a "social" injury and as an *employment*-related issue. Tort law construes it, by contrast, as a "moral" injury, in the liberal sense. Liberalism is here of course identified with a philosophy or ideology of individual (negative) liberty which furnishes a justification for demarcating certain areas of life as private zones of personal discretion, moral (or immoral) choice, etc. and which are *ipso facto* not open to state intervention. It follows that to characterize sexual harassment as a "moral problem" in this sense is to assume that it is essentially a private issue of personal morality and individual responsibility. In making this assumption, tort law "rips . . . injuries to women's sexuality out of the context of women's social circumstances as a whole."[7] In order to capture the "social injury" of sexual harassment this "moral" assumption must be written out of its legal definition. The progressive possibilities of Anti-Discrimination law are seen as a simple function of the extent to which it transfers the problem (at the level of legal and social forms of perception, definition, etc.) from "the" private to "the" public sphere.

This line of argument suffers from a tendency to repeat rather than to challenge simplistic "liberal" philosophical or ideological suppositions of a single neat division between private and public realms of human existence. True, this categorization is assigned to the realm of ideology— "women's place . . ." does not reflect any "natural" abilities or disposition of sexes; "private" relationships do in reality have "political" dimensions and repercussions, etc. However, for MacKinnon, to categorize an activity or domain as private is to imply that it is nonsocial and not subject to regulation; and that if a space can be shown to be crossed by regulation, power relationships, resistance, etc., then this signifies that "really" it has no private dimension at all. "The private is the public for those for whom the personal is the political. In this sense *there is no private,* either normatively or empirically. Feminism confronts the fact that women have no privacy to lose or to guarantee."[8]

It hardly needs stating that this breathtaking MacKinnonesque generalization[9] flies in the face of a substantial corpus of arguments and evidence (from both feminist and nonfeminist sources) of a considerable diversity in the forms, purposes, and, above all, impacts on women of public-private differentiations.[10] To dichotomize "the private" and "the social" is to ignore the extent to which, especially in a liberal style of *government,* as distinct from the simplistic *ideology* with which MacKinnon identifies liberal morality, arenas, agents, or relationships are designated as private for some purposes but not others. They may also function as both effects and instruments of public regulation, ranging from state regulation, through a series of intermediate bodies, to self-regulation. There is therefore no *necessary* incompatability between construing sexual harassment as a "social" problem whilst simultaneously regarding its regulation, to a great or lesser degree, as the responsibility of some "private" body, such as the management of a corporation. The one construction does not cancel out the other. With this suggestion in mind, let us now return to MacKinnon's contention that it is difficult if not impossible in tort law to register the *social* and *employment-related* character of sexual harassment in the workplace. Is MacKinnon right in conflating these two things and counterposing them to the category "private?"

If to categorize an offense as a matter for private law is to exclude the possibility of treating them as employment-related and/or of "social" concern, then what has been described as "one of the principal features of private law in recent years" becomes hard to account for; namely:

> . . . the dramatic increase in the variety of circumstances in which courts are willing to hold that one party owes a duty of care in tort to another . . . the view that categories of relationship attracting duty of care is immutably fixed by precedent, to be extended only by legislation is now seen as quaint.[11]

As if in direct support of this contention, MacKinnon herself has drawn attention to the decision in *Monge* v. *Beebe Rubber* (1974, 316 A2d 549 NH). There, dismissal from employment based on the employee's rejection of sexual harassment was judged in breach of the "duty of care" imposed on employers in the vicarious liability provisions of the employment contract.* Again, MacKinnon's passing mention of affinities between tortious conceptions of emotional distress and the modern medical/psychological concept of work-induced stress will be recalled; together with her suggestion that sexual harassment could be seen as falling under the provisions of health-and-safety legislation or labor contracts.

Even where insistence on the private dimensions of sexual harassment is directly linked to an alleged harasser's legal defense—as in the four initially unsuccessful 1970 cases—this *need* not entail denying that the incident was sexual harassment and justiciable. In *Tomkins* v. *Public Service Electric and Gas Co.* (1976, 422 F Supp 553), the defense sought, initially successfully, to characterize plaintiff's sexual harassment as "a physical attack motivated by sexual desire," and her dismissal as due to her having refused his offer of an affair, not because she was a woman. Differentiation on that basis, it was argued, could happen to "similarly situated" individuals of either sex and therefore fell outside the "Title VII" definition of sex discrimination. Apart from this exploitation of the differences approach, it was also argued that what occurred was a sordid (inter-) *personal* confrontation: "Title VII . . . is not intended to provide a federal tort remedy for what amounts to a private incident which happened to occur in a corporate corridor rather than a back alley."[12] Consequently it was not "Title VII" discrimination.

It is important to be clear about how the appeal to plaintiff's uncontrollable urges and the private and personal character of the incident is actually functioning. According to the generalized view of "the" function of the private-public distinction, to characterize the offense as private and personal ("an unhappy and recurrent feature of our social experience,")[13] is to make its offensive character ethically and legally invisible. Whilst from the defense's standpoint that may be the typical *aim* of that excuse, in the *Tompkins* judgment it actually functioned for questioning the *area* of law—i.e., tort—to which the offense, if there was one, should be assigned. As we have seen, in tort law such an excuse would not, on past precedents, *necessarily* be an acceptable defense. In short, denying that the act was discriminatory, employment-related, and of public interest did not entail that no sexual harassment took place. Moreover, characterizing it as a private incident did *not* prevent the court from treating its repercussions as an employment-related issue. If, according to this original decision, Ms. Tomkins had no right to action, it was also held, even at

---

*"Vicarious liability" applies to employers when they are legally responsible for actions performed by supervisors, managers, or anyone other than the employers themselves. (Ed.)

that point, that, nevertheless, her employer had no right to fire her; on the contrary, he was obliged to investigate her complaint. Not to do so was to exhibit a conscious preference for a male over a female employee.[14] This "sex-based" corporate attitude evidenced by her dismissal was therefore something for which the employer was vicariously liable.[15]

This is the view of a judge who is indulgent about the "fact" that sexual attraction plays a "subtle" part in most personnel decisions.[16] Having shown that in even this "worst case," to attribute a private and moral dimension to sexual harassment does not preclude regarding it as a social and employment-related issue, it now remains to consider MacKinnon's generalized objection to the *language* of sexual torts. The basic objection is of course to the fact that the protections for women afforded by all the sex-related torts are founded on a set of patriarchal attitudes about the ideal structure of household authority and conjugal relations; attitudes which are manifested in the moral idiom of these torts: "A related defect in the vision underlying the sexual tort cases . . . is their disabling and cloying moralism. The aura of the pedestal, more rightly understood as the foundation of the cage, permeates them."[17] The effects of this ideological foundation are manifested, for example, in the tortius treatment of sexual insult. This is only compensible, claims MacKinnon, because a woman's chastity was regarded as defining of her virtue and her virtue defining of her value to her husband, to whom such invasions would amount to loss of consortium. All torts of sexual invasion "blended the enforcement of moral standards with protection for men's possessory interest."[18]

But is it not more by virtue of assertion than argument that MacKinnon assimilates all torts of sexual invasion, such as intentional infliction of emotional distress, to explicitly patriarchal family-related sexual torts? In contemporary resorts to them in legal characterizations of the injury to women entailed in sexual harassment, translations of the intent of anti-discrimination law into the language of tortious injury do not seem to carry the slightest suggestion of paternal-proprietal attitudes to women. Observe the implicit reference to notions of bodily integrity and dignity in an influential legal decision in favor of legal recognition of sexual harassment's constituting a discriminatory, hostile work environment:[19]

Surely the requirement that a man or woman run a gauntlet of sexual abuse in return for the privilege of being allowed to work . . . can be as *demeaning and disconcerting* . . . as the harshest of racial epithets. (*Henson* v. *Dundee,* 1982, 682 F2D 897, 902, emphasis added).

Bundy[20] makes substantially the same point, adding that sexual harassment "always represents an intentional assault on an individual's inner-
most privacy."

The same reasoning underpinning MacKinnon's reluctance to coun-
tenance a positive role for torts in anti-discrimination suits also motivates
the way in which she conceives the overarching purposes and above all
the *limits* of the regulation of sexual harassment. Here is MacKinnon's
response to a proposal for *non*-legal regulation:

> . . . Inventing special rules of morality for the workplace would
> institutionalize new taboos rather than confront the fact that it is women
> who are systematically disadvantaged by the old ones. Resistance to sexual
> harassment is less an issue of right and wrong than an issue of power.
> Women are in no *position* to refuse, which is what makes refusal so moral
> an act . . . the reason these acts can . . . recur . . . is not the breaking of
> a code of good conduct but the relegation of inferiority for which they
> stand. To see sexual harassment as an injury to morality is to turn it into
> an extreme case of bad manners.[21]

If this objection merely went to the idea of "special rules" concerning men's treatment of "ladies"—according to which sexual harassment
would be banned alongside, say, swearing—then this statement might be
unexceptionable. However, as MacKinnon's derogatory reference to "manners" (superficial, gentlemanly . . .) reminds us, her critique of torts of
sexual invasion extends to *any* conceptions of sexual harassment in the
tort idiom; i.e., treating it as involving a moral affront to individuals' bodily integrity. It follows from this general anathema on ethical regulations
*that management action against sexual harassment is out of the question.
If sexual harassment is to be regulated it will be by anti-discrimination
law or not at all.*

Improbable though it may seem, this inference is confirmed by the
striking absence of even so much as a reference in MacKinnon's arguments
to the strategic role of management (including trade-union initiated) policies, both preventive and punitive, in disseminating and institutionalizing
nonsexist norms of conduct in the workplace. The invitation (or goad)
to such initiatives which is built into the vicarious employer liability provisions of the 1964 Civil Rights Act goes unnoticed. MacKinnon's main
references to these provisions[22] are exclusively directed at underlining the
justice of incorporating them in the legislation and of invoking them in
civil suits.[23]

A failure to think strategically about the possibilities of "infralegal" regulation also comes through in her more recent reflections on the limitations of current sexual harassment law. One major qualification to her generally affirmative verdict has to do with women's reluctance to undertake proceedings. One reason for this reluctance, she argues,[24] is their (accurate) anticipation of the fact that "first-person" reiteration of a sexual harassment episode "in the flesh in court" is likely to cast its victim in the humiliating role of a player in a pornographic vignette. This is no doubt a genuine problem. But is this a case of masculinist rituals of adjudication failing to do justice to, indeed exacerbating, women's experience of injury? Or are these problems an unintended consequence of an adversary system of legal process which, among other things, normally requires that all the relevant facts of a case be publicly read into the record? If the pornographic effect of testimony is the result of its public, ceremonial character then that might be one reason to look to alternative judicial or semi-judicial processes. For instance, in the public tribunal hearings at which sexual harassment complaints may be heard under Australian sex discrimination law, where the plaintiff is likely to be seriously embarrassed by verbally rehearsing the details of the harassment, the proceedings at that point may be conducted in camera. The conciliation phase which proceeds (and typically precludes the need for) the tribunal is of course also confidential.[25]

The point of adverting to this "Australian way" of addressing the problem of personal testimony is not to offer a specific alternative (from a very different legal culture, moreover) but simply to draw attention to MacKinnon's silence concerning any alternative form of dispute resolution.[26] What seems to be lacking is any sense that limits to the law's potential might reflect anything other than the entrenchment of structurally reinforced male interests. There are surely quite legitimate reasons to doubt whether law can or should be (re-)made to bear the radical weight of responsibility which in her vision of equality she wishes to place upon it: namely that of serving as the fulcrum of radical social and personal transformation.

This vision of radical social transformation, it could be argued, leads her to place an exaggerated trust in the commanding status of law and concomitantly, in the consciousness-raising impact of legal publicity. It is as if, once the law can be remade so as to embody a feminist structural understanding of what gives rise to sexual harassment; to approximate women's experience of the injury it imposes; and to foreshadow a radical alternative set of relations between the sexes, its traditional majesty could then be invoked in order to provide an Archimedian point of transformation. No wonder MacKinnon has no time for privately conducted alternative dispute resolution procedures. Well-publicized legal cases have an undoubted impact. However, it is unlikely that any impact they might have can be sustained if the significance of sexual harassment law is conceived solely in terms of the exercise of a legal *sovereignty* over sexist conduct. In a liberal political milieu such as the U.S.A., anti-sex-discrimination law is *neither* capable of dramatically changing society either by commanding obedience or by changing hearts *nor* limited to the provision of just remedies to individuals and to symbolizing the general social unacceptablity of sexual harassment. The Civil Rights Act under which it is unlawful is not only an instrument of justice but also an anti-discriminatory social policy and form of governance. The preventative-policing function served by the vicarious liability provisions of the legislation, for example (as an incentive to corporations to initiate their own sexual harassment policies, including complaints procedures) cannot be understood solely in terms of the symbolic, exemplary, and commanding powers of law. Here the effective working of the social policy objectives of the law itself is contingent upon the establishment of infralegal regulatory apparatuses located, not inside the state, but rather in "civil society." They may receive a charter from the law and serve as a means of relaying it but they are not its direct instruments. In this way all sorts of sexual harassment might be addressed which might well slip through the net where full civil litigation is the only avenue of complaints.

In addition to a code of conduct accompanied by a complaints procedure and a range of sanctions and preventative measures, a management policy on sexual harassment may also offer encouragement, training, and advice aimed at encouraging employees in some circumstances to confront it personally and informally. With or without that assistance, where women employees, individually or as a body, take matters into their own hands, this too may be seen as part of the subjection of sexual harassment to a kind of policing or government. This is so even on occasions when direct action may conflict with procedural avenues.

MacKinnon's assumption that in targeting inequitable and gross manners, attempts to modify the ethos of the workplace would *necessarily* have no effects on the balance of power (vis à vis those relations between the sexes which encourage the practice of sexual harassment) is certainly not based upon anything like an examination of the range of measures involved in such attempts.[27] Naturally, putting in place this array of supplementary, infralegal means of regulating sexual harassment is not bound to be effective, but does the mere fact of their affinities to the language of torts or their failure to tackle structural causes guarantee that such measures will be to no avail?

CONCLUSIONS

If one were to formalize the difference between MacKinnon's conception of the progressive potential of law and that hinted at in these paragraphs, one might say that she tends to view law as a *ceremonial and coercive expression of state sovereignty* rather than as one regulatory vehicle among others of a *strategy of liberal social government.* From the latter perspective, the political virtue of Anti-Discrimination (and supporting Affirmative Action) legislation resides in their providing the *legal environment,* including legislation, supportive case law, and sanctions, within which a variegated network of *both* legal measures *and* in some ways less formal "infralegal" initiatives could be instituted and supported. These may be located in enterprises, government departments, educational institutions, and possibly, within limits, other feasible sites, too. These "government" milieus crosscut the divisions between state and society, private and public. Even within the realm of litigation, anti-discrimination legislation need not be seen as a law unto itself. Legal argument on the substance of the offense particularly with respect to its compensible aspects may be nourished rather than stultified by reference to the law of torts. . . .

NOTES

1. C. MacKinnon, *Sexual Harassment of Working Women* (New Haven, Conn.: Yale University Press, 1979), p. 172.
2. C. MacKinnon, "Sexual Harassment: Its First Decade in Court," in C. MacKinnon, *Feminism Unmodified: Discourses on Life and the Law* (Cambridge, Mass.: Harvard University Press, 1987), pp. 104, 105, 116.
3. Ibid. pp. 104–105.
4. J. Attansio, "Equal Justice under Chaos: The Developing Law of Sexual Harassment," *University of Cincinnati Law Review* 1, no. 1 (1982): 51.
5. MacKinnon, *Sexual Harassment of Working Women,* pp. 164, 170–71.
6. Ibid., p. 167.
7. Ibid., p. 171.
8. MacKinnon, "Sexual Harassment: Its First Decade in Court," p. 100, emphasis added.
9. On MacKinnon's sweeping generalizations see B. Brown, "Consciousness Razing" (review of C. MacKinnon), *The Nation,* January 8, 1990, pp. 61–64, and K. Bartlett, "MacKinnon's Feminism: Power on Whose Terms?" *California Law Review* 75 (1987): 1559–70.
10. B. Brown, "Private Faces in Public Places," *I and C* 7 (1980): 3–16, and N. Rose, "Beyond the Public/Private Division: Law, Power, and the Fam-

ily," in P. Fitzpatrick and A. Hunt, eds., *Critical Legal Studies* (Oxford: Basil Blackwell, 1987).

11. J. Logie, "Affirmative Action in the Law of Tort: The Case of the Duty to Warn," *Cambridge Law Review* 48, no. 1 (1989): 115.

12. *Tompkins,* p. 556.

13. Ibid.

14. Ibid., p. 554.

15. Ibid.

16. Ibid., p. 557.

17. MacKinnon, *Sexual Harassment of Working Women,* p. 172.

18. Ibid., p. 169.

19. In the essay "The Justiciability of Sexual Harassment," in J. P. Minson, *Entertaining Ethics: Essays on the Government of Conduct in Liberal Democracies* (London: Macmillan, 1992), a series of Australian cases which illustrate similarly innocuous, or rather positive, mutually supportive crossovers between sex discrimination legislation and torts of sexual invasions are discussed; once again, primarily with respect to the question of compensable damages rather than the legal decision concerning the unlawfulness of the conduct as such.

20. In Bureau of National Affairs, *Sexual Harassment and Labor Relations* (Washington, D.C.: BNA Books, 1981), p. 59.

21. MacKinnon, *Sexual Harassment of Working Women,* p. 173.

22. Ibid., pp. 93–94, 211–13, 237–38.

23. At one point, MacKinnon alludes to the possibility of a management capacity to prevent harassment, but this is once again only in the context of a desire to see the law inscribe women's experience, this time in the form of a desire to see the employer who "winks" at sexual harassment carried out by subordinates "pay" for their collusion (MacKinnon, *Sexual Harassment of Working Women,* p. 57). In this perspective the existence of a company policy appears as an alibi to enable the employer to avoid liability (ibid., p. 62).

24. MacKinnon, "Sexual Harassment: Its First Decade in Court," pp. 111–15.

25. For a dependable account of the way Australian sex-discrimination legislation is implemented in regard to sexual harassment and more generally, see C. Ronalds, *Affirmative Action and Sex-Discrimination Law: A Handbook on Legal Rights for Women* (Sydney: Pluto Press, 1987).

26. Irrespective of the technical portability of such methods into other jurisdictions, one would predict that MacKinnon would strenuously object (1) to their *confidential* character (which privatizes the offense and prevents an appropriate legal signal being sent to the wider community; and (2) to the element of *negotiation* in conciliation which would be seen as compromising harassed women's chances of securing full justice for what they have undergone. For further discussion, see "The Justiciability of Sexual Harassment," in Minson, *Entertaining Ethics.*

27. For a discussion of the possibilities of management policies on sexual harassment, see "Bureaucratic Culture and the Management of Sexual Harassment," in Minson, *Entertaining Ethics.*

12

Sexual Harassment in the Workplace: A View Through the Eyes of the Courts

William L. Woerner and Sharon L. Oswald

Sexual harassment, like pornography, is a phenomenon that is virtually impossible to define or describe, but something on which almost everyone has an opinion. Generally, sexual harassment means "unwanted sexually oriented behavior by someone in the workplace."[1] It is further defined as a form of discrimination and, as such, is covered under Title VII of the Civil Rights Act of 1964. There is little doubt that unwanted physical contact, sexual assaults, threats or promises of advancement tied to sexual favors are obvious acts of sexual harassment in the workplace. It is the less insidious forms that pose a problem (i.e., a pat, verbal abuse, a wink, or a request for a date by a supervisor). The purpose of this [essay] is to examine the evolution of sexual harassment in the courts and clarify its meaning in today's environment.

THE EVOLUTION THROUGH LOWER COURTS

Section 703(a) of Title VII of the Civil Rights Act of 1964 states that:

Reprinted from the November 1990 issue of the *Labor Law Journal,* published and copyrighted 1990 by Commerce Clearing House, Inc., 4025 W. Peterson Avenue, Chicago, Illinois 60646. All Rights Reserved.

It shall be an unlawful employment practice for an employer to fail or refuse to hire or to discharge any individual or otherwise to discriminate against any individual with respect to his compensation, terms, conditions, or privileges of employment, because of such individual's race, color, religion, sex, or national origin.

As Greenbaum and Fraser[2] pointed out, sex discrimination was not included in the original draft of the legislation, but it was a last minute addition aimed at preventing passage of the Act. Thus, the true intent of Congress on the issue of sexual harassment is unknown. In regard to Title VII, Senator Case stated that "it would make it unlawful for a person to discriminate against an individual in regard to employment—hiring, firing, promotion, or *any other matter* (emphasis added)."[3] It is from this wide-open interpretation and "terms and conditions of employment" that courts have included sexual harassment under the Act.

The first case of sexual harassment, *Barnes* v. *Train,*[4] was not litigated until almost ten years after passage of the Civil Rights Act. The plaintiff claimed that she was discharged for refusing to have "an after-hours affair" with her supervisor. The District Court of the District of Columbia found that this was not the type of discrimination purposed by the Act and found no basis for the suit. The court further found that it was "an inharmonious personal relationship" and the discrimination she suffered was not as a result of her gender but rather the business relationship.

The following year in *Corne* v. *Bausch and Lomb, Inc.,*[5] two female employees claimed constructive discharges [i.e., involuntary resignations] as a result of physical and verbal sexual advances by their supervisor. The Arizona Federal District Court said in part that ". . . it would be ludicrous to hold that the sort of activity involved here was contemplated by the Act, because to do so would mean that if the conduct claimed of was directed equally to males there would be no basis for suit . . . an outgrowth of holding such activity actionable under Title VII would be a potential federal lawsuit every time any employee made amorous or sexually oriented advances toward another. The only sure way an employer could avoid such charges would be to have employees who were asexual."[6] Therefore, the court interpreted Title VII to apply to advances or other acts of discrimination made only by upper-level management.

In the 1976 case of *Tomkins* v. *Public Service Electric and Gas Co.,*[7] a federal court strengthened the argument held by the Arizona court. In this case, a secretary alleged she had been propositioned by a supervisor while they were having lunch to discuss her evaluation. The supervisor indicated that her acceptance of his proposal would be required to assure a satisfactory evaluation. Her refusal led to a transfer to a lesser position in a different department, inferior evaluations, and ultimately disciplinary discharge. The court stated that: "An invitation to dinner could become an invitation to a federal lawsuit if a once harmonious relationship turned sour at some later time. And if an inebriated approach by a supervisor at the office Christmas party could form the basis of a federal lawsuit for sex discrimination if a promotion or raise is later denied to the subordinate, we would need 4,000 federal trial judges instead of 400."[8]

During that same year, the often cited survey by *Redbook* magazine was conducted. In a survey of its readership, to which 9,000 responded, 90 percent of the women said they had experienced some form of sexual harassment.[9]

Later that year marked the turning point in the courts' attitudes. In *Williams* v. *Saxbe*,[10] the District of Columbia Federal Court held that sexual harassment was actionable under Title VII and that retaliatory actions on the part of a male supervisor toward a female employee for refusing sexual advances constituted sex discrimination. On appeal, the courts for the first time held the employer responsible for the acts of its supervisory personnel.

The year 1977 brought the previous year's decision full circle. In *Barnes* v. *Costle*,[11] the court held that the plaintiff could establish a prima facie case by showing that sexual favors requested by the supervisor were "an indispensable factor in the job-retention condition."[12] However, the court did leave management with a way to rectify the situation when it said: "But should the supervisor contravene employer's policy without employer's knowledge, and consequences are rectified when discovered, employer may be relieved from responsibility under Title VII."[13]

That same year, *Tomkins* was overturned and the court established two necessary elements for a prima facie case: (1) sexual advances were imposed as a condition of employment and (2) these sexual advances were imposed by the employer in a sexually discriminatory manner. This was the first case to set standards for employer liability.

TITLE VII AND THE EEOC

Making sexual harassment cases actionable under Title VII made it possible for the Equal Employment Opportunity Commission (EEOC) to pursue a case on behalf of the plaintiff, protect plaintiffs from retaliatory action, and reduce the time required to bring action (since it is not intiated in the courts).

The 1980 EEOC guidelines defined sexual harassment with the following statement. "Harassment on the basis of sex is a violation of Section 703 of Title VII. Unwelcome sexual advances, requests for sexual favors, and other verbal or physical conduct of a sexual nature constitute sexual harassment when: (1) submission to such conduct is made either explicitly or implicitly a term or condition of an individual's employment; (2) submission to or rejections of such conduct by an individual is used as the basis for employment decisions affecting such individual; or (3) such conduct has the purpose or effect of unreasonably interfering with an individual's work performance or creating an intimidating, hostile, or offensive environment."[14]

Until 1981, sexual harassment suits had been restricted to tangible losses, and the term "sexual harassment" had seldom been used. The cases were action specific or merely termed as violations of Title VII.[15] In the 1981 landmark case of *Bundy* v. *Jackson*,[16] the plaintiff argued that subjecting female employees to sexual harassment was a violation of Title VII even if no tangible loss was incurred. The case marked the first time a court had recognized that sexual harassment was actionable for a reason other than one of job harm. The U.S. Appeals Court for the District of Columbia held that:

Unless the *Barnes* holding is extended, an employer could sexually harass a female employee with impunity by carefully stopping short of firing the employee or by not taking any other tangible actions against her in response to her resistance. [T]he employer could thus implicitly and effectively make the employee's endurance of sexual intimidation a *condition* of her employment (emphasis added).[17]

The *Bundy* case brought to the attention of the courts a correlation between sexual harassment and "hostile working environments." It had become apparent by then that the attitude of the courts had changed dramatically. The general public, likewise, became more enlightened on the subject of sexual harassment later that year. In a survey of 23,000 civilian government employees conducted by the United States Protection Board Office, 42 percent of the females and 15 percent of the males stated that they had suffered some form of sexual harassment between the years 1978 to 1980.[18]

The EEOC placed further burden on the employer in its 1984 amendment to the sexual harassment guidelines. The amendment states that an employer is responsible for the acts and those of its agents and supervisory employees with respect to sexual harassment regardless of whether the specific acts complained of were authorized or even forbidden by the employer and regardless of whether the employer knew or should have known of the occurrence.[19]

With this amendment, culpability was placed squarely at the feet of the employer, far different from the previous stand of the courts. Until that time, the courts had been using a two-step criteri[on]. First, did the employer have knowledge of the situation, and second, did the employer then fail to investigate and/or remedy the situation. The courts made the assumption that an employer could not remedy a situation of which he had no knowledge. It appears obvious that the courts' guidelines allowed considerably more latitude . . . than those of the EEOC.[20]

THE SUPREME COURT'S LANDMARK DECISION

[The year] 1986 marked the first and only time to date that a sexual harassment case reached the U.S. Supreme Court. *Meritor Savings Bank v. Vinson*[21] not only addressed the issue of employer liability, but the case also gave a clearer definition to hostile environment. What made this case noteworthy to the high court is somewhat of a mystery.

Vinson, an employee of the Northeast Branch of Capital City Federal Savings, alleged that she had acceded to the sexual demands of her supervisor between the years 1975 to 1978 for fear of losing her job. During this period, she advanced from trainee to assistant branch manager. Promotions that she stated were based on merit. She admitted that she was not required to grant sexual favors as a basis for promotion, and despite a bank policy and grievance procedure for dealing with harassment cases, she never notified Capital Savings of her supervisor's behavior. In September 1978, Vinson took indefinite sick leave and was discharged two months later for excessive absences. She sued on the grounds of a constructive discharge [i.e., involuntary resignation] and cited sexual harassment as the reason for her departure. The district court ruled in favor of the bank stating that Vinson was a voluntary participant and, therefore, not the subject of sexual harassment.

On appeal the U.S. Court for the District of Columbia reversed the district court's ruling, finding Capital Savings liable based on the EEOC's guidelines. The court found that the employer and his agent are inseparable, an interpretation that negates any defense on the part of the employer. The court further held that a woman employee need not prove resistance to sexual overtures in order to establish a Title VII claim of sexual harassment.

In June 1986, the U.S. Supreme Court issued its opinion on *Meritor* in a landmark decision that established the principle of employer liability for sexual harassment, while simultaneously limiting the extent of that liability. The Court specifically stated that the issue was not whether the sex-related conduct was voluntary but whether it was "welcomed." The Court additionally held that for sexual harassment to be actionable, it must be ". . . sufficiently severe or pervasive so as to become an abusive working environment; unwelcome in the sense that the plaintiff did not desire that the sex-related conduct take place."[22]

On the issue of employer liability, the Court agreed with the appellate court stating that the employer would be held liable only if it knew or should have known of the alleged harassment. It further held:

> [Does] the mere existence of a grievance procedure and a policy against discrimination, coupled with [the victim's] failure to invoke that procedure . . . insulate [the employer] from liability. . . ? Those facts are plainly relevant. . . . The contention that [the victim's] failure should insulate [the employer] might be substantially stronger if [the employer's] procedure was . . . calculated to encourage victims of harassment to come forward.[23]

The high court thus indicated that the existence of an effective grievance procedure might insulate an employer from liability where a victim fails to use the procedure. . . . As Robinson et al.[24] pointed out, Section 1604.1(d) of the Code of Federal Regulations states that "employers are responsible for all acts of sexual harassment in the workplace unless it can be shown that the employer took immediate and appropriate action." This is interpreted to mean that an employer's defense would hinge on his actions not his intentions.

The importance of a grievance plan was also supported in *Spencer v. General Electric Co.,*[25] when a federal district judge observed that General Electric responded appropriately to the employee's charges of sexual harassment by getting rid of the offending supervisor, transferring the employee to a job of equal grade, and instituting a company-wide policy on sexual harassment.

WHAT IS A HOSTILE ENVIRONMENT?

The Supreme Court clearly established that hostile environment is action-able under Title VII, but it did not define the situation. Thus, the question arises: What is a hostile environment? Burnstein and Vandenberg[26] cite a number of cases subsequent to *Vinson* in which district courts differ greatly on their interpretation. The most interesting of these, *Rabidue* v. *Osceola Refining Company,*[27] and *Yates* v. Avco Corp.,[28] were decided by the 6th Circuit in 1986 and 1987 respectively.

In *Rabidue,* the court held that the plaintiff was not the subject of a hostile environment. The plaintiff alleged that she had been the object of "regularly spewed anti-female obscenities" from a co-worker who sub-jected other females to the same abuse. The court held when it quoted from a lower court ruling that ". . . indeed, it cannot seriously be disputed that in some work environments, humor and language are rough hewn and vulgar. Sexual jokes, sexual conversations, and girlie magazines may abound. Title VII was not meant to, nor can, change this."[29]

The court went on to say that the trier of facts must look at each case individually and "must adopt the perspective of a reasonable per-son's reaction to a similar environment under essentially like or similar circumstances."[30] The question of what reasonable person's perspective the court should use, however, was left unanswered. What is reasonable to one person may be totally offensive to another.

Just one year later, in *Yates* v. *Avco Corp.,*[31] the 6th Circuit adopted a position on that issue when the court made the following statement:

> . . . [I]n a sexual harassment case involving a male supervisor's harassment of a female subordinate, it seems only reasonable that the person standing in the shoes of the employee should be the reasonable woman since the plaintiff in this type of case is required to be a member of a protected class and is by definition female.[32]

The Second Circuit awarded back pay to an employee in *Carrero* v. *New York City Housing Authority*[33] who was demoted after going pub-lic with charges of sexual harassment on the part of her supervisor. The court rejected the defendant's argument that the supervisor's "trivial, sporadic, and innocuous behavior" of "two kisses and three arm strokes" did not rise to the level of conduct necessary to establish a hostile en-vironment. They further stated that female employees should not have to be subjected to extended periods of demeaning and degrading provo-cation before they could receive retribution under Title VII. However, what was considered to be extensive was purely speculative because no guidelines were provided.

In a 1988 case, *Bennett* v. *Corroon & Black Corp.,*[34] the 5th Circuit took up the issue of graffiti (cartoons that depicted both men and women in sexually demeaning postures) as a hostile environment. The lower court held that "while sexually oriented and offensive, they were not based on the sex of the plaintiff."[35] This was ultimately reversed on the basis that "any reasonable person would have to regard these cartoons as highly offensive to a woman who seeks to deal with her fellow employees and clients with professional dignity and without the barrier of sexual differentiation and abuse."[36]

Graffiti was also the issue in *Waltman* v. *International Paper Co.,*[37] where the 5th Circuit said that the presence of sexual graffiti in the plant constituted the existence of a hostile environment. The dissent opinion (2–1 vote) of Justice Jones is noteworthy. He stated that:

> Using evidence of generalized sexual graffiti to bolster an otherwise non-actionable complaint against an employer highlights the subjectivity of the majority's ruling. Sexual mores in our society are in rapid flux. Depictions that were only recently regarded as taboo in movies and television are now *de rigeur* for programs that even children will watch. The public use of lewd and suggestive language is as commonplace on the playgrounds as in the workplace. Against such trends, it is quaint but also naive to rule that employers are legally required to eradicate all sexual graffiti from the establishments. The EEOC guidelines and policy statement never go so far.[38]

Obviously, Justice Jones's interpretation of the "reasonable person" doctrine provides considerably more latitude to the employer.

Regarding the issue of prompt remedial action on the part of the employer, the appellate court in *Bennett* held that the employer failed to take prompt and adequate action because he waited one day to remove offensive cartoons from the men's bathroom. More recently, in *Steele* v. *Offshore Shipbuilding, Inc.,*[39] the court found that despite the fact that a corporate officer's sexual joking and innuendos created a hostile environment for two women employees, the company was not liable because it had taken prompt remedial action in the form of an immediate reprimand. Again, without specific guidelines as to what is considered prompt, the employer may or may not be considered liable.

The 1989 case of *Nelson* v. *Reisher*[40] is noteworthy because it is among the few hostile environment cases, or for that matter sexual harassment cases, involving a male. The plaintiff alleged that unlike his female co-workers, he had been harassed with numerous criticisms and written reprimands from his female supervisor for a period of three years. The court agreed with his charges and awarded him $1,500.

RESPONDEAT SUPERIOR AND SEXUAL HARASSMENT

Another question concerns whether or not the employer is liable if the unwelcome advances are made by an individual who does not have supervisory responsibility over the victim. According to the doctrine of *respondeat superior,* the "master" is liable for the wrongful acts of his servant. This would suggest that the employer would be liable for any "harassing" acts made by any employee. However, the Fourth Circuit Court of Appeals did not see it that way in *Swentek* v. *USAir*.[41] In this highly publicized case, a flight attendant sued USAir alleging she was the victim of sexual harassment by a company pilot. Witnesses described the flight attendant as a vindictive person who was foul-mouthed and often talked about sex. The court stated that: "Plaintiff's use of foul language or sexual innuendo in a consensual setting does not waive her protections against unwelcome harassment."[42]

However, the court further said that USAir was not liable because the pilot was not the attendant's supervisor. The flight attendant was awarded compensatory and punitive damages only on the claims of emotional distress. With the interpretation of respondeat superior, such that it is applicable only in the case of supervisory personnel, relieves some vulnerability from the employer. Given different circumstances, however, specifically, a less colorful plaintiff, it is questionable whether the ruling would have been the same.

CONCLUSION

An assessment of the current environment brings mixed reviews. Terpstra and Baker[43] found an increase of about 3,000 sexual harassment cases reported to the EEOC from 1981 to 1985. They further suggest that this figure could conceivably be much larger since other avenues of retribution are available, such as tort law and collective bargaining agreements. Morgenson[44] found that the trend differed during the period 1984 to 1988 from that reported by Terpstra and Baker, indicating a decrease of about 1,500 cases.

Morgenson further stated that during the study period, only 15 cases were litigated through to a verdict in the state of California. This seems interesting considering California's reputation for being "litigation crazy" and its 5.8 million women in the work force. The decline in sexual harassment cases was further supported by the fact that according to state human rights commission reports, California was the only state that showed an increase in activity. Considering only 15 cases in four years, initial evidence supports Morgenson's contentions. The author further stated that employers are led to believe that harassment cases are on the upswing by anti-harassment consultants who have made an industry out of sexual harassment prevention. If a decrease in cases is indeed a trend in the United States, it is doubtfully due to any actions on the part of the courts.

The lack of consistency in court decisions on how to handle the issue of sexual harassment seems appropriate, given the fact that there is at least as much discrepancy on what constitutes sexual harassment. Unfortunately, the years since *Barnes* v. *Train*[45] have only served to add new terms and provide new angles, without defining the term itself. The decisions seem to overturn so regularly that the entire issue seems to be in a state of chaos. . . .

NOTES

1. F. S. Coles, "Forced to Quit: Sexual Harassment Complaints and Agency Response," *Sex Roles* 14 (1986): 81–95.

2. M. L. Greenbaum and B. Fraser, "Sexual Harassment in the Workplace," *The Arbitration Journal* 36 (1981): 30–41.

3. 110 Cong. Rec. S7253 (1964).

4. 13 FEP 123 (DC D of C 1974).

5. 390 FSupp 163, 9 EPD Par. 10,093.

6. Ibid., p. 163.

7. 422 FSupp 553 (DC NJ 1976) 12 EPD Par. 11,267; rev'd and rem'd (CA-3 1977) 15 EPD Par. 7954.

8. Ibid., p. 5–6.

9. C. Safran, "Sexual Harassment: The View From the Top," *Redbook,* pp. 46–51.

10. 11 EPD Par. 39,106 (DC D of C 1976).

11. 561 F2d 983, 14 EPD Par. 7755 (CA-DC 1977).

12. Ibid., p. 990.

13. Ibid., p. 993.

14. W. B. Nelson, "Sexual Harassment, Title VII, and Labor Arbitration," *The Arbitration Journal* 40 (1985): 55–65.

15. J. B. Attanasio, "Equal Justice under Chaos: The Developing Law of Sexual Harassment," *Cincinnati Law Review* 51 (1982): 1–41.

16. 641 F2d 934, 24 EPD Par. 31,439 (CA-DC 1981).

17. Ibid., p. 945.

18. Attanasio, "Equal Justice under Chaos," pp. 1–41.

19. 29 CFR 1604.11(e).

20. R. K. Robinson, K. Delany, and E. C. Stevens, "Hostile Environment: A Review of the Implications of *Meritor Savings Bank* v. *Vinson,*" *Labor Law Journal* 38 (March 1987): 179.

21. 106 SCt 2399, 40 EPD Par. 36,159 (US 1986).

22. J. S. Monat and A. Gomez, "Sexual Harassment: The Impact of *Meritor Savings Bank* v. *Vinson* on Grievances and Arbitration Decisions," *The Arbitration Journal* 41 (1986): 24–29.

23. Ibid., p. 25.

24. Robinson et al., "Hostile Environment: A Review of the Implications of *Meritor Savings Bank* v. *Vinson,*" p. 182.

25. 894 F2d 651 (CA-41990) 52 EPD Par. 39,583.

26. J. A. Burnstein and W. R. Vandenberg, "Sexual Harassment: Did *Vinson* Make a Difference?" *Employee Labor Relations Journal* 4 (1987): 185–94.

27. 805 F2d 611, 41 EPD Par. 36,643 (CA-6 1986).

28. 819 F2d 630, 43 EPD Par. 37,086 (CA-6 1987).

29. 805 F2d 611, 41 EPD Par. 36,643 (CA-6 1986), p. 620.

30. Ibid.

31. 819 F2d 630, 43 EPD Par. 37,086 (CA-6 1987), p. 637.

32. Ibid.

33. (CA-2 1989), 88-7516, 52 EPD Par. 39,488.

34. 845 F2d 105, 106 (CA-5 1988).

35. Ibid., p. 106.

36. Ibid.

37. 875 F2d 468 (CA-5 1989), 50 EPD Par. 39,106.

38. "Decision of the Fifth Circuit in *Waltman* v. *International Paper Co.,*" *Daily Labor Report* 122 (1989): D1–D10.

39. 867 F2d 1311, 49 EPD Par. 38,839 (CA-11 1989).

40. (CA-4 1989), 88-1133.

41. (CA-4 1987) 44 EPD Par. 37,457.

42. Ibid., p. 1812.

43. D. E. Terpstra and D. D. Baker, "Outcomes of Sexual Harassment Charges," *Academy of Management Journal* 31 (1988): 31,185–94.

44. G. Morgenson, "Watch that Leer, Stifle that Joke," *Forbes* 5 (1989): 69–72.

45. FEP 123 (DC D of C 1974).

13

Vinson v. *Taylor*

(Appellate Court Decision, 1985)

·   ·   ·

Spottswood W. Robinson, III, Chief Judge:

This appeal presents principally the question whether a corporate employer is accountable under Title VII of the Civil Rights Act of 1964, as amended by the Equal Employment Opportunity Act of 1972, for its supervisor's sexual harassment of a woman employee notwithstanding the employer's lack of actual knowledge thereof. The District Court answered in the negative.[1] We conclude that this holding is inconsistent with the intent of Title VII, and accordingly reverse.

I

We launch our review with a summary of the pertinent facts, as they were accepted by the District Court. In 1974, appellant Mechele Vinson met appellee Sidney L. Taylor, who was a vice president of appellee Capital City Federal Savings and Loan Association and the manager of its northeast branch. At Vinson's request, Taylor gave her an application for employment which she completed and returned, and promptly thereafter

---

Federal Reporter 753, 2d Series. Mechele VINSON, Appellant v. Sidney L. TAYLOR, et al. United States Court of Appeals, District of Columbia Circuit. Argued February 16, 1982. Decided January 25, 1985. Rehearing En Banc Denied May 14, 1985. "En banc" refers to the full court (Ed.).

she was hired by Capital City. With Taylor as her supervisor, Vinson began her employment as a teller-trainee, and thereafter was promoted successively to teller, head teller, and finally to assistant branch manager. It is undisputed, and the District Court expressly found, that Vinson's advancement was achieved on merit alone. Vinson worked at the northeast branch for four years, when she took indefinite sick leave, and was discharged two months later for excessive use of that leave.

[1] Vinson brought an action under Title VII against Taylor and Capital City, alleging that she had been victimized by sex discrimination in the form of sexual harassment by Taylor. At trial, the evidence bearing on Taylor's behavior during Vinson's employment was conflicting. Vinson testified that Taylor asked her to have sexual relations with him, claiming that she "owed him" because he had obtained the job for her; that after initially declining his invitation she ultimately yielded, but only because she was afraid that continued refusal would jeopardize her employment. She further testified that thereafter she was forced to submit to sexual advances by Taylor at the northeast branch both during and after business hours, and that often Taylor assaulted or raped her. In addition, she avowed, Taylor caressed her on the job, followed her into the ladies' room when she was there alone, and at times exposed himself to her. . . .

[2] Taylor denied Vinson's accusations of sexual activity and contended that Vinson aired them in retaliation for a business-related dispute. Capital City also controverted Vinson's story, and asserted that any sexual harassment by Taylor was unknown to and unauthorized by it. The District Court rendered judgment for Taylor and Capital City on the grounds that Vinson had not been subjected to sexual harassment or discrimination, and that in any event Capital City would not be accountable. Our interpretation of Title VII leads us to disagree.

II

We first address the District Court's holding that Vinson did make out a case of sex discrimination, even against Taylor. Given due deference to the court's findings of fact, we believe that in critical respects they fatally undermine the legal conclusion that Vinson did not suffer a violation of Title VII.

[3] The District Court found that Vinson "was not required to grant Taylor or any other member of Capital sexual favors as a condition of

either her employment or in order to obtain promotion." That finding would have significance had Vinson been confined to a theory of discrimination based on an imposition of sex-oriented conditions of her employment status. An infringement of Title VII is not, however, necessarily dependent upon the victim's loss of employment or promotion.[2]

Depending upon the particular facts, at least two separate avenues may be open to a Title VII plaintiff for a demonstration of unlawful sex discrimination. The first was recognized in *Barnes* v. *Costle,*[3] where we held that abolition of the job of a female employee because she spurned her male superior's sexual advances was an infringement of Title VII.[4] The second approach is illustrated by *Bundy* v. *Jackson,*[5] decided after the District Court's judgment herein, where we sustained a Title VII cause of action in favor of a woman employee seeking relief simply for pervasive on-the-job sexual harassment by her superiors.[6]

[4, 5] Vinson's grievance was clearly of the latter type and, accordingly, her cause counseled an inquiry as to whether Taylor "created or condoned a substantially discriminatory work *environment,* regardless of whether the complaining employees lost any tangible job benefits as a result of the discrimination."[7] The District Court did not undertake a determination on whether a Title VII violation of this nature had occurred. It follows that we must remand [i.e., order the case back to the District Court] in order that the court may ascertain whether, as in *Bundy,* Vinson was subjected to "sexually stereotyped insults" or "demeaning propositions" that illegally poisoned the "psychological and emotional work environment."

> The District Court further found that [i]f [Vinson] and Taylor did engage in an intimate or sexual relationship during the time of [Vinson's] employment with Capital, that relationship was a voluntary one by [Vinson] having nothing to do with her continued employment at Capital or her advancement or promotions at that institution.

This finding leaves us uncertain as to precisely what the court meant. It could reflect the view that there was no Title VII violation because Vinson's employment status was not affected, an error to which we already have spoken. Alternatively, the finding could indicate that because the relationship was voluntary there was no sexual harassment—no "[u]nwelcome sexual advances, requests for sexual favors, or other verbal or physical conduct of a sexual nature . . . ha[ving] the purpose or effect of unreasonably interfering with an individual's work performance or creating an intimidating, hostile, or offensive working environment." If, however, the evidence warranted a finding of sexual harassment by that standard, Vinson's "voluntar[iness]" had no materiality whatsoever.[8]

[6] *Bundy* held that a woman employee need not prove resistance to sexual overtures in order to establish a Title VII claim of sexual harassment. From that point we take what is hardly a major step by recognizing that a victim's capitulation to on-the-job sexual advances cannot work a forfeiture of her opportunity for redress. If capitulation were dispositive, the "cruel trilemma" identified in *Bundy*—in which a victim must choose among acquiescence in the harassment, opposition to it, or resignation from her job—would be an even more hideous quadrilemma featuring a fourth option—to yield and thereby lose all hope of legal redress for being put in this intolerable position in the first place. We cannot ascribe to Congress a willingness to visit such an unenviable quandary upon an employee. A victim's "voluntary" submission to unlawful discrimination of this sort can have no bearing on the pertinent inquiry: whether Taylor made Vinson's toleration of sexual harassment a condition of her employment.

[7] Another matter, an evidentiary ruling, prompts brief discussion. The District Court refused to allow Vinson to elicit, from other women under Taylor's supervision during her tenure, testimony that assertedly would have established that Taylor sexually harassed them also. Some testimony of this kind was admitted on the issue of notice to Capital City of Taylor's behavior, but Vinson was not permitted to use it in her case-in-chief for other purposes. *Bundy* makes clear that evidence tending to show Taylor's harassment of other women working alongside Vinson is directly relevant to the question whether he created an environment violative of Title VII.[9] Even a woman who was never herself the object of harassment might have a Title VII claim if she were forced to work in an atmosphere in which such harassment was pervasive.[10] The District Court erred when it denied Vinson the opportunity to demonstrate that Taylor had directed his advances toward other women also.

III

The District Court also ruled that Vinson's employer, Capital City, could not be held responsible for any infringements of Title VII by Taylor because it had no notice of the offensive conduct charged to him. To the court, "it seem[ed] reasonable that an employer should not be liable in these unusual cases of sexual harassment where notice to the employer must depend upon the actual perpetrator and when there is nothing else to place the employer on notice."[11] We cannot accept this conclusion or its rationale.

So much as this court has heretofore decided runs counter to the District Court's holding. Nothing before us in *Barnes* suggested that the employer, a federal agency, was aware of the activity of the superior involved, yet we adverted to the general rule that "an employer is chargeable with Title VII violations occasioned by discriminatory practices of supervisory personnel,"[12] and rejected the notion that the superior's conduct insulated the employer merely "because it was a general escapade rather than an agency project." And in *Bundy,* we reaffirmed our continuing allegiance to the proposition that an employer is answerable for discriminatory acts committed by supervisory personnel, though we were not required there to apply that principle to employers without notice, since those having control over personnel practices had full knowledge of the harassment and did virtually nothing to stop it.

Today, however, we are confronted by the question that was not directly and actively litigated in *Barnes* or *Bundy:* Whether Title VII imposes upon an employer without specific notice of sexual harassment by supervisory personnel responsibility for that species of discrimination. We hold that it does.

With exceptions not relevant here, Title VII provides in pertinent part that

[it] shall be an unlawful employment practice for an employer . . . to discriminate against any individual with respect to . . . terms, conditions, or privileges of employment, because of such individual's . . . sex. . . .

"Employer" is defined as "a person engaged in an industry affecting commerce" with a workforce of specified size, "and any agent of such a person . . .," and "person" includes "associations." Taken literally, then, Title VII as much outlaws sex discrimination by an "agent" of an association as by the association itself; put another way, such discrimination by an "agent" of Capital City is as much an affront to Title VII as it would be if engaged in by Capital City as an entity. It is clear that Taylor, as manager of Capital City's Northeast Branch, was Capital City's "agent" with respect to other employees of that branch, and equally clear that the sexual harassment charged to Taylor was forbidden sex discrimination.

We have encountered nothing impugning our reading of the statutory text as meaning that infractions of Title VII by agents are unlawful employment practices attributable to their employers. The legislative history of Title VII is virtually barren of indications, one way or the other, of a vicarious responsibility* for employers. . . .

What the legislative history does not provide can be gleaned, however, from other persuasive indicators of congressional intent. To begin with, the Equal Employment Opportunity Commission (EEOC), has promulgated guidelines which, as "administrative interpretation[s] of the Act by the enforcing agency," are "entitled to great deference," especially when they are supported by the statute and not inconsistent with its legislative history; and EEOC's *Guidelines on Discrimination Because of Sex* are unambiguous on the subject:

> Applying general Title VII principles, an employer . . . is responsible for its acts and those of its agents and supervisory employees with respect to sexual harassment regardless of whether the specific acts complained of were authorized or even forbidden by the employer and regardless of whether the employer knew or should have known of their occurrence.

We attach considerable weight to this interpretation, and we agree that treatment of supervisory personnel as "agents" is in conformity with "general Title VII principles." Our cases have established, as the cornerstone of present analysis, that sexual harassment is a violation of Title VII. Neither the statutory language nor its legislative history suggests that, as a trespass on Title VII, it should be treated any differently from transgressions arising out of racial or religious discrimination. And the caselaw in these latter areas establishes beyond cavil that "an employer is chargeable with Title VII violations occasioned by discriminatory practices of supervisory personnel."

[8, 9] We have no difficulty in concluding that an employer may be held accountable for discrimination accomplished through sexual harassment[13] by any supervisory employee with authority to hire, to promote, or to fire. An employer's delegation of this much authority vests in the supervisor such extreme power over the victimized employee that the supervisor's stature as an "agent" of the employer cannot be doubted. We do not believe, however, that vicarious responsibility is limited to discrimination by supervisors so richly endowed. The mere existence—or even the appearance—of a significant degree of influence in vital job decisions gives any supervisor the opportunity to impose upon employees. That

---

*In this case, "vicarious responsibility" refers to the employer's legal liability for the actions of his corporate agents. (Ed.)

opportunity is not dependent solely upon the supervisor's authority to make personnel decisions; the ability to direct employees in their work, to evaluate their performances, and to recommend personnel actions carries attendant power to coerce, intimidate, and harass. For this reason, we think employers must answer for sexual harassment of any subordinate by any supervising superior. . . .

. . . Confining liability, as the common law* would, to situations in which a supervisor acted within the scope of his authority conceivably could lead to the ludicrous result that employers would become accountable only if they explicitly require or consciously allow their supervisors to molest women employees. While modern courts seem more inclined to treat intentional misconduct on the job as arising out of and in the course of the employment, . . . there simply is no need to confine either the analysis or the solution where Title VII applies.

To hold that an employer cannot be reached for Title VII violations unknown to him is, too, to open the door to circumvention of Title VII by the simple expedient of looking the other way, even as signs of discriminatory practice begin to gather on the horizon. As the Ninth Circuit has said, "[s]uch a rule would create an enormous loophole in the statutes," one we think the courts should strive to seal. Instead of providing a reason for employers to remain oblivious to conditions in the workplace, we think the enlightened purpose of Title VII calls for an interpretation cultivating an incentive for employers to take a more active role in warranting to each employee that he or she will enjoy a working environment free from illegal sex discrimination. . . .

Employer responsiveness to on-the-job discrimination at the supervisory level is an essential aspect of the remedial scheme embodied in Title VII. It is the employer alone who is able promptly and effectively to halt discriminatory practices by supervisory personnel, and only the employer can provide reinstatement, backpay, or other remedial relief contemplated by the Act. Much of the promise of Title VII will become empty if victims of unlawful discrimination cannot secure redress from the only source capable of providing it. . . .

In sum, we hold that Vinson alleged facts sufficient to state a claim of sex discrimination cognizable under Title VII, and that any discriminatory activity by Taylor is attributable to Capital City. Vinson is entitled to an adjudication of that claim on the evidence, considered in light of the legal principles applicable. To that end, we reverse the judgment ap-

---

*The "common law" refers to legal principles, not necessarily mentioned in written laws and statutes, that have evolved over time through judicial opinions. (Ed.)

pealed from and remand the case to the District Court for proceedings consistent with this opinion.

So ordered.

NOTES

1. *Vinson* v. *Taylor,* 23 Fair Empl. Prac. Cas. (BNA) 37, 42 (D.D.C. 1980).

2. *Bundy* v. *Jackson,* 205 U.S. App. D.C. 444, 456, 641 F.2d 934, 946 (1981).

3. 183 U.S. App. D.C. 90, 561 F.2d 983 (1977).

4. Idem at 99, 561 F.2d at 992.

5. *Bundy* v. *Jackson.*

6. 205 U.S. App. D.C. at 453–454, 641 F.2d at 943–944.

7. *Bundy* v. *Jackson,* 205 U.S. App. D.C. at 453–454, 641 F.2d at 943–944 (emphasis in original).

8. The District Court did not elaborate on its basis for the finding of voluntariness, but it may have considered the voluminous testimony regarding Vinson's dress and personal fantasies. . . . Since, under *Bundy,* a woman does not waive her Title VII rights by her sartorial or whimsical proclivities, *Bundy* v. *Jackson,* 205 U.S. App. D.C. at 454, 455–456, 641 F.2d at 944, 945–946, that testimony had no place in this litigation.

9. Such evidence could be critical to a plaintiff's case, for a claim of harassment cannot be established without a showing of more than isolated indicia of a discriminatory environment. *Bundy* v. *Jackson,* 205 U.S. App. D.C. at 453, n. 9, 641 F.2d at 943 n.9.

10. Cf. *EEOC Decision No. 71–909,* Fair Empl. Prac. Cas. (BNA) at 269–270 (maintenance of working environment in which racial insults against blacks are habitual also violation of white employees' statutory rights).

11. *Vinson* v. *Taylor,* 23 Fair Empl. Prac. Cas. (BNA) at 42. Capital City had a grievance procedure whereby a complaint was first to be made to the aggrieved employee's supervisor, and thereafter the grievance was to be resolved by the division head or the president. . . . Vinson contended that management had been notified of Taylor's alleged harassing conduct by various means, but the District Court found that the employer had no knowledge of it. . . . The court held that notice to Taylor would not constitute notice to Capital City. . . .

12. *Barnes* v. *Costle,* 183 U.S. App. D.C. at 100, 561 F.2d at 993.

13. In determining the appropriateness of attribution, enough specificity must be imparted to "harassment" to filter out personal relationships that are not products of employment-related intimidation. For purposes of this case, we are well served by the criteria reflected in the EEOC *Guidelines.* See 29 C.F.R. § 1604.11(a) (1984). . . . The touchstone of these criteria is that sexual advances must be unwelcome, and must in some way amount to an explicit or implicit term or condition of employment in the sense either of job status or work environment.

14

Vinson v. *Taylor*

(Dissenting Opinion)

Appellees' suggestion for hearing *en banc* has been transmitted to the full Court. A majority of the judges of the Court in regular active service have not voted in favor thereof. Upon consideration of the foregoing, it is ordered, by the Court *en banc,* that the suggestion is denied.

A dissenting opinion filed by Circuit Judge Bork is attached and is joined by Circuit Judges Scalia and Starr.

Bork, Circuit Judge, with whom Circuit Judges Scalia and Starr join, dissenting from the denial of rehearing en banc:
This case should be heard en banc. It involves important issues of anti-discrimination law, at least two of which are wrongly decided. The panel's resolutions of the various issues before it, taken in combination, produce an unacceptable result. According to the panel opinion, when an employee charges sexual harassment in the workplace, the supervisor charged may not prove that the sexual behavior, far from constituting harassment, was voluntarily engaged in by the other person, nor may the supervisor show that the charging person's conduct was in fact a solicitation of sexual advances. These rulings seem plainly wrong. By depriving the charged person of any defenses, they mean that sexual dalliance, how-

---

Federal Reporter 753, 2d Series. Mechele VINSON, Appellant v. Sidney L. TAYLOR, et al. United States Court of Appeals, District of Columbia Circuit. May 14, 1985.

ever voluntarily engaged in, becomes harassment whenever an employee sees fit, after the fact, so to charactreize it.

The panel opinion explicitly states that a plaintiff's voluntariness in participating in a sexual relationship with her supervisor "can have no bearing on the pertinent inquiry" in a sexual harassment suit brought under Title VII. *Vinson* v. *Taylor,* 753 F.2d 141, 146 (D.C. Cir. 1985). The panel finds legally insignificant the following factual finding by the district court:

> if [Vinson] and Taylor did engage in an intimate or sexual relationship during the time of [Vinson's] employment with Capital, that relationship was a voluntary one by [Vinson] having nothing to do with her continued employment at Capital or her advancement or promotions at that institution.

. . . This finding may have been irrelevant to enviromental, as opposed to quid pro quo, harassment because it speaks of continued employment and advancement. But the panel did not rest on that distinction and rejected voluntariness as a defense in any kind of case. The panel's reasoning on this point is entirely circular. The opinion states that to allow proof of voluntairness on the part of a woman employee would expose her to what the panel sees fit to characterize as a "hideous quadrilemma" —the victim must acquiesce in the harassment, oppose it, resign, or yield and lose all hope of legal redress. . . . Passing the point that yielding and acquiescing would seem to be the same thing, the argument succeeds only because the defendant is denied the right to prove that the "victim" is not that but a willing participant. The rules of evidence are rigged so that dalliance is automatically harassment because no one is allowed to deny it.

The harmfulness of the panel decision is augmented by additional rulings on what evidence is to be admissible in Title VII sexual harassment cases. On the one hand, the panel holds that plaintiffs must be allowed to introduce evidence of their supervisor's behavior toward other employees in an effort to establish a pattern or practice of sexual harassment. . . . On the other hand, the panel also holds that a supervisor must not be allowed to introduce similar evidence of an employee's dress or behavior in an effort to prove that any sexual advances were solicited or welcomed. . . . In this case, evidence was introduced suggesting that the plaintiff wore provocative clothing, suffered from bizarre sexual fantasies, and often volunteered intimate details of her sex life to other employees at the bank. While hardly determinative, this evidence is relevant to the question of whether any sexual advances by her supervisor were solicited or voluntarily engaged in. Obviously, such evidence must be evaluated critically and in the light of all the other evidence in the case, but it is astonishing that it should be held inadmissible.[1] Added to the elimination of any voluntariness defense, these rulings make certain that to be charged is to be guilty.

But it is not the supervisor alone who is deprived of essential defenses. The panel decision makes the employer vicariously liable for the acts of the supervisor even though those facts were wholly unknown to the employer and were directly contrary to his instructions.[2] Of course, the employer is also prohibited from demonstrating that the alleged harassment was instead voluntary participation or that advances made were solicited. The result is that the employer is virtually converted into an insurer that all relationships between supervisors and employees are entirely asexual. Though the employer has no way of preventing sexual relationships, he is defenseless and must pay if they occur and are then claimed to be harassment.[3]

The Supreme Court has never addressed the question of an employer's vicarious liability under Title VII. I would, however, not suggest that we sit en banc to decide that issue were it not clear that the evidentiary rulings already discussed should be reconsidered en banc. That being so, we ought to take up the difficult and important question of an employer's vicarious liability under Title VII for conduct he knows nothing of and has done all he reasonably can to prevent. In doing this, we cannot necessarily import wholesale notions of vicarious liability which are evolving in lower court Title VII cases involving racial discrimination. We have previously recognized that various Title VII doctrines may require some modification before they can be applied in sexual harassment cases.[4] *Bundy v. Jackson,* 641 F.2d 934, 951 (D.C. Cir. 1981). The doctrine of vicarious liability may be one such doctrine since it is extremely unlikely that a supervisor would harass an employee for the purpose of furthering his employer's business. Indeed, supervisors engaging in such harassment (whether or not in violation of an explicit company policy) would ordinarily be aware that their employer disapproved of their actions.

Therefore, whatever the proper rule in cases involving racial discrimination, it would be appropriate for the en banc court to reexamine the vicarious liability issue in the unique context presented by sexual harassment claims. The panel's rule is at odds with traditional practice which was not to hold employers liable at all for their employee's intentional torts involving sexual escapades. In addition, the panel's rule is at odds with, or is at least a substantial extension of, the prior case law in this circuit. The two prior decisions of this court upon which the panel relied were both cases where the employer was fully aware of the acts of sexual harassment perpetrated by its supervisory employees. *Bundy* v. *Jackson,* 641 F.2d at 943; *Barnes* v. *Costle,* 561 F.2d 983, 1001 (D.C. Cir. 1977) (MacKinnon, J., concurring). Indeed, we qualified our holdings in both cases by indicating that if "a supervisor contravene[s] employer policy without the employer's knowledge and the consequences are rectified when discovered, the employer may be relieved from responsibility under Title VII." *Barnes,* 561 F.2d at 993; *Bundy,* 641 F.2d at 943. Accordingly, the panel in the present case has apparently gone well beyond *Barnes* and *Bundy* in holding this employer vicariously liable for its supervisor's alleged sexual harassment when the employer was not even made aware of and given the chance to rectify the consequences of the harassment alleged. . . .

Perhaps some of the doctrinal difficulty in this area is due to the awkwardness of classifying sexual advances as "discrimination." Harassment is reprehensible, but Title VII was passed to outlaw discriminatory behavior and not simply behavior of which we strongly disapprove. The artificiality of the approach we have taken appears from the decisions in this circuit. It is "discrimination" if a man makes unwanted sexual overtures to a woman, a woman to a man, a man to another man, or a woman to another woman. But this court has twice stated that Title VII does *not* prohibit sexual harassment by a "bisexual superior [because] the insistence upon sexual favors would . . . apply to male and female employees alike." *Barnes* v. *Costle,* 561 F.2d at 990 n. 55; *Bundy* v. *Jackson,* 641 F.2d at 942 n. 7. Thus, this court holds that only the differentiating libido runs afoul of Title VII, and bisexual harassment, however blatant and however offensive and disturbing, is legally permissible. Had Congress been aiming at sexual harassment, it seems unlikely that a woman would be protected from unwelcome heterosexual or lesbian advances but left unprotected when a bisexual attacks. That bizarre result suggests that Congress was not thinking of individual harassment at all but of discrimination in conditions of employment because of gender. If it is proper to classify harassment as discrimination for Title VII purposes, that decision at least demands adjustments in subsidiary doctrines. *See, e.g., Bundy* v. *Jackson,* 641 F.2d at 951.

NOTES

1. The panel cited no evidentiary rules or authorities in defense of its statement that this evidence should be suppressed. The sole reason given for excluding the evidence was that "under *Bundy* [v. *Jackson,* 641 F.2d 934 (D.C. Cir.

1981)], a woman does not waive her Title VII rights by her sartorial or whimsical proclivities." [chapter 13, n. 8]. I am not aware of anything in Title VII or the Federal Rules of Evidence that authorizes a court to suppress evidence that may be relevant to the presence of discriminatory intent. The panel has thus failed to perform the analysis required before relevant evidence may be excluded.

2. In this case, employer Capital City had an official policy of nondiscrimination. *Vinson v. Taylor,* 23 Fair Empl. Prac. Cas. (BNA) 37, 43 (findings of fact Par. 15) (D.D.C. 1980). Accordingly, any acts of harassment by supervisor Taylor were unauthorized and against company policy.

3. In this case, the employer could not have done more to avoid liability without actually monitoring or policing his employees' voluntary sexual relationships. Aside from the very outrageousness of such policing, it would be a very high-cost way, undoubtedly the highest-cost way, of solving the problem. *But cf. Horn* v. *Duke Homes,* 755 F.2d 599 mem. op. (7th Cir. 1985) (Swygert, J.) (holding employer strictly liable in Title VII sexual harassment case in part because "the employer is a more efficient cost avoider than is the injured employee").

4. We recognized in *Bundy* v. *Jackson,* 641 F.2d 934 (D.C. Cir. 1981), for example, that the "literal" *McDonnell-Douglas* test, *see McDonnell Douglas Corp.* v. *Green,* 411 U.S. 792, 802, 805, 93 S. Ct. 1817, 1824, 1825, 36 L.Ed.2d 668 (1973), which normally governs Title VII actions, does not apply "precisely" to Title VII sexual harassment claims. As we explained in *Bundy,* this is because

> the *McDonnell* formula presumes the standard situation where the alleged discrimination is due to the bare fact of the claimant's membership in a disadvantaged group. It therefore . . . fails to fit with precison the very unusual, perhaps unique, situation of sexual harassment, where the alleged basis of discrimination is not the employee's gender *per se,* but her refusal to submit to sexual advances which she suffered in large part because of her gender.

641 F.2d at 951 (emphasis in original). Accordingly, it was necessary to modify the *McDonnell* test in *Bundy* so that it would fit the unique situation of the sexual harassment claim.

15

Gender Dilemmas in Sexual Harassment Policies and Procedures

Stephanie Riger

Sexual harassment—unwanted sexually oriented behavior in a work context—is the most recent form of victimization of women to be redefined as a social rather than a personal problem, following rape and wife abuse. A sizeable proportion of women surveyed in a wide variety of work settings reported being subject to unwanted sexual attention, sexual comments or jokes, offensive touching, or attempts to coerce compliance with or punish rejection of sexual advances. In 1980, the U.S. Merit Systems Protection Board[1] conducted the first comprehensive national survey of sexual harassment among federal employees: About four out of ten of the 10,648 women surveyed reported having been the target of sexual harassment during the previous 24 months. A recent update of this survey found that the frequency of harassment in 1988 was identical to that reported earlier: 42 percent of all women surveyed in 1988 reported that they had experienced some form of unwanted and uninvited sexual attention compared to exactly the same percentage of women in 1980.[2]

Women ranging from blue-collar workers[3] to lawyers[4] to airline personnel[5] have reported considerable amounts of sexual harassment in surveys. Among a random sample of private sector workers in the Los Angeles

From the *American Psychologist* 46, no. 5 (1991): 497–505. Copyright © 1991 by the American Psychological Association. Reprinted by permission.

area, more than one half of the women surveyed by telephone reported experiencing at least one incident that they considered sexual harassment during their working lives.[6] Some estimate that up to about one third of women in educational institutions have experienced some form of harassment.[7] Indeed, Garvey stated that "Unwanted sexual attention may be the single most widespread occupational hazard in the workplace today."[8]

It is a hazard faced much more frequently by women than men. About 40 percent of the women in the original U.S. Merit Systems Protection Board survey reported having experienced sexual harassment, compared with only 15 percent of the men.[9] Among working people surveyed in Los Angeles, women were nine times more likely than men to report having quit a job because of sexual harassment, five times more likely to have transferred, and three times more likely to have lost a job.[10] Women with low power and status, whether due to lower age, being single or divorced, or being in a marginal position in the organization, are more likely to be harassed.[11]

Sex differences in the frequency of harassment also prevail in educational environments.[12] A mailed survey of more than 900 women and men at the University of Rhode Island asked about a wide range of behavior, including the frequency of respondents' experience of sexual insult, defined as an "uninvited sexually suggestive, obscene, or offensive remark, stare, or gesture."[13] Of the female respondents, 40 percent reported being sexually insulted occasionally or often while on campus, compared with 17 percent of the men. Both men and women reported that women are rarely the source of such insults. Similar differences were found in a survey of social workers, with two and one-half times as many women as men reporting harassment.[14]

Despite the high rates found in surveys of sexual harassment of women, few complaints are pursued through official grievance procedures. Dzeich and Weiner[15] concluded, after reviewing survey findings, that 20 to 30 percent of female college students experience sexual harassment. Yet academic institutions averaged only 4.3 complaints each during the 1982–1983 academic year,[16] a period roughly consecutive with the surveys cited by Dzeich and Weiner. In another study conducted at a university in 1984, of 38 women who reported harassment, only one reported the behavior to the offender's supervisor and two reported the behavior to an adviser, another professor, or employer.[17] Similar findings have been reported on other college campuses.[18]

Low numbers of complaints appear in other work settings as well. In a survey of federal workers, only about 11 percent of victims reported the harassment to a higher authority, and only 2.5 percent used formal complaint channels.[19] Similarly, female social workers reacted to harassment by avoiding or delaying the conflict or attempting to defuse the situation rather than by adopting any form of recourse such as filing a grievance.[20] The number of complaints alleging sexual harassment filed with the Equal Employment Opportunity Commission in Washington, D.C., has declined since 1984, despite an increase in the number of women in the workforce during that time,[21] and surveys that suggest that the rate of sexual harassment has remained relatively stable.[22]

It is the contention of this [essay] that the low rate of utilization of grievance procedures is due to gender bias in sexual harassment policies that discourages their use by women. Policies are written in gender-neutral language and are intended to apply equally to men and women. However, these policies are experienced differently by women than men because of gender differences in perception of harassment and orientation toward conflict. Although victims of all forms of discrimination are reluctant to pursue grievances,[23] women, who are most likely to be the victims of sexual harassment, are especially disinclined to pursue sexual harassment grievances for at least two reasons. First, the interpretation in policies of what constitutes harassment may not reflect women's viewpoints, and their complaints may not be seen as valid. Second, the procedures in some policies that are designed to resolve disputes may be inimical to women because they are not compatible with the way that many women view conflict resolution. Gender bias in policies, rather than an absence of harassment or lack of assertiveness on the part of victims, produces low numbers of complaints.

GENDER BIAS IN THE DEFINITION OF SEXUAL HARASSMENT

The first way that gender bias affects sexual harassment policies stems from differences between men and women in the interpetation of the definition of harassment. Those writing sexual harassment policies for organizations typically look to the courts for the distinction between illegal sexual harassment and permissible (although perhaps unwanted) social interaction (see Cohen[24] for a discussion of this distinction in legal cases). The definition of harassment in policies typically is that provided by the U.S. Equal Employment Opportunity Commission guidelines:

> Unwelcome sexual advances, requests for sexual favors, and other verbal or physical conduct of a sexual nature constitute sexual harassment when (1) submission to such conduct is made either explicitly or implicitly a term or condition of an individual's employment; (2) submission to or rejection

of such conduct by an individual is used as the basis for employment decisions affecting such individual; or (3) such conduct has the purpose or effect of unreasonably interfering with an individual's work performance or creating an intimidating, hostile, or offensive working environment.[25]

The first two parts of the definition refer to a quid pro quo relationship involving people in positions of unequal status, as superior status is usually necessary to have control over another's employment. In such cases bribes, threats, or punishments are used. Incidents of this type need happen only once to fall under the definition of sexual harassment. However, courts have required that incidents falling into the third category, "an intimidating, hostile, or offensive working environment," must be repeated in order to establish that such an environment exists;[26] these incidents must be both pervasive and so severe that they affect the victim's psychological well-being.[27] Harassment of this type can come from peers or even subordinates as well as superiors.

In all three of these categories, harassment is judged on the basis of conduct and its effects on the recipient, not the intentions of the harasser. Thus, two typical defenses given by accused harassers—"I was just being friendly," or "I touch everyone, I'm that kind of person"—do not hold up in court. Yet behavior may have an intimidating or offensive effect on some people but be inoffensive or even welcome to others. In deciding whose standards should be used, the courts employ what is called the *reasonable person rule,* asking whether a reasonable person would be offended by the conduct in question. The dilemma in applying this to sexual harassment is that a reasonable woman and a reasonable man are likely to differ in their judgments of what is offensive.

Definitions of sexual harassment are socially constructed, varying not only with characteristics of the perceiver but also those of the situational context and actors involved. Behavior is more likely to be labeled harassment when it is done by someone with greater power than the victim;[28] when it involves physical advances accompanied by threats of punishment for noncompliance;[29] when the response to it is negative;[30] when the behavior reflects persistent negative intentions toward a woman;[31] the more inappropriate it is for the actor's social role;[32] and the more flagrant and frequent the harasser's actions.[33] Among women, professionals are more likely than those in secretarial-clerical positions to report the more subtle behaviors as harassment.[34]

The variable that most consistently predicts variation in people's definition of sexual harassment is the sex of the rater. Men label fewer behaviors at work as sexual harassment.[35] Men tend to find sexual overtures from women at work to be flattering, whereas women find similar approaches from men to be insulting.[36] Both men and women agree that certain blatant behaviors, such as sexual assault or sexual bribery, constitute harassment, but women are more likely to see as harassment more subtle behavior such as sexual teasing or looks or gestures.[37] Even when they do identify behavior as harassment, men are more likely to think that women will be flattered by it.[38] Men are also more likely than women to blame women for being sexually harassed.[39]

These gender differences make it difficult to apply the reasonable person rule. Linenberger[40] proposed ten factors that permit an "objective" assessment of whether behavior constitutes sexual harassment, regardless of the perception of the victim and the intent of the perpetrator. These factors range from the severity of the conduct to the number and frequency of encounters, and the relationship of the parties involved. For example, behavior is less likely to be categorized as harassment if it is seen as a response to provocation from the victim. But is an objective rating of provocation possible? When gender differences are as clear-cut and persistent as they are in the perception of what behavior constitutes sexual harassment, the question is not one of objectivity, but rather of which sex's definition of the situation will prevail. Becker asserted that there is a "hierarchy of credibility" in organizations, and that credibility and the right to be heard are differentially distributed: "In any system of ranked groups, participants take it as given that members of the highest group have the right to define the way things really are."[41] Because men typically have more power in organizations,[42] Becker's analysis suggests that in most situations the male definition of harassment is likely to predominate. As MacKinnon put it, "objectivity—the nonsituated, universal standpoint, whether claimed or aspired to—is a denial of the existence or potency of sex inequality that tacitly participates in constructing reality from the dominant point of view."[43] "The law sees and treats women the way men see and treat women."[44] This means that men's judgments about what behavior constitutes harassment, and who is to blame, are likely to prevail. Linenberger's ten factors thus may not be an objective measure, but rather a codification of the male perspective on harassment. This is likely to discourage women who want to bring complaints about more subtle forms of harassment.

SEX DIFFERENCES IN THE ATTRIBUTION OF HARASSMENT

Attribution theory provides an explanation for the wider range of behaviors that women define as harassment and for men's tendency to find women at fault.[45] Attribution theory suggests that people tend to see their own behaviors as situationally determined, whereas they attribute the behaviors of others to personality characteristics or other internal causes.[46] Those who see sexual harassment through the eyes of the actor are likely to be male. As actors are wont to do, they will attribute their behaviors to situational causes, including the "provocations" of the women involved. They will then not perceive their own behaviors as harassment. In fact, those who take the perspective of the victim do see specific behaviors as more harassing than those who take the perspective of the actor.[47] Women are more likely to view harassment through the eyes of the victim; therefore, they will label more behaviors as harassment because they attribute them to men's disposition or personality traits. Another possibility is that men, as potential harassers, want to avoid blame in the future, and so shift the blame to women[48] and restrict the range of behaviors that they define as harassment.[49] Whatever the cause, a reasonable man and a reasonable woman are likely to differ in their judgments of whether a particular behavior contitutes sexual harassment.

Men tend to misinterpret women's friendliness as an indication of sexual interest.[50] Acting on this misperception may result in behavior that is harassing to women. Tangri, Burt, and Johnson stated that "Some sexual harassment may indeed be clumsy or insensitive expressions of attraction, while some is the classic abuse of organizational power."[51] Gender differences in attributional processes help explain the first type of harassment, partially accounting for the overwhelming preponderance of sexual harassment incidents that involve a male offender and a female victim.

GENDER BIAS IN GRIEVANCE PROCEDURES

Typically, procedures for resolving disputes about sexual harassment are written in gender-neutral terms so that they may apply to both women and men. However, men and women may react quite differently to the same procedures.

Analyzing this problem requires looking at specific policies and procedures. Educational institutions will serve as the context for this discussion for three reasons. First, they are the most frequent site of surveys about the problem, and the pervasive nature of harassment on campuses has been well documented.[52] Second, although sexual harassment is harmful to women in all occupations, it can be particularly devastating to those in educational institutions, in which the goal of the organization is to nurture and promote development. The violation of relationships based on trust, such as those between faculty and students, can leave long-lasting and deep wounds, yet many surveys find that those inpositions of authority in educational settings are often the source of the problem.[53] Third, educational institutions have been leaders in the development of sexual harassment policies, in part because of concern about litigation. In *Alexander* v. *Yale University*[54] the court decided that sexual harassment constitutes a form of sex discrimination that denies equal access to educational opportunities, and falls under Title IX of the Educational Amendments of 1972. The Office of Civil Rights in the U.S. Department of Education now requires institutions that receive Title IX funds to maintain grievance procedures to resolve complaints involving sexual discrimination or harassment.[55] Consequently, academic institutions may have had more experience than other work settings in developing procedures to combat this problem. A survey of U.S. institutions of higher learning conducted in 1984[56] found that 66 percent of all responding institutions had sexual harassment policies, and 46 percent had grievance procedures specifically designed to deal with sexual harassment complaints, with large public schools more likely to have them than small private ones. These percentages have unquestionably increased in recent years, given the government funding regulations. Although the discussion here is focused on educational contexts, the problems identified in sexual harassment policies exist in other work settings as well.

Many educational institutions, following guidelines put forward by the American Council on Education[57] and the American Association of University Professors,[58] have established policies that probihit sexual harassment and create grievance procedures. Some use a formal board or hearing, and others use informal mechanisms that protect confidentiality and seek to resolve the complaint rather than punish the offender.[59] Still others use both types of procedures. The type of procedure specified by the policy may have a great impact on victims' willingess to report complaints.

Comparison of Informal and Formal Grievance Procedures

Informal attempts to resolve disputes differ from formal procedures in important ways. . . . First, their goal is to solve a problem, rather than to judge the harasser's guilt or innocence. The assumptions underlying these processes are that both parties in a dispute perceive a problem (although they may define that problem differently); that both share a common interest in solving that problem; and that together they can negotiate an agreement that will be satisfactory to everyone involved. Typically, the goal of informal processes is to end the harassment of the complainant rather than judge (and punish, if appropriate) the offender. The focus is on what will happen in the future between the disputing parties, rather than on what has happened in the past. Often policies do not specify the format of informal problem solving, but accept a wide variety of strategies of reconciliation. For example, a complainant might write a letter to the offender,[60] or someone might talk to the offender on the complainant's behalf. The offender and victim might participate in mediation, in which a third party helps them negotiate an agreement. Many policies accept a wide array of strategies as good faith attempts to solve the problem informally.

In contrast, formal procedures generally require a written complaint and have a specified procedure for handling cases, usually by bringing the complaint to a group officially designated to hear the case, such as a hearing board. The informal process typically ends when the complainant is satisfied (or decides to drop the complaint); the formal procedure ends when the hearing board decides on the guilt or innocence of the alleged harasser. Thus, control over the outcome usually rests with the complainant in the case of informal mechanisms, and with the official governance body in the case of a hearing. Compliance with a decision is usually voluntary in informal procedures, whereas the decision in a formal procedure is binding unless appealed to a higher authority. Formal procedures are adversarial in nature, with the complainant and defendant competing to see whose position will prevail.

A typical case might proceed as follows: A student with a complaint writes a letter to the harasser (an informal procedure). If not satisfied with the response, she submits a written complaint to the sexual harassment hearing board, which then hears both sides of the case, receives available evidence, and decides on the guilt or innocence of the accused (a formal procedure). If the accused is found guilty, the appropriate officer of the institution decides on punishment.

Gender Differences in Orientation to Conflict

Women and men may differ in their reactions to dispute resolution in procedures for at least two reasons. First, women typically have less power than men in organizations.[61] Using a grievance procedure, such as appearing before a hearing board, may be inimical because of the possibility of retaliation for a complaint. Miller suggested that differences in status and power affect the way that people handle conflict:

> As soon as a group attains dominance it tends inevitably to produce a situation of conflict and . . . it also, simultaneously, seeks to suppress conflict. Moreover, subordinates who accept the dominant's conception of them as passive and malleable do not openly engage in conflict. Conflict . . . is forced underground.[62]

This may explain why some women do not report complaints at all. When they do complain, however, their relative lack of power or their values may predispose women to prefer informal rather than formal procedures. Beliefs about the appropriate way to handle disputes vary among social groups.[63] Gilligan's[64] distinction between an orientation toward rights and justice compared with an emphasis on responsibilities to others and caring is likely to be reflected in people's preferences for ways of handling disputes.[65] Neither of these orientations is exclusive to one sex, but according to Gilligan, women are more likely to emphasize caring. Women's orientation to caring may be due to their subordinate status.[66] Empirical support for Gilligan's theories is inconclusive.[67] Yet the fact that most victims of sexual harassment state that they simply want an end to the offending behavior rather than punishment of the offender[68] suggests a "caring" rather than "justice" perspective (or possibly, a fear of reprisals).

In the context of dispute resolution, an emphasis on responsibilities and caring is compatible with the goals of informal procedures to restore harmony or at least peaceful coexistence among the parties involved, whereas that of justice is compatible with formal procedures that attempt to judge guilt or innocence of the offender. Thus women may prefer to use informal procedures to resolve conflicts, and indeed most cases in educational institutions are handled through informal mechanisms.[68] Policies that do not include an informal dispute resolution option are likely to discourage many women from bringing complaints.

Problems With Informal Dispute-Resolution Procedures

Although women may prefer informal mechanisms, they are problematic for several reasons.[69] Because they do not result in punishment, offenders suffer few negative consequences of their actions and may not be deterred from harassing again. In institutions of higher learning, the most common form of punishment reported is a verbal warning by a supervisor, which is given only "sometimes."[70] Dismissal and litigation are almost never used. It seems likely, then, that sexual harassment may be viewed by potential harassers as low-risk behavior, and that victims see few incentives for bringing official complaints.

The confidentiality usually required by informal procedures prevents other victims from knowing that a complaint has been lodged against a multiple offender. If a woman knows that another woman is bringing a complaint against a particular man who has harassed both of them, then she might be more willing to complain also. The secrecy surrounding informal complaint processes precludes this information from becoming public and makes it more difficult to identify repeat offenders. Also, complaints settled informally may not be included in reports of the frequency of sexual harassment claims, making these statistics underestimate the scope of the problem. Yet confidentiality is needed to protect the rights of the accused and may be preferred by those bringing complaints.

These problems in informal procedures could discourage male as well as female victims from bringing complaints. Most problematic for women, however, is the assumption in informal procedures that the complainant and accused have equal power in the process of resolving the dispute. This assumption is likely to put women at a disadvantage. Parties involved in sexual harassment disputes may not be equal either in the sense of formal position within the organization (e.g., student versus faculty) or status (e.g., female versus male students), and position and status characteristics that reflect levels of power do not disappear simply because they are irrelevant to the informal process. External status characteristics that indicate macrolevel social stratification (e.g., sex and age) help explain the patterns of distribution of sexual harassment in the workplace.[71] It seems likely that these external statuses will influence the interpersonal dynamics within a dispute-resolution procedure as well. Because women are typically lower than men in both formal and informal status and power in organizations, they will have less power in the dispute resolution process.

When the accused has more power than the complainant (e.g., a male faculty member accused by a female student), the complainant is more vulnerable to retaliation. Complainants may be reluctant to use grievance procedures because they fear retaliation should the charge be made public. For example, students may fear that a faculty member will punish them for bringing a complaint by lowering their grades or withholding recommendations. The person appointed to act as a guide to the informal resolution process is usually expected to act as a neutral third party rather than advocate for the complainant, and may hold little formal power over faculty: "Relatively few institutions have persons empowered to be (non-legal) advocates for the complainants; a student bringing a complaint has little assurance of stopping the harassment and avoiding retaliation."[72] The victim then is left without an advocate to face an opponent whose formal position, age, and experience with verbal argument is often considerably beyond her own. The more vulnerable a woman's position is in her organization, the more likely it is that she will be harassed;[73] therefore, sexual harassment, like rape, involves dynamics of power and domination as well as sexuality. The lack of an advocate for the complainant who might equalize power between the disputing parties is particularly troubling. However, if an advocate is provided for the complainant in an informal process, fairness and due process require that the defendant have an advocate as well. The dilemma is that this seems likely to transform an informal, problem-solving process into a formal, adversarial one.

OTHER OBSTACLES TO REPORTING COMPLAINTS

Belief That Sexual Harassment of Woman Is Normative

Because of differences in perception of behavior, men and women involved in a sexual harassment case are likely to have sharply divergent interpretations of that case, particularly when a hostile environment claim is involved. To women, the behavior in question is offensive, and they are likely to see themselves as victims of male actions. The requirement that an attempt be made to mediate the dispute or solve it through informal processes may violate their perception of the situation and of themselves as victims of a crime. By comparison, a victim of a mugging is not required to solve the problem with the mugger through mediation.[74] To many men, the behavior is not offensive, but normative. In their eyes, no crime has been committed, and there is no problem to be solved.

Some women may also consider sexual harassment to be normative. Women may believe that these sorts of behaviors are simply routine, a commonplace part of everyday life, and thus not something that can be challenged. Younger women—who are more likely to be victims[75]—are more tolerant of harassment than are older women.[76] Indeed, Lott et al. concluded that "younger women in particular have accepted the idea that prowling men are a 'fact of life.' "[77] This attitude might prevent women from labeling a negative experience as harassment. Surveys that ask women about sexual harassment and about the frequency of experiencing specific sexually harassing behaviors find discrepancies in responses to these questions.[78] Women report higher rates when asked if they have been the target of specific harassing behaviors than when asked a general question about whether they have been harassed. Women are also more willing to report negative reactions to offensive behaviors than they are to label those behaviors as sexual harassment.[79]

Normative beliefs may deter some male victims of harassment from reporting complaints also, because men are expected to welcome sexual advances if those advances are from women.

Negative Outcomes for Victims Who Bring Complaints

The outcome of grievance procedures does not appear to provide much satisfaction to victims who bring complaints. In academic settings, despite considerable publicity given to a few isolated cases in which tenured faculty have been fired, punishments are rarely inflicted on harassers, and the punishments that are given are mild, such as verbal warnings.[80] Among federal workers, 33 percent of those who used formal grievance procedures to protest sexual harassment found that it "made things worse."[81] More than 65 percent of the cases of formal charges of sexual harassment filed with the Illinois Department of Human Rights involved job discharge of the complainant.[82] Less than one third of those cases resulted in a favorable settlement for the complainant, and those who received financial compensation got an average settlement of $3,234.[83] Similar findings in California were reported by Coles,[84] with the average case settlement there of $973, representing approximately one month's pay. Although a few legal cases have resulted in large settlements,[85] these studies suggest that typical settlements are low. Formal actions may take years to complete, and in legal suits the victim usually must hire legal counsel at considerable expense.[86] These settlements seem unlikely to compensate victims for the emotional stress, notoriety, and financial costs involved in filing a public complaint. Given the consistency with which victimization falls more often to women than men, it is ironic that one of the largest settlements awarded to an individual in a sexual harassment case ($196,500 in damages) was made to a man who brought suit against his female supervisor,[87] perhaps because sexual aggression by a woman is seen as especially [outrageous].

Emotional Consequences of Harassment

In academic settings, harassment can adversely affect students' learning, and therefore their academic standing. It can deprive them of educational and career opportunities because they wish to avoid threatening situations. Students who have been harassed report that they consequently avoid taking a class from or working with a particular faculty member, change their major, or leave a threatening situation.[88] Lowered self-esteem follows the conclusion that rewards, such as a high grade, may have been based on sexual attraction rather than one's abilities.[89] Decreased feelings of competence and confidence and increased feelings of anger, frustration, depression, and anxiety all can result from harassment.[90] The psychological stress produced by harassment is compounded when women are fired or quit their jobs in fear or frustration.[91]

Meek and Lynch[92] proposed that victims of harassment typically go through several stages of reaction, first questioning the offender's true intentions and then blaming themselves for the offender's behavior. Women with traditional sex-role beliefs are more likely to blame themselves for being harassed.[93] Victims then worry about being believed by others and about possible retaliation if they take formal steps to protest the behavior. A victim may be too frightened or confused to assert herself or punish the offender. Psychologists who work with victims of harassment would do well to recognize that not only victims' emotional reactions but also the nature of the grievance process as discussed in this [essay] may discourage women from bringing formal complaints. . . .

NOTES

1. U.S. Merit Systems Protection Board, *Sexual Harassment in the Federal Workplace: Is It a Problem?* (Washington, D.C.: U.S. Government Printing Office, 1981).

2. U.S. Merit Systems Protection Board, *Sexual Harassment in the Federal Government: An Update* (Washington, D.C.: U.S. Government Printing Office, 1988).

3. E. LaFontaine and L. Tredeau, "The Frequency, Sources, and Correlates of Sexual Harassment among Women in Traditional Male Occupations," *Sex Roles* 15 (1986): 433–42, and D. E. Maypole and R. Skaine, "Sexual Harassment of Blue-Collar Workers," *Journal of Sociology and Social Welfare* 9 (1982): 682–95.

4. N. Burleigh and S. Goldberg, "Breaking the Silence: Sexual Harassment in Law Firms," *ABA Journal* 75 (1989): 46–52.

5. S. Littler-Bishop, D. Seidler-Feller, and R. E. Opaluck, "Sexual Harassment in the Workplace as a Function of Initiator's Status: The Case of Airline Personnel," *Journal of Social Issues* 38 (1982): 137–48.

6. B. A. Gutek, *Sex and the Workplace* (San Francisco: Jossey-Bass, 1985).

7. S. Kenig and J. Ryan, "Sex Differences in Levels of Tolerance and Attribution of Blame for Sexual Harassment on a University Campus," *Sex Roles* 15 (1986): 535–49.

8. M. S. Garvey, "The High Cost of Sexual Harassment Suits," *Labor Relations* 65 (1986): 75.

9. U.S. Merit Systems Protection Board, *Sexual Harassment in the Federal Workplace: Is It a Problem?*

10. A. M. Konrad and B. A. Gutek, "Impact of Work Experiences on Attitudes toward Sexual Harassment," *Administrative Science Quarterly* 31 (1986): 422–38.

11. T. C. Fain and D. L. Anderton, "Sexual Harassment: Organizational Context and Diffuse Status," *Sex Roles* 5/6 (1987): 291–311; LaFontaine and Tredeau, "The Frequency, Sources, and Correlates of Sexual Harassment among Women in Traditional Male Occupations," pp. 433–42; W. L. Robinson and P. T. Reid, "Sexual Intimacy in Psychology Revisited," *Professional Psychology: Research and Practice* 16 (1985): 512–20.

12. L. F. Fitzgerald et al., "The Incidence and Dimensions of Sexual Harassment in Academia and the Workplace," *Journal of Vocatonal Behavior* 32 (1988): 152–75.

13. B. Lott, M. E. Reilly, and D. R. Howard, "Sexual Assault and Harassment: A Campus Community Case Study," *Signs: Journal of Women in Culture and Society* 8 (1982): 309.

14. D. E. Maypole, "Sexual Harassment of Social Workers at Work: Injustice Within?" *Social Work* 31 (1986): 29–34.

15. B. Dziech and L. Weiner, *The Lecherous Professor* (Boston: Beacon Press, 1984).

16. C. Robertson, C. E. Dyer, and D. Campbell, "Campus Harassment: Sexual Harassment Policies and Procedures at Institutions of Higher Learning," *Signs: Journal of Women in Culture and Society* 13 (1988): 792–812.

17. M. E. Reilly, B. Lott, and S. Gallogly, "Sexual Harassment of University Students," *Sex Roles* 15 (1986): 333–58.

18. J. W. Adams, J. L. Kottke, and J. S. Padgitt, "Sexual Harassment of University Students," *Journal of College Student Personnel* 23 (1983): 484–90; D. J. Benson and G. Thomson, "Sexual Harassment on a University Campus: The Confluence of Authority Relations, Sexual Interest and Gender Stratification," *Social Problems* 29 (1982): 236–51; J. B. Brandenburg, "Sexual Harassment in the University: Guidelines for Establishing a Grievance Procedure," *Signs: Journal of Women in Culture and Society* 8 (1982): 320–36; L. P. Cammaert, "How Widespread Is Sexual Harassment on Campus?" *International Journal of Women's Studies* 8 (1985): 388–97; R. M. Meek and A. Lynch, "Establishing an Informal Grievance Procedure for Cases of Sexual Harassment of Students," *Journal of the National Association for Women Deans, Administrators, and Counselors* 46 (1983): 30–33; B. E. Schneider, "Graduate Women, Sexual Harassment, and University Policy," *Journal of Higher Education* 58 (1987): 46–65.

19. J. A. Livingston, "Responses to Sexual Harassment on the Job: Legal, Organizational, and Individual Actions," *Journal of Social Issues* 38, no. 4 (1982): 5–22.

20. Maypole, "Sexual Harassment of Social Workers at Work: Injustice Within?" pp. 29–34.

21. G. Mayerson, "Watch That Leer, Stifle That Joke," *Forbes,* May 1989, pp. 69–72.

22. U.S. Merit Systems Protection Board, *Sexual Harassment in the Federal Workplace: Is It a Problem?* and idem, *Sexual Harassment in the Federal Government: An Update.*

23. K. Bumiller, "Victims in the Shadow of the Law: A Critique of the Model of Legal Protection," *Signs: Journal of Women in Culture and Society* 12 (1987): 421–39.

24. C. F. Cohen, "Legal Dilemmas in Sexual Harassment Cases," *Labor Law Journal* (November 1987): 681–89.

25. U.S. Equal Employment Opportunity Commission, "Final Amendment to Guidelines on Discrimination Because of Sex under Title VII of the Civil Rights Act of 1964, as Amended, 29 CFR Part 1604," *Federal Register* 45 (November 10, 1980): 74675–74677.

26. D. E. Terpstra and D. D. Baker, "Outcomes of Sexual Harassment Charges," *Academy of Management Journal* 31 (1988): 185–94.

27. T. B. Trager, "Legal Considerations in Drafting Sexual Harassment Policies," in J. Van Tol, ed., *Sexual Harassment on Campus: A Legal Compendium* (Washington, D.C.: National Association of College and University Attorneys, 1988), pp. 181–90.

28. B. A. Gutek, B. Marasch, and A. G. Cohen, "Interpreting Social-Sexual Behavior in a Work Setting," *Journal of Vocational Behavior* 22 (1985): 30–48; Kenig and Ryan, "Sex Differences in Levels of Tolerance and Attribution of Blame for Sexual Harassment on a University Campus," pp. 535–49; D. Lester et al., "Judgments about Sexual Harassment: Effects of the Power of the Harasser," *Perceptual and Motor Skills* 63 (1986): 990; P. M. Popovich et al., "Assessing the Incidence and Perceptions of Sexual Harassment Behavior among American Undergraduates," *Journal of Psychology* 120 (1987); 387–96.

29. P. H. Rossi and W. Weber-Rudin, "Sexual Harassment on the Campus," *Social Science Research* 12 (1983): 131–58.

30. T. J. Jones, M. S. Remland, and C. C. Brunner, "Effects of Employment Relationship, Response of Recipient and Sex of Rater on Perceptions of Sexual Harassment," *Perceptual and Motor Skills* 65 (1987): 55–63.

31. J. B. Pryor and J. D. Day, "Interpretations of Sexual Harassment: An Attributional Analysis," *Sex Roles* 18 (1988): 405–17.

32. J. B. Pryor, "The Lay Person's Understanding of Sexual Harassment," *Sex Roles* 13 (1985): 273–86.

33. D. A. Thomas and R. L. Weiner, "Physical and Psychological Causality as Determinants of Culpability in Sexual Harassment Cases," *Sex Roles* 17 (1987): 573–91.

34. D. I. McIntyre and J. C. Renick, "Protecting Public Employees and Employers from Sexual Harassment," *Public Personnel Management Journal* 11 (1982): 282–92.

35. Kenig and Ryan, "Sex Differences in Levels of Tolerance and Attribu-

tion of Blame for Sexual Harassment on a University Campus," pp. 535–49; Konrad and Gutek, "Impact of Work Experiences on Attitudes toward Sexual Harassment," pp. 422–38; Lester et al., "Judgments About Sexual Harassment," p. 990; G. N. Powell, "Effects of Sex Role Identity and Sex on Definitions of Sexual Harassment," *Sex Roles* 14 (1986): 9–19; Rossi and Weber-Burdin, "Sexual Harassment on the Campus," pp. 131–58.

36. Gutek, *Sex and the Workplace.*

37. Adams et al., "Sexual Harassment of University Students," pp. 484–90; E. G. C. Collins and T. B. Blodgett, "Some See It . . . Some Won't," *Harvard Business Review* 59 (1981): 76–95; Kenig and Ryan, "Sex Differences in Levels of Tolerance and Attribution of Blame for Sexual Harassment on a University Campus," pp. 535–49; U.S. Merit Systems Protection Board, *Sexual Harassment in the Federal Workplace: Is It a Problem?*

38. D. Kirk, "Gender Differences in the Perception of Sexual Harassment," paper presented at the Academy of Management National Meeting, Anaheim, Calif., August 1988.

39. Kenig and Ryan, "Sex Differences in Levels of Tolerance and Attribution of Blame for Sexual Harassment on a University Campus," pp. 535–49.

40. D. Linenberger, "What Behavior Constitutes Sexual Harassment?" *Labor Law Journal* (April 1983): 238–47.

41. H. S. Becker, "Whose Side Are We On?" *Social Problems* 14 (1967): 241.

42. R. M. Kanter, *Men and Women of the Corporation* (New York: Basic Books, 1977).

43. C. A. MacKinnon, "Feminism, Marxism, Method, and the State: Toward Feminist Jurisprudence," in S. Harding, ed., *Feminism and Methodology: Social Science Issues* (Bloomington: Indiana University Press, 1987), p. 136.

44. Ibid., p. 140.

45. Kenig and Ryan, "Sex Differences in Levels of Tolerance and Attribution of Blame for Sexual Harassment on a University Campus," pp. 535–49; Pryor, "The Lay Person's Understanding of Sexual Harassment," pp. 273–86; Pryor and Day, "Interpretations of Sexual Harassment: An Attributional Analysis," pp. 405–17.

46. E. E. Jones and R. E. Nisbett, *The Actor and the Observer: Divergent Perceptions of the Causes of Behavior* (Morristown, N.J.: General Learning Press, 1971).

47. Pryor and Day, "Interpretations of Sexual Harassment: An Attributional Analysis," pp. 405–17.

48. I. W. Jensen and B. A. Gutek, "Attributions and Assignment of Responsibility in Sexual Harassment," *Journal of Social Issues* 38 (1982): 321–36.

49. Kenig and Ryan, "Sex Differences in Levels of Tolerance and Attribution of Blame for Sexual Harassment on a University Campus," pp. 535–49.

50. A. Abbey, "Sex Differences in Attributions for Friendly Behavior: Do Males Misperceive Females' Friendliness?" *Journal of Personality and Social*

Psychology 42 (1982): 830–38; A. Abbey and C. Melby, "The Effects of Non-verbal Cues on Gender Differences in Perceptions of Sexual Interest," *Sex Roles* 15 (1986): 283–98; F. E. Saal, C. B. Johnson, and N. Weber, "Friendly or Sexy? It May Depend on Whom You Ask," *Psychology of Women Quarterly* 13 (1989): 263–76; R. L. Shotland and J. M. Craig, "Can Men and Women Differentiate between Friendly and Sexually Interested Behavior?" *Social Psychology Quarterly* 51 (1988): 66–73.

51. S. S. Tangri, M. R. Burt, and L. B. Johnson, "Sexual Harassment at Work: Three Explanatory Models," *Journal of Social Issues* 38 (1982): 51. [See Part Two above.]

52. Dziech and Weiner, *The Lecherous Professor.*

53. Benson and Thomson, "Sexual Harassment on a University Campus," pp. 236–51; Fitzgerald et al., "The Incidence and Dimensions of Sexual Harassment in Academia and the Workplace," pp. 152–75; R. D. Glaser and J. S. Thorpe, "Unethical Intimacy: A Survey of Sexual Conduct and Advances between Psychology Educators and Female Graduate Students," *American Psychologist* 41 (1986): 43–51; Kenig and Ryan, "Sex Differences in Levels of Tolerance and Attribution of Blame for Sexual Harassment on a University Campus," pp. 535–49; N. Maihoff and L. Forrest, "Sexual Harassment of Social Workers at Work: An Assessment Study," *Social Work* 31 (1983): 9–15; Robinson and Reid, "Sexual Intimacy in Psychology Revisited," pp. 512–20; K. R. Wilson and L. A. Krause, "Sexual Harassment in the University," *Journal of College Student Personnel* 24 (1983): 219–24.

54. *Alexander et al.* v. *Yale University,* 459 F. Supp. 1 (D. Conn. 1977), affirmed 631 F. 2d (2nd Cir. 1980).

55. M. Wilson, "Sexual Harassment and the Law," *The Community Psychologist* 21 (1988): 16–17.

56. Robertson et al., "Campus Harassment: Sexual Harassment Policies and Procedures at Institutions of Higher Learning," pp. 792–812.

57. American Council on Education, *Sexual Harassment on Campus: Suggestions for Reviewing Campus Policy and Educational Programs* (Washington, D.C.: American Council on Education, 1986).

58. American Association of University Professors, "Sexual Harassment: Suggested Policy and Procedures for Handling Complaints," *Academe* 69 (1983): 15a–16a.

59. See, e.g., J. B. Brandenburg, "Sexual Harassment in the University: Guidelines for Establishing a Grievance Procedure," *Signs: Journal of Women in Culture and Society* 8 (1982): 320–36, and Meek and Lynch, "Establishing an Informal Grievance Procedure for Cases of Sexual Harassment of Students," pp. 30–33.

60. M. P. Rowe, "Dealing with Sexual Harassment," *Harvard Business Review,* May–June 1981, pp. 42–46.

61. Kanter, *Men and Women of the Corporation.*

62. J. B. Miller, *Toward a New Psychology of Women* (Boston: Beacon Press, 1976), p. 127.

63. S. E. Merry and S. S. Silbey, "What Do Plaintiffs Want? Reexamining the Concept of Dispute," *Justice System Journal* 9 (1984): 151–78.

64. C. Gilligan, *In a Different Voice: Psychological Theory and Women's Development* (Cambridge, Mass.: Harvard University Press, 1982).

65. D. M. Kolb and G. G. Coolidge, *Her Place at the Table: A Consideration of Gender Issues in Negotiation* (Working Paper Series 88–5) (Cambridge, Mass.: Harvard Law School, Program on Negotiation, 1988).

66. Miller, *Toward a New Psychology of Women.*

67. See, e.g., M. T. Mednick, "On the Politics of Psychological Constructs: Stop the Bandwagon, I Want to Get Off," *American Psychologist* 44 (1989): 1118–23, for a summary of criticisms.

68. Robertson et al., "Campus Harassment: Sexual Harassment Policies and Procedures at Institutions of Higher Learning," pp. 792–812.

69. J. Rifkin, "Mediation from a Feminist Perspective: Promise and Problems," *Mediation* 2 (1984): 21–31.

70. Robertson et al., "Campus Harassment: Sexual Harassment Policies and Procedures at Institutions of Higher Learning," pp. 792–812.

71. Fain and Anderton, "Sexual Harassment: Organizational Context and Diffuse Status," pp. 291–311.

72. Robertson et al., "Campus Harassment: Sexual Harassment Policies and Procedures at Institutions of Higher Learning," pp. 792–812.

73. Robinson and Reid, "Sexual Intimacy in Psychology Revisited," pp. 512–20.

74. B. Sandler, personal communication, 1988.

75. Fain and Anderton, "Sexual Harassment: Organizational Context and Diffuse Status," pp. 291–311; LaFontaine and Tredeau, "The Frequency, Sources, and Correlates of Sexual Harassment among Women in Traditional Male Occupations," pp. 433–43; McIntyre and Renick, "Protecting Public Employees from Sexual Harassment," pp. 282–92.

76. Lott et al., "Sexual Assault and Harassment: A Campus Community Case Study," pp. 296–319, and Reilly, Lott, and Gallogly, "Sexual Harassment of University Students," pp. 333–58.

77. Lott et al., "Sexual Assault and Harassment: A Campus Community Case Study," p. 318.

78. Fitzgerald et al., "The Incidence and Dimensions of Sexual Harassment in Academia and the Workplace," pp. 152–75.

79. M. Brewer, "Further beyond Nine to Five: An Integration and Future Directions," *Journal of Social Issues* 38 (1982): 149–57.

80. Robertson et al., "Campus Harassment: Sexual Harassment Policies and Procedures at Institutions of Higher Learning," pp. 792–812.

81. Livingston, "Responses to Sexual Harassment on the Job," pp. 5–22.

82. D. E. Terpstra and S. E. Cook, "Complainant Characteristics and Reported Behaviors and Consequences Associated with Formal Sexual Harassment Charges," *Personnel Psychology* 38 (1985): 559–74.

83. Terpstra and Baker, "Outcome of Sexual Harassment Charges," pp. 185–94.

84. F. S. Coles, "Forced to Quit: Sexual Harassment Complaints and Agency Response," *Sex Roles* 14 (1986): 81–95.

85. M. S. Garvey, "The High Cost of Sexual Harassment Suits," *Labor Relations* 65 (1986): 75–79.

86. Livingston, "Responses to Sexual Harassment on the Job," pp. 5–22.

87. M. B. Brewer and R. A. Berk, "Beyond Nine to Five: Introduction," *Journal of Social Issues* 38 (1982): 1–4.

88. Adams et al., "Sexual Harassment of University Students," pp. 484–90, and Lott et al., "Sexual Assault and Harassment: A Campus Community Case Study," pp. 296–319.

89. A. McCormack, "The Sexual Harassment of Students by Teachers: The Case of Students in Science," *Sex Roles* 13 (1985): 21–32.

90. Cammaert, "How Widespread Is Sexual Harassment on Campus?" pp. 388–97; P. Crull, "The Stress Effects of Sexual Harassment on the Job," *American Journal of Orthopsychiatry* 52 (1982): 539–43; J. A. Hamilton et al., "The Emotional Consequences of Gender-Based Abuse in the Workplace: New Counseling Programs for Sex Discrimination," *Women and Therapy* 6 (1987): 46–65.

91. Coles, "Forced to Quit: Sexual Harassment Complaints and Agency Response," pp. 81–95.

92. Meek and Lynch, "Establishing an Informal Grievance Procedure for Cases of Sexual Harassment of Students," pp. 30–33.

93. Jensen and Gutek, "Attributions and Assignment of Responsibility in Sexual Harassment," pp. 121–36.

16

Perceptions of Sexual Harassment: A Reexamination of Gender Differences

Douglas D. Baker, David E. Terpstra,
and Bob D. Cutler

A number of researchers have begun to examine factors influencing the perception of sexual harassment.[1] One of the most common variables examined in these studies has been the gender of the respondents. Typically, the findings indicate that women perceive more types of behaviors to be sexual harassment than do men.[2] Presumably, these findings are due to different sex roles or the fact that women are more frequently the victims of harassment.

There has been at least one investigation, however, which indicates that these gender differences in perceptions of sexual harassment may be overstated. Terpstra and Baker[3] reported a study in which a sample of student women, student men, and working women indicated their perceptions of eighteen scenarios portraying examples of potential sexual harassment situations. Terpstra and Baker's findings indicated that the rank order of the incidents' severity was very similar for all three groups in the study and that there were few gender differences between student women's and student men's perceptions of the individuial scenarios. A higher percentage of the working women perceived four of the scenarios

From *The Journal of Psychology* 124, no. 4 (1990): 409–416. Reprinted with permission of the Helen Dwight Reid Educational Foundation. Published by Heldref Publications, 1319 Eighteenth Street, N.W., Washington, D.C. 20036–1802. Copyright © 1990.

to be sexual harassment, however. Thus, the perceptual differences that existed were between students and workers, not between women and men.

The perceptual differences found between the workers' and students' perceptions may have been affected by the respondents' personal and organizational backgrounds. For example, an academic setting, populated with individuals who are relatively young and predominantly single, may have a different code of conduct for interactions between women and men than is found in most work organizations. Because Terpstra and Baker used a relatively small sample of working women ($n = 48$), however, these differences must be interpreted with some caution. In addition, their findings are limited by the lack of a comparative sample of working men.

Terpstra and Baker's findings also may be related to their reliance on a student sample. The students' relative youth may have limited their contact with workplace harassment and its consequences. Such a restricted range of experiences, in turn, may have attenuated the students' perceptions of harassment's severity and consequences.

Another potential cause of the limited gender effects may be related to the amount and type of information contained in Terpstra and Baker's scenarios. Their instrument portrayed relatively specific situations. For example, one of their scenarios read: "Although Ms. X had indicated that she was not interested, Mr. Y persisted in propositioning her. Mr. Y had indicated that her job status might be enhanced if she would have an affair with him." Such a description is relatively unambiguous about the gender of the parties involved and the characteristics of the situation, factors that are important to its interpretation.[4]

In contrast, some of the previous studies examining perceptual differences asked less specific questions that provided limited contextual information. For example, one of the questions used by Gutek et al.[5] was: "Would you consider verbal comments and remarks of a sexual nature that were perceived to be positive as sexual harassment?" Similarly, Popovich et al.[6] asked student subjects if it was harassment if a supervisor or co-worker "makes sexual remarks" or "tells sexual jokes." Potentially, these more general types of questions result in greater ambiguity, which in turn may lead to greater gender differences in the responses. Support for this argument is suggested by the findings of Gutek[7] and Gutek et al.,[8] whose studies indicated that men tend to interpret ambiguous social-sexual cues more positively than do women. Thus, the previously reported gender differences in perceptions of sexual harassment may have been overstated because of the general nature of the questions that researchers used.

One purpose of the present study was to clarify the conflicting evidence on the effects of gender on perceptions of sexual harassment. A second goal was to compare the sexual harassment perceptions of students and workers to determine whether previous differences could be replicated with a larger and more diverse sample of workers. We gave the Terpstra and Baker questionnaire to a sample of working women and working men and compared our results to those of the earlier study.

METHOD

Subjects and Procedure

A questionnaire was distributed by state personnel officers to 800 employees of a state government in the western United States. Five departments were surveyed: Highways, Administration, Natural Resources, Social and Rehabilitation Services, and Institutions. Sampling was stratified on a departmental basis, and personnel officers were instructed to distribute the questionnaires to equal numbers of men and women. The questionnaires were voluntarily completed and returned to state personnel offices without respondent identification. They were then forwarded to us for analysis.

Four hundred sixteen questionnaires were returned, a response rate of 52 percent. Missing data reduced the usable number of questionnaires to 409. The final sample was composed of 59 percent women and 41 percent men, indicating that women had a slightly higher response rate. The average age of the respondents was 38.6 years, and they possessed an average of 15.8 years of work experience. Ninety-eight percent had at least a high school education, 31 percent also held bachelors degrees, and 10 percent held graduate degrees.

Instrument

The survey instrument contained demographic questions on age, gender, marital status, and education, as well as the eighteen situational scenarios of Terpstra and Baker's hierarchy of sexual harassment questionnaire. For each of the eighteen scenarios, subjects were asked to indicate whether or not they personally considered the depicted incident to be sexual harassment. Terpstra and Baker developed the eighteen situational incidents from cases and examples of sexual harassment published in the *Fair Employment Practices Guidelines*.[9] The incidents were selected to represent the spectrum of major types of sexual harassment. The eighteen incidents were randomly ordered in the survey instrument and standardized as to length and format to limit extraneous cues.

Results . . .

A summary of the percentage of workers and students perceiving each scenario to be sexual harassment is illustrated in Figure 1. On the horizontal axis of the figure are the eighteen scenarios, rank ordered from most to least harassing on the basis of Terpstra and Baker's findings for student subjects. The vertical axis represents the percentage of subjects perceiving each incident to be sexual harassment. Consistent with the regression analysis, the figure indicates that workers and students similarly ordered the severity of the scenarios. Workers, however, perceived a slightly higher proportion of the incidents to be harassment (63.3 percent) than did the students (58.3 percent). . . . In particular, workers perceived a higher percentage of the less severe scenarios (Incidents 9 to 18) to be sexual harassment.

DISCUSSION

The sexual harassment perceptions of working women and working men were very similar. Both their relative ordering of the incidents' severity and their perceptions of each specific scenario indicated a high degree of agreement. A number of factors may have led to this lack of gender differences. First, the responses of the current sample may reflect a change in general societal perceptions regarding sexual harassment; such a shift in opinions may reflect the increasing percentage of women in the workforce or the high level of media attention sexual harassment has received in recent years. This argument may be somewhat questionable, however, given the similar lack of gender differences found by Terpstra and Baker with their student sample.

A second potential explanation is related to the specificity of the scenarios portrayed in Terpstra and Baker's survey instrument. Their scenarios provide information about the actors' gender and the type of behavior that occurred. Such scenarios may decrease ambiguity, resulting in a more reliable measurement of perceptual differences between women and men. As Gutek[10] noted, men tend to see the ambiguous social-sexual situations more positively than do women. Thus, the gender differences reported by previous researchers may have been inflated by artifacts of the instruments employed. Similarly, Hyde[11] argued that there are rela-

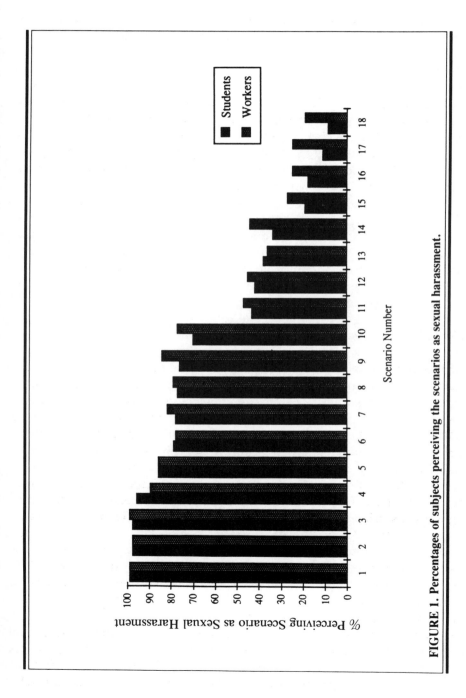

FIGURE 1. Percentages of subjects perceiving the scenarios as sexual harassment.

tively few cognitive gender differences and those that have been reported are overstated because of the methods and statistics used to analyze the data.

We also found significant agreement between the current sample of workers and Terpstra and Baker's student sample as to the order of the scenarios' relative severity. A higher percentage of the workers perceived some of the less severe incidents to be sexual harassment than did the students, however.

Several factors may have led to these differences in perceptions. First, there may have been a cohort effect influencing both students' and workers' sex role norms. Each group learned norms for social-sexual behavior at different times and under different social conditions.[12] A second potential cause of the perceptual differences between the workers and the students may relate to the differing organizational norms for social-sexual behaviors that existed in the university and state bureaucracy at the time the questionnaires were administered. Universities, which are populated by young individuals who are single and very socially active, may have codes of conduct that are more accepting of sexually oriented behaviors (e.g., requesting dates). Furthermore, students have probably experienced less harassment simply because of their relative youth and limited work experience. As they grow older, come into contact with harassing situations, and experience the negative outcomes of such behavior, their perceptions may change to more closely match those of the current worker sample.[13]

The findings of the current study indicate that the major differences in perceptions of sexual harassment may occur between individuals with different organizational backgrounds. Thus, individuals new to an organization may have different perceptions of appropriate social-sexual behaviors than do individuals who have been with the organization for many years. Organizations may want to focus a portion of their training programs for new employees on sexual harassment issues to help clarify differences in perceptions and forestall problems of sexual harassment. Such problems, if not dealt with, can lead to a loss of productivity, decreased worker satisfaction, turnover, and legal penalties.[14]

NOTES

1. E.g., E. G. C. Collins and T. B. Blodgett, "Sexual Harassment: Some See It . . . Some Won't," *Harvard Business Review* 59 (1981): 76–95; B. A. Gutek et al., "Sexuality and the Workplace," *Basic and Applied Social Psychology* 1 (1980): 255–65; G. N. Powell, "Definitions of Sexual Harassment and Sexual

Attention Experienced," *Journal of Psychology* 113 (1983): 113–17; G. N. Powell et al., "Sexual Harassment as Defined by Working Women," paper presented at the 41st Annual Meeting of the Academy of Management, San Diego, Calif., August 1981; T. Reilly et al., "The Factorial Survey: An Approach to Defining Sexual Harassment on Campus," *Journal of Social Issues* 38 (1982): 99–110; E. Weber-Burdin and P. H. Rossi, "Defining Sexual Harassment on Campus: A Replication and Extension," *Journal of Social Issues* 38 (1982): 111–19.

2. B. A. Gutek, *Sex and the Workplace* (San Francisco: Jossey-Bass, 1985).

3. D. E. Terpstra and D. D. Baker, "A Hierarchy of Sexual Harassment," *Journal of Psychology* 121 (1987): 599–605.

4. B. A. Gutek, B. Marasch, and A. G. Cohen, "Interpreting Social-Sexual Behavior in a Work Setting," *Journal of Vocational Behavior* 22 (1983): 30–48.

5. Gutek et al., "Sexuality and the Workplace," pp. 255–65.

6. P. M. Popovich et al., "Assessing the Incidence and Perceptions of Sexual Harassment Behaviors among American Undergraduates," *Journal of Psychology* 120 (1986): 387–96.

7. Gutek, *Sex and the Workplace.*

8. Gutek et al., "Sexuality and the Workplace," pp. 255–65.

9. *Fair Employment Practices Guidelines* (Waterford, Conn.: Bureau of Business Practices, 1978–1982).

10. Gutek, *Sex and the Workplace.*

11. J. S. Hyde, "How Large Are Cognitive Gender Differences?" *American Psychologist* 36 (1981): 892–901.

12. K. O. Mason, J. Czajka, and S. Arber, "Changes in U.S. Women's Sex-Role Attitudes, 1954–1974," *American Sociological Review* 41 (1976): 573–96, and K. F. Slevin and C. R. Wingrove, "Similarities and Differences among Three Generations of Women in Attitudes Toward the Female Role in Contemporary Society," *Sex Roles* 9 (1983): 609–24.

13. A. Konrad and B. A. Gutek, "Impact of Work Experiences on Attitudes toward Sexual Harassment," *Administrative Science Quarterly* 31 (1986): 422–38.

14. D. E. Terpstra and D. D. Baker, "Predictors of Sexual Harassment Case Settlements," *Academy of Management Journal* 31 (1988): 185–94.

17

Talking Dirty

The Editors, *The New Republic*

For all its luridness, absurdity, and brutality, the television trial of Clarence Thomas had at least one laudable side effect. It raised the public's awareness of sexual harassment in the workplace, and may even serve to discourage it in the future. As senators not previously known for their concern about women fell over each other to show their sensitivity to the nuances of sexual harassment, men around the country wondered whether they might be guilty of inappropriate conduct themselves. But by also revealing the elasticity of the legal definition of sexual harassment, the hearings could have another effect as well. They could ultimately cause harassment charges to be taken less seriously. Because the legal definition includes any unwanted "verbal conduct" that contributes to an "intimidating, hostile, or offensive working environment," it may lead to an outpouring of charges based less upon legitimate claims of harm than upon an increasingly powerful impulse to censor speech merely because it is offensive.

Invented in the 1970s by the feminist legal theorist Catharine MacKinnon, and endorsed in 1986 by the Supreme Court, the "hostile environment" test threatens to trivialize legitimate claims of sexual harassment by equating sexual assaults with pin-up calendars, and by diverting attention from genuine, harmful sex discrimination. It represents a radical new exception to the First Amendment axiom that speech cannot be punished just because it is offensive. Like restrictions on "hate speech," it punishes expression where it should punish harm. This would present a dilemma for civil libertarians if there weren't any other way to protect victims of real harassment. But there is.

The Civil Rights Act of 1964 says nothing about sexual harassment, and before the 1970s, courts dismissed the idea that offensive words—without physical, psychological, or economic harm—could add up to sex discrimination under Title VII. But in 1980, influenced by Professor MacKinnon's arguments, the Equal Employment Opportunity Commission adopted three tests for deciding whether "unwelcome verbal or physical conduct" violates the Civil Rights Act: first, is it "quid pro quo" behavior that makes submission to sex an implicit or explicit condition of advancement? Second, is it behavior that "unreasonably interferes with an individual's job performance"? And third, is it behavior that creates an "intimidating, hostile, or offensive working environment"?

We have no problems with the first two tests. But the third one is another matter. It relies heavily on the ambiguous term "verbal conduct," obscuring the most important distinction in First Amendment doctrine, which insists that the line between speech and conduct be drawn as precisely as possible. And in upholding the test, the Supreme Court never explained why unpleasant speech that *didn't* interfere with job performance could be regulated in any way. The ambiguous test then became unintelligible. Courts decided that legality of speech would depend, in retrospect, on whether a "reasonable woman" would have found that it created an "intimidating, hostile, or offensive" environment. This turns the First Amendment on its head. The Supreme Court has traditionally protected offensive speech because "one man's vulgarity is another man's lyric." Under the new rules, speech can be banned whenever one man's lyric becomes a reasonable woman's vulgarity. The fact that men and women often find different things funny (not to mention the fact that women themselves find different things funny) makes the "reasonable woman" standard even more perverse.

To prove the point, a federal appeals court found last January [1991] that even "well-intentioned compliments" from officemates can count as sexual harassment. An IRS agent in San Mateo, California, asked a fellow agent out to lunch twice, and after she declined, he declared his love in a poignant note praising her "style and elan," but promising to leave her alone if she asked. She sued and—because the court found that a "reasonable woman" would have found the note unwelcome—won. Days later a Florida district judge ordered the owner of a shipyard to stop his male welders from displaying pin-up calendars and telling dirty jokes. His logic:

"[B]anning sexist speech in the workplace does not censor such speech everywhere and for all time."

These cases are disturbing on two levels. First, they suggest that harassment claims tend to be trivial or imagined, when clearly most of them are not. It is impossible to wade through sexual harassment cases without being shocked by the sordidness—and the extent—of the abuse that many women experience at work. The scatology that runs throughout the opinions would make Long Dong Silver blush. But if men are enjoined by courts from writing unwanted love letters, they will find it much harder to take real harassment seriously.

Second, it's scary to suggest that the rights of expression (including the right to ask for dates) should be less protected at work than at home. Work is where most Americans spend most of their waking hours; they must be free to express themselves verbally without fear of prosecution. Professor MacKinnon is correct when she argues that the logic of the "hostile environment" exception cannot be limited to the workplace, which is why it should apply neither in the office nor outside of it.

The solution to this mess is a definition of sexual harassment that excludes verbal harassment that has no other effect on its recipient than to create an unpleasant working environment. Sexual harassment, as the ACLU [American Civil Liberties Union] argues, should be limited to expression that is directed at a specific employee and that "demonstrably hinders or completely prevents his or her continuing to function as an employee." This would refine the existing test for "unreasonable interference." Either version would cover legitimate claims. As a 1989 note in the *Yale Law Journal* points out, *all* women who have successfully sued their supervisors (not their co-workers) for creating a "hostile environment" have also suffered some tangible economic harm, such as being fired. Dropping the hostile environment standard wouldn't permit real harassment by co-workers either. Even though it rarely presents an economic threat, such assaults often interfere with job performance. The law against sexual harassment would be strengthened, not weakened.

Assume, for example, that Anita Hill's charges are true. She would not need a "hostile environment" test to make her case. She might have trouble proving "quid pro quo" harassment, which occurs, according to the EEOC [Equal Employment Opportunity Commission], when submission to (or rejection of) sexual advances is used as the basis for employment decisions. She concedes that her refusal to date Mr. Thomas and to watch bestiality videos didn't stop her from being promoted on schedule. Ms. Hill could argue, however, that Mr. Thomas's advances "unreasonably interfered" with her job performance. She was sent to the hospital with nervous cramps, told her friends she had become depressed, and eventually left the EEOC because she felt unable to continue. The judge in her case would still have to make a difficult, subjective decision about how much the harassment had interfered with her job, and how much interference is "reasonable." But these are the kinds of murky decisions that judges make every day, and they are far more appropriate than decisions about what a reasonable woman would find offensive.

What would be excluded from the legal definition of sexual harassment if the "hostile environment" test were abandoned? Only sexual expression that is offensive but that has no detectable effect on job performance. That would include most pin-up calendars, most well-intentioned compliments, and even some gross remarks. But trivial complaints like these are unusual. Sexual harassment lawyers say that cases of verbal harassment where the woman cannot prove physical or psychological damage are rarely successful in court, even under the "hostile environment" test.

Abandoning the "hostile environment" test is in the best interest of feminists as well as civil libertarians. The only realistic way to narrow the gap between what reasonable women and men perceive as harassment is to persuade men that unwanted advances can hurt women in tangible ways. A definition of harassment that diverts attention from that question makes relief for women all the more remote.

18

Pluralist Myths and Powerless Men: The Ideology of Reasonableness in Sexual Harassment Law

Nancy S. Ehrenreich

.   .   .

I. INDIVIDUALISM, PLURALISM, AND REASONABLENESS . . .

Reasonableness in Anti-Discrimination Law

In the sexual harassment context—specifically, in hostile environment cases—the reasonable person standard serves . . . [the] function of identifying regulable behavior. Under Title VII, conduct that unreasonably interferes with the plaintiff's ability to work constitutes prohibited discrimination.[1] For this reason, a discussion of the role of the reasonableness test in sexual harassment law necessarily devolves into a discussion of the role of the concept of discrimination in anti-discrimination law more generally. . . .

Two Sides of the Traditional Model of Discrimination

In the following sections, I will discuss the concept of discrimination as it is traditionally understood in American ideology.[2] . . . [T]hat model,

Reprinted by permission of The Yale Law Journal Company and Fred B. Rothman & Company from *The Yale Law Journal* 99, no. 6 (April 1990): 1177–1234.

which has dominated judicial decisions for decades, considers actions based on factors such as race or sex to be presumptively illegitimate. Although the model is primarily concerned with protecting the interests of the individual, I will argue here that it also expresses a commitment to group-based pluralism—to a society which preserves the diversity of social groups, and a government that gives no group preferential treatment. It is this latter, group-based dimension of the traditional concept of discrimination that will be the focus of my concern here.

Protecting the Individual

It has often been noted that the traditional model of discrimination, sometimes called the equality of opportunity model, focuses on the individual rather than the group. Concerned with protecting the individual from treatment based on group stereotypes, it views the role of the law as assuring that all people are judged on their own merits, free from consideration of their group affiliations. The assumption is that once society is freed of group-based bias, each individual's progress in the world will reflect nothing more or less than her own abilities and effort.

Protecting the Group

In contrast to the individual-oriented notion of rewarding personal merit is the other side of the traditional model—a concern with protecting groups and perpetuating cultural and political diversity. I will call this concern the pluralist view of discrimination.

The fact that an allegation of membership in a protected group is a prerequisite to a successful discrimination claim under both Title VII and the equal protection clause suggests that the preservation of groups has always been one concern underlying anti-discrimination efforts. If protecting individuals from irrational prejudice were the only purpose that such efforts were designed to serve, then someone fired because of the length of his hair or the manner in which he dressed would have a viable claim of discrimination. The fact that claims do not succeed (unless the trait possessed can be proven to be a proxy for some forbidden category) suggests that American ideology sees something particularly pernicious about discrimination that affects certain groups.

Of course, the concern with protecting groups would still reflect an ultimately individualist purpose. That is, it could reflect a desire to protect individual members of such groups from the loss of self-esteem produced by an awareeess of both the discrimination experienced by others in the group (because of their group membership) and the general low status of the group itself. However, I would suggest that this concern also reflects a pluralist purpose of maintaining the diversity of American society, as well as a conviction that government, in attempting to accomplish that purpose, must avoid favoring one group over another. . . .

It should be apparent at this point that the concern with group protection represented in this pluralist view of discrimination is somewhat different from the group focus found in the "quality of result" model of discrimination that is often advocated in the scholarly literature. Under the latter model, which has not been widely followed by the courts, the concern is neither with protecting individuals for specific acts of discrimination (although it would bar such acts) nor with assuring the neutral governmental treatment of groups themselves, but rather with eliminating the conditions of inequality under which groups exist. In contrast, the traditional ideology lacks this concern with assuring equality of results and does not conceive of discrimination as the perpetuation of structures of inequality.

To better understand the pluralist view of discrimination—to understand why a positive value would attach to the idea of preserving groups per se, why judicial neutrality would seem to be required to attain such preservation, and how such neutrality could nevertheless still be thought of as an effective tool for the elimination of inequality—it will be helpful to describe briefly the ideology of political and cultural pluralism underlying that view.

Pluralist Ideology

Pluralism is based on the assumption that the success of a democratic society depends upon its ability to sustain a relativistic culture—one "that denie[s] absolute truths, remain[s] intellectually flexible and critical, value[s] diversity, and [draws] strength from innumerable competing subgroups.[3] Under this view, pluralistic tolerance of diversity protects a nation from the absolutist ideas that lead to totalitarianism. Rather than being viewed as a dangerous, nihilistic belief system that prevents us from judging others, cultural relativism is seen as a positive good, a guaranty of democracy.

Furthermore, in pluralist ideology, not only is tolerance of groups necessary to democracy, but diversity *itself* improves the success of a democratic society. The existence of a variety of competing viewpoints works as a set of social checks and balances, preventing any one perspective from gaining dominance, and thereby curbing any tendencies toward absolutist thought and totalitarian government. Just as the marketplace of ideas in the social arena and voluntary competition in the economic realm are equated with (and thought to guarantee) individual freedom in liberal individualist thought, so the unencumbered interplay of different perspectives and the competing demands of different interest groups are associated with democracy in pluralist thought.

Finally, cultural relativism is not solely thought of as a prescriptive ideal; it is also seen as a descriptive reality—as an accurate depiction of existing American society. What holds the widely diverse American population together, it is thought, is a universally held pluralism, a spirit of open-minded debate and tolerance for diversity that crosses all ethnic boundaries. . . . The heterogeneity of the population poses the possibility of conflict among groups (just as self-interestedness potentially produces conflict among individuals in the individualist vision), but an overarching culture (and practice) of pluralism mediates that conflict within the private sphere (just as economic competition and growth do in the other model).

The role of government, therefore, is to refrain from interfering in the private world of interest-group politics, unless someone uses illegitimate tactics to undermine a group's ability to participate, thereby threatening the public interest. Instances justifying intervention are thought to be the exception rather than the rule, not only because the democratic culture makes intolerant conduct rare, but also because the potential of state power to transform a particular viewpoint into a totalitarian creed means that government itself probably poses the greatest threat to democracy. Thus, it is seen as essential that the government take a relativistic stance to different groups in society, in order to preserve the heterogeneous private sphere that is needed to curb dangerous state power.

For the courts, this relativism translates into neutrality, a refusal to ground judicial decisions on personal preferences for particular perspectives or political judgments about the importance of certain group interests. Only by remaining neutral in the struggle among interest groups can the courts preserve the cultural and political pluralism that is the essence of democracy.

Reasonableness in the Pluralist Vision of Anti-Discrimination Law . . .

The Public/Private Dichotomy

Anti-discrimination law can be seen as (at least in part) an exercise of government power to regulate the world of interest group pluralism, eliminating both the coercive use of group power and the illegitimate reliance upon group stereotypes that, by disadvantaging the members of the stereotyped groups, impair those groups' abilities to engage in the open dialogue and competitive pursuit for self-interest necessary to democracy. Title VII, for example, is designed to secure equal employment opportunity for women and other groups by prohibiting discrimination against them by private employers. In so doing, it assures their effective participation in both the economic and the political realms, thereby furthering not only their interest in equality but the general societal interest in pluralistic democracy (not to mention productivity) as well.

Reasonableness as Mediator

The role of the courts in this scheme . . . is to determine when conduct has gone beyond the exercise of private freedom and thus imperils the public interest in democratic pluralism. By exerting a counter-majoritarian influence, the judiciary is supposed to prevent the tyranny of the majority (or of a minority) that would ultimately threaten the liberty interests of all. But again, in regulating the private sphere it must act neutrally, so that its decisions will not represent merely a delegation of state power to one group or another. Thus, courts should base their decisions on the principle of tolerance for diversity and a concern for the protection of minorities, rather than on the substantive content of the views or needs of different groups.

Here . . . the central contradiction between individual liberty and collective security that the courts are supposed to resolve is articulated through groups, not individuals. Thus, in the pluralist view of discrimination, the individual's interests are not of particular concern; rather, it is the contradiction between the liberty and security interests of groups that the legal doctrine must mediate.

And . . . doctrinal terms like reasonableness and discrimination are recognized to be indeterminate. Given that indeterminacy, they should be defined (so the argument goes) to implement policy decisions about what types of group-based interests should be protected. The role of the courts, then, is again seen as one of linedrawing—identifying a point along a continuum of conduct that separates (prohibited) discrimination from (protected) freedom—and judges are again supposed to perform this task neutrally, deriving the policies that they implement from other, politically legitimate sources.

It is for these reasons that the test for hostile environmental sexual harassment can be phrased as that which violates societal norms about how people should be treated in the workplace (and, implicitly, how groups should be treated in society). Here . . . the private world of free cultural expression by groups that the courts are seeking to protect is itself seen as providing the solution to the problem of government neutrality. After all, if pluralism both relies upon and reproduces a culture of democracy— a moral consensus voluntarily arrived at and untainted by governmental power—then that culture can provide the neutral standard with which the government can determine when intervention is necessary.

. . . [W]hat constitutes reasonable behavior is recognized to be a political question of where to draw the line between group and social interests—that is, between diversity and conformity—and it is society, not the court, that makes that judgment. Thus, it is not so much that the reasonableness test is itself a neutral standard, but rather that it serves as a vehicle for importing an already-arrived-at (and legitimate) political solution into the law.

In summary . . ., the reasonableness standard, . . . in sexual harassment law, supposedly serves as a mechanism with which courts can distinguish protected exercises of freedom from regulable interferences with collective security. Furthermore, it is thought to allow courts to draw that line neutrally, by basing their decision on a neutral principle (efficiency, tolerance for diversity) or on a preexisting policy preference arrived at through freely willed interactions in the private sphere (societal consensus). However, as my discussion of the *Rabidue* case will illustrate, the reasonable person standard in operation merely contains and suppresses the contradiction between diversity and conformity, rather than overcoming it.

II. *RABIDUE* V. *OSCEOLA REFINING COMPANY*: REASONABLENESS IN THE SEXUAL HARASSMENT CONTEXT

This Part examines the role that the reasonable person standard plays in the specific doctrinal context of sexual harassment law. It does so through a close reading of a recent sexual harassment case that applies the reasonable person standard. Before turning to that discussion, however, two points deserve mention. First, in focusing my analysis on one case, I am treating the judicial opinions that comprise that case as a cultural text. That is, I am assuming that the analyses engaged in by the judges were informed by culturally based notions that can be discovered through a careful reading of those opinions. In addition, I am assuming that an exploration of those notions in the context of a particular judicial decision can not only increase one's understanding of that decision but also contribute insights that might be more broadly applicable to other cases and legal contexts. In addition, such an exploration can yield an understanding of law's role in reproducing culture, for the subtle messages residing in a judicial opinion not only reflect existing ideology, but also reinforce, legitimate, and transform it.

Second, in the following discussion I take as given certain things that others might be inclined to debate. Thus, I assume not only that contemporary society is characterized by systematic and significant inequalities —between women and men, lower and upper classes, people of color and whites, etc.—but also that how one perceives a particular social situation or interaction, such as an alleged act of harassment, will be a function both of one's personal psychological makeup and of social factors, such as one's race, sex, class, etc. Thus, while I do not mean to suggest that all women or men think the same way,[4] I do believe that the formidable differences in the material conditions and socialization processes that women and men face will tend to produce broad commonalities of perspective within each sex. (Differences of class, race, sexual orientation and the like, as well as personality factors, will of course cut across and dilute the sex-based similarities.)

Given these assumptions, it should be clear that I would not want to suggest that I am approaching the issue of sexual harassment "objectively." Rather, I believe that anyone dealing with this (or any other) issue will bring to it a particularized perspective, so that a "neutral" assessment is simply not possible. I come to the issue of sexual harassment as a white, upper-middle class woman, and as a feminist—as one who believes both that women are subordinated to men in our society and that the law should be directed towards rectifying that imbalance. I also believe that some men who engage in (what I would call) harassing behavior do so with neither conscious hostility towards women nor an awareness of the effect of their conduct, and I have no doubt that such men would feel personally wronged by judgments declaring their conduct harassment. (Other men, of course, are perfectly aware of what they are doing.) Nevertheless, I am convinced, as will become clear below, that while the elimination of inequality in society inevitably makes some people feel wronged—entailing, as it does, a reduction in the social status and privilege of those on the top of the hierarchy, regardless of whether they harbor personal hostility toward those beneath them—that fact does not justify its perpetuation.

The Case in Brief

Vivienne Rabidue was an administrative assistant at Osceola Refining Company—the sole woman in a salaried management position in the company.[5] After her discharge in 1977, she filed a sexual harassment claim against her employer,[6] charging that its refusal to stop the display of pornographic posters in private offices and common work areas at the company plant, as well as the stream of anti-female obscenities directed at her and other women by a co-worker in another department,[7] constituted sex discrimination in violation of Title VII. She also introduced evidence that she had been denied various managerial privileges accorded to male employees (free lunches and gasoline, entertainment privileges, etc.) and in other ways had been given secondary status in the company.[8]

The conduct of which Rabidue complained was hardly mild or ambiguous. One of the posters displayed at the plant depicted a prone woman with a golf ball on her breasts, straddled by a man holding a golf club and yelling, "Fore."[9] The comments that her co-worker, Douglas Henry, directed at her and her fellow female workers included such epithets as "whores," "cunt," "pussy," "tits," and "fat ass."[10] Henry once remarked of the plaintiff: "All that bitch needs is a good lay."[11] He also engaged in generally uncooperative behavior that impaired Rabidue's ability to perform her job effectively.[12]

Judge Krupansky, writing for the majority of the court and applying the reasonableness standard traditionally used in hostile work environment cases,[13] held that the conduct complained of had not unreasonably interfered with Rabidue's ability to work. The court characterized that conduct as a legitimate expression of the cultural norms of workers at the employer's plant and suggested that the prevailing depictions of women in the media indicated that such conduct was not unreasonably offensive in any case. In so doing, the majority treated its solution as promoting pluralism and neutrally reflecting preexisting norms. In dissent, Judge Keith advocated the use of a reasonable woman (or reasonable victim) standard, rejecting the majority's approach as enforcing an essentially male viewpoint under the guise of universality.

The majority relied upon three distinct arguments in concluding that the conduct at Osceola had not been unreasonably offensive: (1) the plaintiff had "voluntarily" and knowingly entered the Osceola workplace and therefore could not complain about the conditions she encountered there;[14] (2) the court should not interpret Title VII as mandating that it transform working class culture, and therefore should not interfere with the Osceola environment (and, implicitly, such noninterference did not constitute discrimination against women because the plaintiff was merely an overly sensitive, aberrational individual);[15] and (3) the Osceola environment was not unreasonably offensive in any case because it was no different from the rest of society.[16] The court presented each of these arguments as a neutral ground for its decision—as a vehicle for distinguishing between legitimate individual or group freedom and illegitimate discrimination. However, as the discussion below will demonstrate, each argument ultimately fails at this enterprise, for each ignores or minimizes the conflict between men's and women's viewpoints that the case presented and thus only "solves" the problem by avoiding it.

Reasonableness as Meditator: The Messages Conveyed by the Majority Opinion . . .

There are at least two ways to understand the social interaction with which the court grappled in the *Rabidue* case. One way is to see it as posing a fundamental conflict between two unequal groups—men and women—about how they should relate to each other in the workplace, with women saying they should be allowed to be free from (and define) demeaning treatment and men saying they should not. Under such a reading, the court would seem to be faced with no choice but to make a value-laden decision about which group's approach was preferable. Moreover, its rejection of the plaintiff's claim could seem to be nothing more than judicial enforcement of a powerful group's subordination of the less powerful.

It is also possible, however, to see the case as not involving a conflict between men and women at all. This second vision is the vision that Judge Krupansky's opinion relies upon (and creates). In this section, I examine the rhetorical messages through which such a vision of the case is conveyed. As the discussion will demonstrate, the combined effect of the three aspects of the majority opinion addressed here—its "privatization" of the plaintiff, its recasting of the group conflict in the case, and its equation of reasonableness with consensus—is to make it seem as if Vivienne Rabidue, not Douglas Henry or Osceola Refining Company, was attempting to engage in discrimination, and as if workers and their employers, not women, need the protection of the court.

"Privatization" of the Plaintiff: Erasing Group Conflict

Both by describing the plaintiff as an atypical woman and by suggesting that her situation was the product of her own personal choice, the majority opinion conveyed the impression that Vivienne Rabidue's complaint represented a personal, individual claim. Because such a depiction effectively eliminated the plaintiff's group identity (she became an unreasonable, idiosyncratic woman, not a reasonable, typical one), I call it "privatization." This erasing of Rabidue's group membership both allowed the court to avoid visualizing the case as a conflict between men and women, and undermined the legitimacy of the plaintiff's claim by making it seem not to implicate pluralism concerns (since she did not represent the interests of women as a group). Moreover, it legitimated the role of the court in the case, obscuring the value judgments inherent in its application of the "voluntariness" label by making that application seem to be an objective determination of fact.

The "Abrasiveness" and Oversensitivity of the Plaintiff

The majority's description of the *Rabidue* situation presented the plaintiff as an overly sensitive, obnoxious woman,[17] incapable of getting along with others,[18] and trivialized the conduct to which she was subjected.[19] Through emphasizing the plaintiff's "abrasiveness" and minimizing the harmfulness of the harasser's conduct, the court subtly suggested that something was wrong with Rabidue for having been offended by Henry's behavior. Depicting the case as a situation in which an abnormally sensitive and difficult individual sought to label as sexist what was merely harmless joking, the court reduced Rabidue's complaint from a serious charge of sex discrimination that raised questions of public power[20] and group hierarchy to merely the peevish protest of an unreasonably oversensitive woman.

Her Private "Choice" to Enter the Workplace

The majority opinion further privatized Rabidue's claim through emphasizing her "voluntary" entry into the workplace. Stating that the factors to be considered in a hostile environment case include "the lexicon of obscenity that pervaded the environment of the workplace both before and after the plaintiff's introduction into its environs, [and] the reasonable expectation of the plaintiff upon voluntarily entering that environment,"[21] Judge Krupansky seemed to suggest that the plaintiff could have avoided the situation had she so desired. In concluding that Vivienne Rabidue essentially had assumed the risk of harassment,[22] the court ignored the possibility that her situation was the product of structural inequities in society that she was powerless to overcome. Treating her situation as the product of individual choice, rather than an instance of group-based discrimination, the court effectively erased Rabidue's group identity, making her seem to be responsible for her own mistreatment.

Moreover, by accepting the trial court's reliance on the "fact" that Rabidue had voluntarily entered the workplace, the court obscured the value choices that such a conclusion required. . . . Judge Krupansky's conclusion that Rabidue "voluntarily" submitted to Henry's verbal abuse is subject to the same criticism. The judge's effort to use private, individual "choice" as his neutral benchmark necessarily assumes that all such choices are themselves freely arrived at—that is, that they are the product of (protected) freedom rather than of (regulable) coercion.

But to decide whether Rabidue's choice was "voluntary," one must decide whether to consider the impact on that choice of current social arrangements—arrangements that severely limit the number and nature of economic opportunities open to women as well as constrain their ability to affect the conditions under which they work. Given current economic realities, Judge Krupansky's conclusion that women can choose between, on the one hand, accepting workplaces where the derogation of women is taken to be humor (my characterization, not his) and, on the other hand, working elsewhere constitutes a decision that women must accept domination by men in order to achieve equal economic opportunity. It "locks the vast majority of working women into workplaces which tolerate anti-female behavior."[23]

Thus, the court's reliance on choice is circular, for it assumes that choice is a preexisting "thing" in the world that can simply be "identified" by a judge and thus ignores the fact that the definition of that term is itself a subject of controversy between groups. Given that conflict, the court's ruling necessarily reflects a political decision—a decision that the freedom of employers and male workers is more important than the security of women faced with unwelcome and demeaning treatment (or, if they leave work, unemployment). . . .

Tolerance and Consensus as Neutral Grounds for Decision: Minimizing the Choice Between Groups

Although at one level, as described above, the majority opinion in *Rabidue* seems to deny the plaintiff's group status altogether, at another level the court implicitly acknowledges that the case requires a choice between two groups, simultaneously minimizing its own role in making that choice. The act of choice is minimized through the court's reliance upon two seemingly neutral grounds for choosing between groups: the principle of tolerance for diversity and the concept of societal consensus.

Tolerance for Diversity: Protecting Minorities as a Neutral Policy

The *Rabidue* court grounded its conclusion about the reasonableness of the behavior at Osceola in the principle of tolerance for diversity, depicting its ruling as a prudent refusal to intrude into private sphere group relations on the side of a powerful group. In refusing to find the conduct engaged in at Osceola unreasonable, the court quoted with approval the following passage from the trial court's opinion:

> [I]t cannot seriously be disputed that in some work environments, humor and language are rough hewn and vulgar. Sexual jokes, sexual conversations and girlie magazines may abound. Title VII was not meant to—or can [sic]—change this. It must never be forgotten that Title VII is the federal court mainstay in the struggle for equal employment opportunity for the female workers of America. But it is quite different to claim that Title VII was designed to bring about a magical transformation in the social mores of American workers.[24]

The court thus portrayed the defendant's employees as members of a prototypically American social class ("American workers") with their own distinct "social mores" deserving of protection. In so doing, it presented its decision to allow Henry's conduct as a refusal to enter the private sphere in order to impose one group's views on another. By emphasizing Henry's group identity, the court precluded a conclusion that he was a deviant individual engaging in bad acts, and transformed the case into one of group conflict in which the court could properly refuse to interfere.

In addition, the court's association of Henry's conduct with the working class (and its ignoring of his sex) conveyed the impression that its decision worked to the benefit of a low-status, relatively powerless group. Had the court presented the plaintiff's claim as challenging *men's* right to express their "mores," it would of course have highlighted the fact that those mores were being expressed to the disadvantage of women. In short, it would have drawn attention to the plaintiff's membership in a less powerful group. In contrast, the majority's representation of the case as one of socioeconomic rather than sex discrimination (a vision that was supported by its privatization of Vivienne Rabidue) made its decision seem to be a defense of the weak against the powerful, a refusal to delegate state power to private forces of domination. Thus, by redrawing the group lines in the case, Judge Krupansky's opinion reinforced the impression that the court's inaction served to preserve the pluralism of the private sphere, protecting a minority rather than enforcing one group's domination of the other.

Moreover, the majority's redrawing of those group lines obscured the choices that underlay its ruling. That ruling clearly entailed political judgments, not only about the relative importance of elite and worker values (assuming for the moment that the court's attribution of views to these two groups was accurate), but also—given that the only workers whom the opinion's "class" analysis favored anyway were males—about the relative validity of men's and women's perspectives as well. . . .

Consensus: The Private Sphere as Source of Neutral Grounds

Besides invoking the principle of tolerance of diversity to ground his reasonableness determination, Judge Krupansky also relied upon the notion of societal consensus to provide him with a definition of reasonableness. Like the tolerance of diversity argument, the judge's equating of reasonableness with consensus simultaneously acknowledged the group conflict in the case and minimized the court's role in choosing between the groups.

Concluding that the conduct engaged in at Osceola, "although annoying, [was] not so startling as to have affected seriously the psyches of the plaintiff or other female employees,"[25] Judge Krupansky stated further:

> The sexually oriented poster displays had a *de minimis* effect on the plaintiff's work environment when considered in the context of a society that condones and publicly features and commercially exploits open displays of written and pictorial erotica at the newsstands, on prime-time television, at the cinema, and in other public places.[26]

In other words, Judge Krupansky seemed to view Rabidue's objections as unreasonable on the grounds that the prevailing consensus in American society is that conduct like Henry's is not offensive. As with the voluntary entry argument, the question was treated as one of fact: either society accepts behavior such as Henry's or it does not. The judge treated societal consensus, like choices, as a preexisting, neutral mediator, a mechanism for distinguishing between legitimate demands for protection of group interests and illegitimate demands for enforcment of group (or individual) prejudices. Consensus fails to fulfill that purpose, however, for both the selection and the application of that construct entail value choices. . . .

Discrimination as Individual Bad Acts

The court's choice of consensus to give content to the reasonableness standard reflects underlying political judgments about what discrimination itself—the very concept that "consensus" is supposed to be defining—actually is, and about how discrimination should be eliminated. In equating "reasonableness" with societal consensus (that is, in defining discrimination as deviation from the status quo), the *Rabidue* court (like all courts using this definition of reasonableness) necessarily assumes that the status quo itself is egalitarian, pluralistic, and nondiscriminatory. This in turn shifts the focus to the individual, obscuring the possibility of structural inequalities and creating the impression that only a small number of deviant people fail to conform to society's pluralistic norms (that is, engage in discrimination). Thus, in focusing on whether the particular conduct engaged in by Douglas Henry was generally acceptable (that is, whether it violated social norms) rather than, for example, on whether it perpetuated conditions of inequality,[27] the *Rabidue* majority implicitly assumed that sexual discrimination is merely deviant behavior by individuals, rather than a structural problem inherent in American ideology and institutions. This narrow definition of discrimination favors liberty over security, diversity over conformity, the individual group to society at large (and the powerless groups society seeks to protect).[28] . . .

Hidden Messages: Reinforcing the Status Quo

Despite the fact that its decision superficially seems to be a pluralistic one, refusing to support dominant groups and neutrally enforcing existing societal norms, the *Rabidue* court's opinion is not pluralistic at all. While Judge Krupansky suggests that he disapproves of the harassment of women in the workplace, he nevertheless subtly rejects women's views about such conduct and denies them the means to resist it. And, while the articulated basis for his ruling is deference to worker culture, the rhetoric of the opinion actually derogates that culture. Rather than being pluralistic, the court's opinion privileges one narrow, elite viewpoint and silences others.

Disavowing Sexism While Reinforcing Patriarchal Views of Women

Despite the fact that Judge Krupansky seems to condemn Henry's sexist behavior and to endorse equal employment opportunity for all, his discussion reflects very patriarchal attitudes. At the most obvious level, the judge's trivializing of the sexual comments and visual displays at Osceola is consistent with the attitude of many men, who tend to view "milder" forms of harassment, such as suggestive looks, repeated requests for dates, and sexist jokes, as harmless social interactions to which only overly sensitive women would object.[29] It completely ignores the fact that persistent behavior of this "milder" sort is just as disturbing to many women as is overt quid pro quo harassment.[30]

The judge's assertion that a "proper assessment" of a hostile environment claim will include evidence on "the personality of the plaintiff"[31] suggests that he minimized the conduct involved in *Rabidue* because he shares a common male attitude that the victim of harassment is in some sense to blame for her mistreatment.[32] Many men believe, for example, that women can avoid harassment if they behave properly, and that the tactful registering of a complaint is usually an effective way of dealing with harassment when it occurs.[33] Women, in contrast, harbor no such illusions.[34]

These views about harassment are consistent, of course, with a general distrust of women that has been widely criticized by feminists. Thus, just as rapists' stories have been believed over their victims' on the grounds that women can be expected to "cry rape" in retaliation for the slightest rejection,[35] so too some men worry that female employees will use false harassment allegations as a "smoke screen" to hide poor job performance.[36] Judge Krupansky's focus on the character of the victim echoes these attitudes, belying the "neutrality" of his analysis. While seeming to criticize anti-female behavior, the judge actually expresses and reinforces the very attitudes that produce such behavior. It was these attitudes that led the dissent to criticize the majority for having taken the male viewpoint as the universal norm, and to conclude that "unless the outlook of the reasonable woman is adopted, the defendants as well as the courts are permitted to sustain ingrained notions of reasonable behavior fashioned by the offenders, in this case, men."[37]

Disavowing Elitism While Criticizing Workers as Sexist

The majority opinion not only reinforces existing male attitudes toward women but also reinforces existing elite attitudes toward the working class. While Judge Krupansky explicitly presents his finding that Douglas Henry's behavior was reasonable as a principled defense of worker culture, a tolerant and pluralistic decision, he simultaneously derogates that culture, devaluing workers' norms while claiming to protect them. Thus, for example, his opinion conveys an attitude of profound disrespect for the working class when it endorses the trial court's description of "some work environments" as the arena of "rough-hewn" "humor."[38] This language reveals a patronizing distaste for such humor, strongly suggesting that it is much inferior to Judge Krupansky's own, more refined variety. Furthermore, as Judge Keith notes in dissent, there is a strong classist dimension to the majority's argument: "[A] disturbing implication of considering defendants' backgrounds [in deciding such cases] is the notion that workplaces with the least sophisticated employees are the most prone to anti-female environments."[39] The majority's implicit message is: "They might be sexist—unlike [us] civilized people—but boys will be boys!" Thus, Judge Krupansky's effort to be tolerant of workers nevertheless conveys a disparaging attitude toward those not of his own class.

In short, while seeming to follow the neutral principle of tolerance for diversity, the court's opinion in fact reinforces an ideology that disempowers and devalues the very workers of whom it claims to be tolerant. It conveys a specific viewpoint, one that accepts a class hierarchy in which workers are devalued, while simultaneously seeming not to convey any viewpoint at all.

To summarize, by seeming to condemn the harasser's sexist conduct and views at the same time that it both protects and reproduces them, the opinion seems sympathetic to women while actually perpetuating sexist attitudes and reducing women's power in the workplace. Similarly, by seeming to defend the social class with which the harasser is identified while subtly derogating that class, the majority opinion seems to defend workers while actually reinforcing the existing class hierarchy that devalues and subordinates them.

Moreover, by relying on apparently objective concepts such as choice, consensus, and tolerance for diversity (as well as by disassociating his personal opinions from those of the class and gender groups involved in the case), Judge Krupansky conveys the distinct impression (and might even have believed himself) that he has been able to make the choice between diversity and conformity without resorting to personal political judgments. Transforming the case from one raising questions of gender roles and social hierarchy to one about pluralistic culture and societal consensus, the judge protects male power by treating it as worker powerlessness and reinforces class hierarchy by presenting it as tolerance for diversity. Relying on apparently neutral constructs to resolve the group conflict in the case, the majority's opinion obscures the fact that its ruling actually enforces (and reinforces) a particular, identifiable perspective— that of upperclass men. . . .

III. PLURALISM AND THE APPEAL OF REASONABLENESS

This Part argues that the *Rabidue* majority's belief in the reasonable person standard derives, at least in part, from certain pluralist assumptions that underlie its analysis. Moreover, to the extent that the dissent in the case also relied upon the notion of reasonableness, its analysis seems to depend upon a comparable belief in pluralist ideology. After briefly describing the dissenting opinion, it will be possible to compare the pluralist assumptions underlying both its and the majority's reasonableness analysis.

The Dissenting Opinion's Reasonable Woman Standard

Delivering a trenchant critique of the majority opinion, Judge Keith argued in dissent that the court's supposedly neutral analysis actually contained a hidden male perspective. Apparently attributing that problem to the use of the reasonable person test, he concluded that a reasonable woman standard should have been used instead. Because he justified the use of such a standard in terms of the concrete effect of sexual harassment on women, Judge Keith's position illustrates the value of a jurisprudence that directly addresses the intergroup conflicts raised by legal cases. Because of the reasonableness language in which he articulated his position, however, the judge's opinion also illustrates the tenacity of the idea that courts should not engage in explicitly political decision making.

The Reasonable Woman Standard as a Rejection of the Search for Neutrality

To Judge Keith, *Rabidue* clearly represented a conflict between the sexes over how they should relate in the workplace, and the Osceola Refining Company was clearly the site of persistent and significant degradation of women by men.[40] Moreover, as far as the dissenter was concerned, all three of the means that Judge Krupansky used to give content to the reasonable person standard were unacceptable. First, the tolerance for diversity argument did not work because the defendant's class was simply irrelevant.[41] Furthermore, the court was wrong to suggest "that such work environments somehow have an innate right to perpetuation."[42] Second, the court's reliance upon plaintiff's "choice" to enter the workplace suggested "that a woman assumes the risk of working in an abusive, anti-female environment."[43] Third, the "society" whose views the majority claimed to be enforcing "must primarily refer to the unenlightened." Wrote Judge Keith, "I hardly believe reasonable women condone the pervasive degradation and exploitation of female sexuality perpetuated in American culture."[44]

The dissenter's analysis implicitly rejects the role of courts as neutral arbiters of disputes. Challenging the idea of a homogeneous consensus in society, Judge Keith's opinion openly acknowledges that what constitutes appropriate behavior toward the opposite sex is a subject of dispute between women and men. Moreover, arguing that the reasonableness standard should be based on the viewpoint of the oppressed group, rather than on that of those doing the oppressing, he implicitly recognizes as well that the consensus view itself (to the extent that one exists) might simply be wrong. This recognition implicitly criticizes the idea that discrimination should or can be defined in terms of an external referent derived from the private sphere. If societal views about concepts like discrimination, reasonableness, etc., are the product of a discriminatory status quo, then the private sphere cannot provide a neutral, external definition of those concepts to guide judicial decisions. Judge Keith thus quite explicitly bases his conclusion about *Rabidue* on a value judgment: "As I believe no woman should be subjected to an environment where her sexual dignity and reasonable sensibilities are visually, verbally, or physically assaulted as a matter of prevailing male prerogative, I dissent."[45]

The Reasonable Woman Standard as a Neutral Mediator

As the discussion above indicates, at one level Judge Keith's opinion can be read as rejecting the idea that the private sphere can provide a neutral basis for the definition of discrimination and as offering instead an explicitly political argument for chooosing Rabidue's security over Henry's freedom. However, his depiction of the reasonable woman standard as itself a neutral construct seems to belie that position. In that respect, Judge Keith's formulation, like Judge Krupansky's, engages in a futile effort to overcome the contradiction between diversity and conformity.

In addition to using the traditional "reasonableness" terminology to describe his test, Judge Keith invokes the idea of neutrality in his statement that the reasonable woman standard "simultaneously allows courts to consider salient sociological differences as well as shield employers from the neurotic complainant."[46] In short, he seems to believe that the doctrinal construct itself will determine whether a particular woman's complaint is legitimate. Just as the majority conceives of the reasonable person test as a vehicle for identifying where an individual group's right to freedom ends and society's interest in the security of other groups begins, so the dissenter views the reasonable woman test as distinguishing between regulable "neurotic" women and protected "reasonable" women. And just as the majority uses consensus as the neutral mediator between diversity and conformity, so the dissent uses consensus among women as a similar mediator.

This position is subject to a critique similar to that directed at the majority's reasonable person test: Both in deciding to use the reasonable woman standard to begin with and in identifying the consensus view among women that will give it content, a court must necessarily make choices between freedom and security, the individual (or individual group) and the collectivity. The reasonable woman construct itself does not constrain judges' discretion in making these choices. Thus, Judge Keith's apparent conclusion that substituting his standard for the reasonable person test would assure fairer results for women seems unjustified.[47]

Moreover, in treating the resolution of sexual harassment cases as a matter of neutral decision making, Judge Keith's approach obscures the fact that his standard, like Judge Krupansky's (or any other standard, for that matter), necessarily requires a court to make substantive judgments about what kind of conduct should be allowed in the workplace. Encouraging a formalistic reliance on doctrine, his reasonable woman test obscures the fact that doctrinal constructs like consensus are merely vehicles for articulating value choices, not determinants of results.

In short, the discourse of reasonableness can create a false sense of security, lulling one into believing that a result is inherently fair regardless of its specific content, and reinforcing the idea that legal analysis can be neutral and objective. For example, to the extent that a reasonable woman standard fails to draw the court's attention to issues of race and class, it may perpetuate existing inequities based on those factors in the same way that the reasonable person standard does when it fails to consider women's point of view.[48]

Of course, one might argue that the result of this critique is an infinite regress, for a "reasonable black woman" standard would still ignore differences of class, a "reasonable lower-class black woman" standard would ignore differences of sexual orientation, etc. But that both misses the point and is the point. As one analysis of the use of the reasonableness test in criminal law concluded, "It is the reasonableness part of the standard that is faulty, not merely the sex or class of the mythical person. . . . By emphasizing individual responsibility in the abstract form, the reasonable man standard . . . ignores the social reality of the individual. . . ."[49] As a result, any unequal social conditions that affect an individual's situation are both perpetuated and condoned by such a standard. In short, the goal of employing an "objective" test that is unaffected by the judge's (or any other) worldview and that is sufficiently general to apply to all people is simply an illusory one.[50]

So you will never be satisfied? a reader might ask at this point. Surely the reasonable woman standard is a step in the right direction, for it draws attention to the hidden bias in the reasonable person test and directs the decision maker to consider the viewpoint of the woman, thus allowing the oppressed to define their own oppression (or at least endorsing the idea that they should be allowed to do so). Moreover, Judge Keith employs a very political tone, justifying his resolution in terms of the concrete effect that would have on people's daily lives. What more, one might ask, could he have done?

Such objections are without merit; Judge Keith's formulation is certainly a distinct improvement over the traditional one. However, as I will discuss in the next Section, I am still troubled by the messages that his formulation conveys, and by the assumptions that underlie it.

Pluralism and the Problem of Conflicting Liberties

How, one might ask, did Judge Keith apparently fall into the same traps that he recognized in the majority opinion? How did he find it so easy to accept (and endorse) Vivienne Rabidue's characterization of the Osceola environment and yet simultaneously believe that he was acting neutrally? Why did he fail to address the impact his ruling might have on the sense of dignity and validity that the men at Osceola might feel? In short, why did he seem not to be concerned with the fact that he was ruling not only for women but against men—that he was making a political choice between groups? The answer, I believe, lies in his implicit acceptance of the ideology of pluralism, in both its descriptive and its normative manifestations. It is to the law of that ideology, and its implications for anti-discrimination law, that I now turn.

Descriptive Pluralism

Both the majority and dissenting opinions in *Rabidue* reveal a belief, varying considerably in strength between the two opinions, that current American society is pluralistic and egalitarian. Judge Krupansky's belief in a broadly pluralistic society is easy to see; Judge Keith's pluralistic assumptions are narrower and more subtle.

As the above discussion of *Rabidue* illustrates, Judge Krupansky's presentation of his opinion as neutral and apolitical is only convincing if one accepts a pluralistic vision of the world. Equating reasonableness with the status quo, the majority opinion necessarily assumes that American society is not fundamentally hierarchical, and that what gets called the societal consensus represents a truly general view, rather than the viewpoint of a single, powerful group. Relying upon the private sphere for the normative content of his decision, Judge Krupansky must assume that sphere is not itself tainted by illegitimate inequality. Only by believing in the descriptive accuracy of pluralist ideology can he believe in his ability to reach neutral decisions through use of the reasonable person construct.

In contrast, Judge Keith clearly does not conceive of society as a whole as pluralistic, rejecting the reasonable person standard as merely governmental enforcement of the male point of view. However, his reliance upon a reasonable woman test suggests that, at least among women, he assumes equal ability to contribute to the formation of a consensus, ignoring differences of power due to class, race, etc. Indeed, only by ascribing to this partial descriptive pluralism could Judge Keith logically conclude, as he apparently does, that a reasonable woman test would allow courts to reach nonpolitical decisions unaffected by either the judges' own values or existing power differences among women.[51]

Normative Pluralism

The judges' shared belief that the reasonableness test can provide an apolitical ground for decision—as well as their apparent conviction that judges should strive for such apolitical grounds—stems also from their acceptance of pluralism as a normative ideal. To reiterate, pluralism basically means diversity, having a culture in which many different groups can peacefully coexist. Implicit in this idea, however, is the need to prohibit conduct that so harms other groups as to destroy pluralism itself —that is, a commitment to protecting minorities. In short, the ideology of pluralism defines group freedom as the freedom to act self-interestedly, but only as long as such conduct does not unduly harm other groups (and, implicitly, the societal interest in pluralism). Thus, it implies that it is possible to be tolerant of group diversity and still prohibit discrimination.

Applying this concept to the *Rabidue* case, it can be seen that the majority's emphasis on the need to be tolerant of worker culture and to protect workers against the elite's efforts to impose its own values invokes the ideal of a pluralistic society in which all groups can coexist. Similarly, the dissenter's failure to address the possibility that his desired ruling would have harmed the men at Osceola suggests that he ascribes to the view that women can be accommodated without injuring men—that is, that pluralism is a viable ideal.

This Section argues that the notion that pluralism is an unproblematic goal is logically incoherent and disconsonant with the reality of irresolvable conflicts between groups. As such, that notion discourages courts from recognizing the existence of such conflicts and encourages them to articulate their decisions in the mystifying discourse of neutrality.

Conflicting Liberties

It is logically incoherent to say that a group is free to pursue its own interest and express its own norms unless that conduct harms other groups. That is so because *all* acts by any one group (or individual) are inevitably harmful to others. One side's freedom can always be seen as the other side's loss of security, one side's equal treatment can seem like the other's unequal treatment, one group's pursuit of its own interest can always be called intolerance of any other group that is affected by that pursuit. In the *Rabidue* situation, for example, either side's conduct can be characterized as discrimination, and, as a result, a ruling either way could be called either governmental regulation *of* discrimination or government engaging *in* discrimination.

Let me expand to illustrate. Assuming for the moment that sexism actually is an important norm among American (male) workers—an important source of their identity and component of their worldview— Douglas Henry's conduct can be seen as an exercise of his group's freedom to follow its own norms. One way to assess that freedom would be to argue that, since it also harmed Vivienne Rabidue, limiting her freedom to work and subjecting her to public humiliation, it had to be constrained. Under this analysis, Henry's conduct constituted discrimination and can be prohibited by the state.

It makes just as much *logical* sense, however, to say that Rabidue's claim is an attempt to exercise *her* freedom to engage in remunerative employment under conditions she finds acceptable, and that the exercise of her right to freedom harmed Douglas Henry. Under this view, Rabidue's insistence that Henry refrain from displaying pornography would have prevented him from following a fundamental tenet of his group's philosophy and undermined the sense of identity, of maleness, that the act of displaying pornography affirms. Therefore, the argument would go, it was actually Rabidue who tried to discriminate against Henry, not he who discriminated against her.

In other words, although Henry's freedom impinges upon Rabidue's security (and freedom), Rabidue's freedom also reduces Henry's security (and freedom). Each side's liberty is in conflict with the other's. It is impossible for either to act without discriminating, and no matter which side the court rules for, it will be subject to the accusation that it has allowed discrimination against the other side.[52] . . .

The Relational Construction of Groups

The ideal of pluralism is logically incoherent not only because the concepts of freedom and security are relational (one group's liberty is another's injury), but also because group identities themselves are relationally and hierarchically constructed in current American society. As a result of that construction, individual groups' fates are inextricably linked: One group's benefit will almost always be another's loss.

By saying that group identities are relationally constructed, I mean that groups attain their identity in contrast with other groups, in the same way that words attain their meaning in contrast with other words:

> [T]he meaning generated by linguistic conventions is negative and differential rather than positive and fixed. The meaning of the word "tree" is *artificial* in that it does not flow from anything in the nature of the word itself. Instead the meaning flows from the word's relationship to other words within the socially created representational practice. It acquires its meaning from not being another word, say "bush" or "woods."[53]

In a similar way, to be "male" is defined in part as to be "not female," "black" attains its meaning in contrast to "white," "rich" in contrast to "poor," and so forth.

Perhaps more importantly, group identities are hierarchized, as feminist scholarship has amply demonstrated. The categories of male and female, for instance, are socially constructed in a relationship of domination and submission, such that what makes a man "masculine" (i.e., truly male) is his ability (and desire) to dominate women and what makes a woman "feminine" (truly female) is her susceptibility to (and apparent desire of) domination by a man. Extending the analysis to a more general level, one could say that maleness is defined, at least in part, as superiority to women, and femaleness as inferiority to men.[54]

The briefest consideration of popular ideology about sex difference confirms this interdependence and hierarchization of male and female identities.[55] Consider, for example, the fact that a man who is "feminine" in demeanor or clothing is considered unmanly (think of how most people would react to a man in a skirt); that the worst epithet to hurl at a male is a charge of homosexuality, that is, of having "female" sexual urges; and that a man who cannot "control" his woman is often considered emasculated. Similarly, to be attractive as a woman is to be pretty (read: pleasing as a sexual object) and soft (read: vulnerable, incapable of self-protection), while to be unattractive is to be overly strong, harsh, or aggressive—that is, to be like (and able to resist) a man. And of course, the worst epithet to fire at a woman is to call her a lesbian (like a man in sexual urges), or, perhaps ugly (unable to serve as a sex object for men).

Similarly, part of the definition of class identity involves contrasting oneself with other social classes. Suntans indicate wealth precisely because those who work all day lack the leisure time needed to acquire them; unblemished hands mark the professional since laborers' hands get calloused. Part of each group's identity is its awareness of its position in a hierarchy of groups. Because groups are mutually defined in this way, it is simply impossible to accommodate one group without in some way affecting others. And, since one group's gain will virtually inevitably be another's loss, any judicial decision, even one that attempts merely to bring one group up to another's level of power or status, inevitably constitutes a decision that favors one group and harms another.

In this light, it can be seen that the display of pornography in which women are demeaned and threatened reaffirms the male identity of the displayer, underlining his ability to subordinate women. Simultaneously, of course, such displays affirm the construction of women as willing victims. Thus, a judicial decision that bars pornography in the workplace, rejecting the notion that women exist as sexual objects for men, also rejects and undermines a definition of men as beings who can objectify and subordinate women. Because the sexes are mutually defined, Judge Keith's approach would necessarily harm men, just as Judge Krupansky's harms women.

In summary, given that any action by one group produces some sort of harm to others, the ideal of a pluralistic coexistence of all groups is unrealistic, especially within existing social arrangements. Neither the principle of tolerance for diversity nor the concept of societal consensus can provide neutral grounds upon which to resolve cases, for choices among conflicting groups cannot be avoided. By relying on such concepts, both Judge Krupansky and Judge Keith reached the mistaken conclusion that doctrine could overcome inter-group conflicts—that a reasonableness test could assure fair results to all. In so doing, they failed to recognize that liberty is necessarily the freedom *to* harm others, and courts must decide whose liberty wins. . . .

Transforming the Discourse

The discussion thus far suggests that both reasonableness and pluralism are problematic concepts which hide the power struggles behind legal issues and mystify the court's role in resolving such struggles. Moreover, both Judge Krupansky's and Judge Keith's opinions reveal that the two concepts are mutually enforcing: To protect his conviction that his reasonableness analysis was neutral, each judge had to assume an (at least somewhat) egalitarian, pluralistic society,[56] and, to affirm his vision of an egalitarian and pluralistic world, each judge had to perceive himself as making nonpolitical, neutral decisions. It is worth exploring briefly, therefore, whether either of these constructs can be salvaged—whether our understanding of either reasonableness or pluralism can be sufficiently transformed to eliminate those constructs' harmful effects and still retain their usefulness.

There are both risks and benefits to retaining and redefining problematic legal and political constructs rather than discarding them altogether. The major risk is that, even when used by the disempowered, the constructs will continue to hide power relationships and thereby legitimate a fundamentally unequal system. Especially if new formulations of old constructs are presented as neutral themselves, the redefined constructs will still merely reinforce and legitimate an unequal status quo. The primary benefit of retaining problematic concepts like reasonableness and pluralism is that their immense symbolic power can serve to legitimate the demands for social transformation that they are used to articulate, while their very vagueness and abstractness can allow them to serve as valuable vehicles for generating dialogue on national values. In this respect, the problem is not with the terms themselves, but with the meanings that we give them. The question, then, becomes essentially one of transition. To the extent that concepts can be infused with new meaning, they can be valuable tools for reform. To the extent that they resist such redefinition, they will continue to legitimate inequality.

The Futility of Retaining Reasonableness

In this light, it seems futile to attempt a transformation of the concept of reasonableness. While it might be possible to reconceptualize the reasonable person (or woman) standard as merely shorthand for something like "the judge's considered judgment about the inappropriateness of the conduct in question," such a revised vision seems unlikely to succeed. Reasonableness in legal ideology is simply too closely tied to the idea of objectivity —to the notion that the law can resolve legal conflicts without reflecting or reinforcing any personal perspsective—to allow for such a transformation. And the homogeneous image of society that results from the traditional equation of reasonableness with societal consensus is simply too harmful, excluding all but the dominant elite, to justify retention.

Toward a Transformed Vision of Pluralism

In contrast, the concept of pluralism seems to have the potential for articulating valuable and meaningful ideals. While the idea that judicial decisions can be dictated by a principle of pluralistic tolerance of all groups is unrealistic,[57] this does not mean that the whole notion of a tolerant and diverse nation is bankrupt. Rather than be seen as a guaranty of judicial neutrality, however, pluralism and tolerance for diversity should be viewed as part of an expanded commitment to the true sharing of social power. While it would no doubt be helpful to see pluralism as requiring an in-depth, empathic exploration of social problems, and as mandating that we not ignore the group identification of each individual, these changes in attitude are not enough. It is also essential that we think more expansively about the need for the redistribution of power, and be willing to accept the hard choices—and losses—that true redistribution would entail. Such expansive thinking and acting is crucial for the success of any effort to eliminate inequality. For as the preceding Section demonstrates, behavior like that of Douglas Henry can be neither understood nor eradicated without addressing the other hierarchies of power and status that contribute to male assertions of dominance over women through harassment, intimidation, and violence.

IV. CONCLUSION

. . . [T]he prevailing ideology systematically ignores differences among the citizenry as a whole, promoting a homogeneous vision of American society that both excludes those groups who do not fit the accepted American model and elevates a small but powerful elite to the status of universal "type." The history of the exclusion of women and African Americans from American culture and politics[58] is only the most striking example of this pervasive privatization and depoliticization of powerless groups. Rendering such groups invisible by ignoring their differences (or even their existence) and assimilating everyone into a purportedly general type, American ideology conceals the conflict created by those differences and thus allows us to avoid the hard decisions that such conflict requires. Only by denying diversity have we been able to see ourselves as tolerant of it.

   The reasonable person standard both reflects and reproduces this mystifying ideology. Perceived as a mediating construct that allows group diversity without sacrificing collective security, it suggests that pluralism is both a descriptively accurate and a normatively viable vision of American society. Creating the impression that judges can rely on abstract tolerance and private orderings to resolve questions of group conflict, it obscures the political decisions that inevitably underlie such resolutions.

Conversely, the concept of pluralism legitimates the reasonable person standard, affirming its message of objectivity. Descriptive pluralism, by presenting contemporary society as egalitarian, affirms that the societal consensus the reasonableness test relies upon is a meaningful concept, reflecting a true and voluntary agreement among groups. Normative pluralism, by suggesting that the coexistence of all groups is not only morally right but also logically possible, validates the idea that the reasonableness test allows courts to avoid political choices between litigants by simply being tolerant of all.

Of course, the concepts of reasonableness and cultural pluralism need not of necessity be vehicles for denying difference and obscuring choices. But as long as reasonableness means abstract neutrality and pluralism means limitless tolerance, each concept will reinforce the other, and both will perpetuate an unequal status quo.

NOTES

1. See *Meritor Savings Bank* v. *Vinson,* 447 U.S. 57 (1986).

2. While I realize that some subtleties inevitably will be lost as a result, in this Section I will draw on discussions of both race and sex discrimination to make my points. Although there are important differences between the life situations and legal treatments of women, on the one hand, and racial minorities on the other (not to mention the further differences in the experiences of minority women), the various conceptions of discrimination present in each area of thought are nevertheless sufficiently similar to be treated together for this brief description of anti-discrimination ideology.

In describing that ideology, I will focus primarily on examples from political and legal ideology, but it is part of my position—and, indeed, part of the problem I seek to redress—that the assumptions I will be discussing are prevalent in the general culture (that is, are held, consciously, or not, by many but not necessarily all Americans) as well.

3. E. Purcell, *The Crisis of Democratic Theory* (Lexington: University of Kentucky Press, 1973), p. 211.

4. The thought-provoking work of Carol Gilligan, *see, e.g.,* C. Gilligan, *In a Different Voice* (1982), has greatly improved our understanding of women's situation. It has also, unfortunately, generated much reductionist and essentialist discussion of women's differences from men. Nevertheless, the presence of such crude overgeneralizations about the sexes should not produce the equally crude

reaction of totally ignoring the ways in which many women's social and epistemological world—partly because it is *itself* a product of patriarchy—is genuinely different from that of many men.

5. *Rabidue* v. *Osceola Ref. Co.*, 805 F.2d 611, 623 (6th Cir. 1986) (Keith, J., dissenting), *cert. denied*, 48 U.S. 1041 (1987).

6. She also filed a discriminatory discharge claim. At the time the claims were filed, Osceola was a division of Texas-American Petrochemicals, Inc., which had acquired Osceola on September 1, 1976. The Sixth Circuit affirmed the district court's ruling that Texas-American could not be held liable for any alleged discriminatory acts that occurred prior to that date, because, given that charges had not been filed with the Equal Employment Opportunity Commission at or before the time of acquisition, Texas-American, as successor, had no notice of contingent charges when it acquired the company. 805 F.2d at 616 (citations omitted). Apparently because at least some of the conduct complained of had occurred after September 1, 1976, the court went on to address the substantive merits of plaintiff's claims. Id . at 615, 618.

7. Id. at 615.

8. Id. at 624 (Keith, J., dissenting).

9. Id.

10. Id.

11. Id.

12. Id. at 625.

13. "[A] plaintiff . . . must assert and prove that . . . the charged sexual harassment had the effect of *unreasonably* interfering with the plaintiff's work performance and creating an intimidating, hostile, or offensive working environment . . . ." 805 F.2d at 619 (emphasis added).

14. *Rabidue*, 805 F.2d at 620 ("the reasonable expectation of the plaintiff upon voluntarily entering [an] environment" pervaded by "a lexicon of obscenity" is relevant factor for court to consider).

15. Id. at 620–22.

16. Id. at 622.

17. The court's description of her as "a capable, independent, ambitious, aggressive, intractable, and opinionated individual" with "an abrasive, rude, antagonistic, extremely willful, uncooperative, and irascible personality," *Rabidue*, 805 F. 2d at 615, effectively obscured the possibility that Rabidue's complaint represented the viewpoint of women in general.

18. Noting that the plaintiff's claim arose primarily out of the "acrimonious working relationship" between her and another employee and concluding that she was fired, in part, because of her "inability to work harmoniously with co-workers and customers," id., the court conveyed the distinct impression that the dispute in the case was primarily attributable to Rabidue's difficult personality.

19. Calling the Osceola posters "calendar type office wall displays," id. at 622 n.7, comparing them to "erotica," id. at 622, and describing Henry's epithets as "off-color language," id. at 622 n.7, Judge Krupansky's opinion trivialized

the injury that Rabidue alleged, and thereby suggested that only an unusually sensitive woman would find the conduct at Osceola offensive. His comment that the plaintiff and others were merely "annoyed" by Henry's behavior, id. at 615, further suggested that such behavior did not justify Rabidue's supposedly irascible reaction.

20. It raised questions of public power because, to the extent that the court's decision gave Henry the "right" to engage in his harassing conduct, it constituted government enforcement of such conduct.

21. *Rabidue*, 805 F.2d at 620.

22. I have taken this "assumption of risk" paraphrasing from the dissent. Id. at 626 (Keith, J., dissenting). . . .

23. *Rabidue*, 805 F.2d at 627 (Keith, J., dissenting). Having to decide between submitting to sexual harassment and quitting one's job hardly constitutes a choice. In fact, it is exactly this sort of tying of job benefits to sexual demands that the harassment cause of action was designed to prevent. See C. MacKinnon, *Sexual Harassment of Working Women: A Case of Sex Discrimination* (New Haven, Conn.: Yale University Press, 1979), pp. 40–47; cf. *Rabidue*, 805 F.2d at 626 (Keith, J., dissenting) ("In my view, Title VII's precise purpose is to prevent [vulgar] behavior and attitudes from poisoning the work environment of classes protected under the Act."). Since their subordinate position in an employment market that restricts their job opportunities and devalues their work is precisely what makes women vulnerable to harassment in the first place (MacKinnon, *Sexual Harassment of Working Women,* pp. 41–42), the view that Rabidue's position was voluntarily entered into can be seen as a virtual rejection of the very concept of sexual harassment itself. At a minimum, such a view certainly reflects value judgments about whether and under what circumstances women should be allowed to work in our society. In addition, the recent Supreme Court case of *Meritor Sav. Bank* v. *Vinson,* 477 U.S. 57, 68 (1986), which held that unwelcome conduct constitutes harassment even if "consented" to, raises questions about the continued vitality of such reasoning.

24. *Rabidue*, 805 F.2d at 620–21 (quoting *Rabidue* v. *Osceola* Ref. Co., 584 F. Supp. 419, 430 (E.D. Mich. 1984) (Newblatt, J.)).

25. *Rabidue*, 805 F.2d at 622.

26. Id.

27. This test is MacKinnon's, and she contrasts it with what she calls the "differences approach" of traditional equal protection jurisprudence, under which the question is whether the plaintiff is similarly situated to, yet treated differently than, members of other groups. MacKinnon, *Sexual Harassment of Working Women,* pp. 101–102. Like the differences approach, a focus on consensus fails to consider that the supposedly neutral criterion ("real" sex difference, consensus) might be exactly what sex discrimination law should be addressing—that is, might itself be discriminatory. Ibid., p. 227 (focusing on sex difference "allow[s] the very factors the law against discrimination exists to prohibit to be the reason not to prohibit them").

28. Cf. Freeman, "Legitimizing Racial Discrimination through Anti-Discrimination Law: A Critical Review of Supreme Court Doctrine," *Minnesota Law Review* 62 (1978): 1049. Freeman describes two different ways of approaching the concept of racial discrimination. The first, which he identifies with traditional Supreme Court jurisprudence, is the "perpetrator perspective," which "sees racial discrimination not as conditions, but as actions, or series of actions, inflicted on the victim by the perpetrator," ibid., p. 1053, and thus views discrimination "not as a social phenomenon, but merely as the misguided conduct of particular actors." Ibid., p. 1054. In contrast, the "victim perspective" sees discrimination as

> those conditions of actual social existence as a member of a perpetual underclass. This perspective includes both the objective conditions of life—lack of jobs, lack of money, lack of housing—and the consciousness associated with those objective conditions—lack of choice and lack of human individuality in being forever perceived as a member of a group rather than as an individual.

Ibid., pp. 1052–53 (footnotes omitted). It recognizes that discrimination will not be eliminated "until the conditions associated with it have been eliminated." Ibid., p. 1053.

29. See L. Finley, "A Break in the Silence: Including Women's Issues in a Torts Course," *Yale Journal of Law and Feminism* 60 (1985): 60; see also A. Astrachan, *How Men Feel Their Response to Women's Demands for Equality and Power* (Garden City, N.Y.: Doubleday, 1988), p. 88 (reporting that many men believe their sexual propositions are just jokes); E. G. C. Collins and T. B. Blodgett, "Sexual Harassment . . . Some See It . . . Some Won't," *Harvard Business Review* (March–April 1981): 81, 82–93 (noting that three times as many women as men think "eye[ing] the woman up and down" is harassment); Cohen, "What's Harassment? Ask the Woman," *Washington Post,* July 5, 1988, p. A19, col. 1 (commenting on this tendency of men to trivialize certain forms of harassment).

30. See Collins and Blodgett, "Sexual Harassment . . . Some See It . . . Some Won't," pp. 78, 80.

31. *Rabidue,* 805 F.2d at 620.

32. Collins and Blodgett, "Sexual Harassment . . . Some See It . . . Some Won't," p. 90.

33. Ibid. Thus, for example, I have heard a university official speaking to a group of women employees about how to prevent sexual harassment urge those women to help matters by making sure that they do not engage in "ambiguous" conduct. One wonders if he also met with male employees to tell them how *they* could help prevent harassment.

34. Ibid. (78 percent disagree with statements that a woman who dresses and behaves properly will not be subjected to harassment). It is a testament to the strength of the male power of naming that even some women do, however, hold the woman responsible. Collins and Blodgett, "Sexual Harassment . . . Some See It . . . Some Won't," p. 90; see also MacKinnon, *Sexual Harassment of*

Working Women, p. 47 (many victims of harassment feel guity and somehow to blame for what happened).

35. See generally S. Brownmiller, *Against Our Will: Men, Women and Rape* (New York: Simon and Schuster, 1975), pp. 348, 413; 1132 (describing and criticizing that view of rape victims).

36. Collins and Blodgett, "Sexual Harassment . . . Some See It . . . Some Won't," p. 92. Of course, I am not saying that this would never happen. But such occurrences would be so rare that their possibility simply does not justify failing to condemn the conduct, any more than the same possibility would justify rejecting any other type of discrimination complaint (or legal claim in general, for that matter).

37. *Rabidue,* 805 F.2d at 626 (Keith, J., dissenting) (citation omitted) "Rape," *Yale Law Journal* 95 (1986).

38. Id. at 620 (quoting *Rabidue,* 584 F. Supp. at 430 (Newblatt, J.)).

39. Id. at 627 (Keith, J., dissenting). That attitude is also conveyed in a remark that Henry's supervisor made to him, exhorting him to learn to become more of "an executive-type person." Id. at 624 (Keith, J., dissenting).

40. Judge Keith repeatedly labeled behavior of the type that occurred at Osceola in gender terms—"anti-female obscenity," *Rabidue* v. *Osceola Ref. Co.,* 805 F.2d 611, 624 (6th Cir. 1986) (Keith, J., dissenting), *cert. denied,* 481 U.S. 1041 (1987); "misogynous language," id. at 625; "primitive views of working women," id.—and concluded that Rabidue had received "sex-based disparate treatment," id.

41. Id. at 627.

42. Id. at 626.

43. Id.

44. Id. at 627.

45. Id. at 626–27.

46. Id. at 626.

47. In fact, Judge Keith's unfortunate choice of terms in which to articulate the role of his standard—that is, his comment that it allows courts to distinguish between "reasonable" and "neurotic" women—suggests that even in his own hands that standard might not always produce desirable results, for women's efforts to articulate their views and object to their disempowerment have often been dismissed as mere neurotic worrying.

48. As Lucinda Finley points out, because the reasonable woman standard merely replaces one stereotype with another, it would still be unfair to any woman who failed to conform to traditionally female standards of conduct, as would be the reasonable person standard to untraditional men. Finley, "A Break in the Silence," pp. 63–64. In addition, "substituting a reasonable woman standard to judge the conduct of women, but not going further to question the inclusiveness of the norms informing the reasonable person standard, implies that women's experiences and reactions are something for women only, rather than normal human responses." Ibid., p. 64.

49. Donovan and Wildman, "Is the Reasonable Man Obsolete? A Critical Perspective on Self-Defense," *Harvard C.R.-C.L. Law Review* 623 (1980): 437, 465.

50. . . . [I]t is important that judges engage in an analysis that is self-consciously aware both of their own perspectives and of the concrete circumstances and varying viewpoints involved in any dispute. While no judge will be able to completely escape his or her own cultural blinders, such an effort would still be a vast improvement over a purportedly neutral reasonableness analysis that unquestioningly (and often unknowingly) replicates the views of a powerful elite.

51. Judge Keith's position also assumes that women exist in a hermetically sealed environment unaffected by male power. That is, his advocacy of a reasonable woman standard ignores the extent to which women's views are themselves constructed by patriarchy. The extent to which "false consciousness" can or should be identified as such is, of course, a huge and difficult issue in feminist thought, but further discussion of it is beyond the scope of this essay.

52. To the extent that they recognize that helping one group inevitably entails harming others, those who label affirmative action measures "reverse discrimination" are logically correct (*if* you define discrimination as the exercise of group freedom in a way that harms others). Where they go wrong is in viewing a *refusal* to engage in such programs as neutral, rather than as reinforcing existing inequalities which *also* raise one group over another.

53. Peller, "The Metaphysics of American Law," *California Law Review* 73 (1985): 1164.

54. See F. Olsen, "The Sex of Law" (unpublished manuscript).

55. I take my terminology from Olsen, "The Sex of Law," 1223.

56. The dissenter had to assume at least equality among women. . . .

57. It is incoherent to think that the principle of tolerance for diversity can provide the ground for a neutral methodology. Pluralism simply cannot provide an external referent that will assure the neutrality of judicial decisions; to ignore that fact is merely to clothe a particularized perspective in the false veneer of objectivity.

58. On the history of the exclusion of women from culture and politics, see E. Flexner, *Century of Struggle* (Cambridge, Mass.: Belknap Press, 1959), and B. Hooks, *Ain't I A Woman: Black Women and Feminism* (Boston: South End Press, 1981). On the arguably even more severe exclusion of blacks, see E. Genovese, *Roll, Jordan, Roll: The World the Slaves Made* (New York: Pantheon Books, 1974); T. Gossett, *Race: The History of an Idea in America* (New York: Random House, 1989); B. Hooks, *Ain't I A Woman;* R. Kluger, *Simple Justice: The History of* Brown v. Board of Education *and Black America's Struggle for Equality* (New York: Random House, 1976); and C. Woodward, *The Strange Career of Jim Crow* 3d ed. (New York: Oxford University Press, 1974).

Contributors

DOUGLAS D. BAKER, Department of Management and Systems, Washington State University, Pullman.

SHERRY B. BORGERS, Department of Counseling Psychology, University of Kansas, Lawrence.

MARTHA R. BURT, Human Resources Policy Center, Urban Institute, Washington, D.C.

BOB D. CUTLER, Department of Marketing, University of North Texas, Denton.

NANCY S. EHRENREICH, College of Law, University of Denver.

JOHN C. HUGHES, Department of Political Science, Saint Michaels College, Winooski, Vermont.

LEANOR B. JOHNSON, Department of Psychology, Howard University, Washington, D.C.

ALAN CHARLES KORS, Department of History, University of Pennsylvania, Philadelphia.

CATHARINE A. MACKINNON, School of Law, University of Michigan, Ann Arbor.

LARRY MAY, Department of Philosophy, Washington University, St. Louis, Missouri.

J. P. MINSON, School of Humanities, Griffith University, Queensland, Australia.

SHARON L. OSWALD, Department of Management, Auburn University, Atlanta, Georgia.

CAMILLE PAGLIA, Department of Humanities, University of the Arts, Philadelphia, Pennsylvania.

ELLEN FRANKEL PAUL, Social Philosophy and Policy Center, Bowling Green State University, Ohio.

STEPHANIE RIGER, Department of Psychology and Women's Studies and Director, Women's Studies Program, University of Illinois, Chicago.

LINDA J. RUBIN, Department of Counseling Psychology, University of Kansas, Lawrence.

SANDRA S. TANGRI, Department of Psychology, Howard University, Washington, D.C.

DAVID E. TERPSTRA, Department of Management and Marketing, University of Mississippi.

NANCY TUANA, Department of Humanities and Fine Arts, University of Texas at Dallas.

EDMUND WALL, Department of Philosophy, Santa Barbara City College.

WILLIAM L. WOERNER, engineering consultant, Silver Spring, Maryland.